IT'S A
FAR CRY TO
LOCH
AWE

Charlie Mitchell

DALMALLY
HISTORICAL ASSOCIATION

To Lynn,
a special friend

An Historical and Nostalgic Tour Around Loch Awe

In the following pages, I have tried to give an interesting historical and contemporary account of the places, past events, people and stories that are to be found in a trip around my home country of Loch Awe-side.

I have started from Glennan, at the south-west end and gone clockwise around the loch but have also diverted off, to include Loch Avich, Glen Orchy, Glen Lochy and other parts that I feel should be included in the Loch Awe area.

The road mileage of the full journey completed in 2010, is well over a hundred miles.

Charlie Mitchell

ISBN 978 1 5262 0548 3
Published by Dalmally Historical Association
Copyright © The Estate of Charlie Mitchell 2016
The moral right of the author has been asserted

Printed in Malta by Gutenberg Press Ltd

CONTENTS

Dan and Jessie Stuart turning hay at Glennan circa 1952.

CHAPTER ONE

GLENNAN TO FORD AND TORRAN

We start our journey at Glennan Cottage, which is built on the watershed between Loch Awe and Kilmartin Glen. It is said that the rain falling on one side of its roof runs into the sea at Crinan but the rain falling on the other side runs into Loch Awe and eventually the sea north of Oban. Glennan Cottage is mentioned in the 1841 census as having nine inhabitants. It is an old house and for most of its life appears to have been a croft and during much of the 1900's it was home to 'Neilly Ban' and his family.

His son Dan Stuart was a well-known, larger-than-life character and it was from Dan, who was commonly known as 'the Bohunk', I heard many stories about the loch-side that had come down from generations past. I have used a good number of his stories in this book. Although Glennan Cottage is no longer a croft some South American alpacas are reared there and a small number of them can be seen beside the house.

By the roadside, about a hundred yards south of the house, is a large broken standing stone with its leaning stump still embedded in the ground and the rest of it lying down flat. It is said to have been broken in the 1879 gale that destroyed the Tay Bridge. This stone must have been one of the tallest ones around as it was a good five metres in height. Near the standing stone are a few remains of Tigh-a-Charr or House by the Stone, which is mentioned in the 1790's Statistical Account for Kilmartin Parish. For this is part of the Kilmartin Parish, which stretches up the west side of Loch Awe almost to Kilmaha and that is the way that we will be going on the early part of our journey.

There once flowed a mighty river from Glennan down Kilmartin Glen to the sea, which was fed by melting ice at the end of the Ice Age. This was once the outlet from the Loch Awe catchment area that stretches as far as Rannoch Moor. Why the water in Loch Awe later changed to flowing out by the Pass of Brander is not clear. I think the likeliest explanation is simply that it had flowed out at the Glennan end for centuries, because the Pass of Brander was blocked by a glacier fed by the ice from Ben Cruachan, and when that had melted and the Pass of Brander was scoured out lower than the Glennan watershed, the water simply flowed out the other way.

Glennan Cottage is situated opposite the junction of the Kilmichael Glen road with the B840 and across from the Carrier's Field. We will follow the B840 past a modern house built at the foot of the towering and precipitous Craigantairb (Crag of the Bull) or as it is known locally as 'the Bull Rock' after a bull fell over the edge. In the past this was home to a pair of peregrine falcons.

The B840 road runs alongside the small Dog-Head Loch. Just before this the old Ford road can be seen running up and across the hillside. It goes past the ruins of an old Free Church building, which was situated in what is a very pleasant and idyllic spot at the edge of the trees and looking out over the Dog-Head Loch. This does not seem consistent with the Free Church's austere image, but this site would probably have been chosen as central to both the Ford and Kilmartin areas. The old road then goes past Auchinellan and re-joins the B840. When walking the road I found an old lime-kiln, which was built into the banking below the road and had made use of the lime-rich rock nearby. The lime-kiln dates from the big agricultural improvement time, which started in the late 1700's and carried on through the 1800's, and involved liming, land-draining, enclosing land with stone dykes and growing new kinds of crops. The road above would have given easy access for charging the kiln with fuel and broken up limestone. There was also water nearby to slake and disintegrate the burned limestone and complete the chemical process of lime-making. Although sometimes it seems the burned limestone was simply carted out to the fields and left for nature to finish the job.

As we continue alongside Loch Ederline a small stony man-made islet can be seen a short distance from the shore, and this would once have been the foundation for a crannog building, which was supported on piles and would have risen high above the water and provided a refuge and home for a large extended family and their livestock. This would probably have been built and occupied for many centuries around the early AD years and would appear to have had a causeway connecting it to the shore. I was told a much later tale of how someone fleeing for his life had swum out to this islet for refuge, but had been killed by an arrow fired from the shore.

The Kilmartin Parish Statistical Account from the 1840's says that 'freshwater mussels containing pearls of great value have been found in Loch Ederline'. I do not know whether the loch still has mussels with pearls but freshwater mussels are now an endangered and protected species and pearl fishing is banned. Loch Ederline is a popular pike-fishing loch and a favourite haunt of ospreys. Ospreys on Lochaweside and elsewhere had died out through persecution and egg collecting in the 1800's, but after their return to Scotland a pair were persuaded to set up home at Ederline in 1987 when a man-made nest-platform was built on a tree-top. Since then the ospreys from there have returned yearly, multiplied and spread, and with a bit of help by man providing other nest sites on tree-tops, there are now a good number of pairs nesting around Loch Awe. The number of young ospreys being reared yearly is now into the high teens. Osprey chicks are almost all ringed by the RSPB and a ring from an Ederline reared bird was found in the stomach of a crocodile in Africa.

Pike were, I believe, introduced into Loch Ederline by a laird from

Ederline, possibly Henry Bruce, or maybe his angling wife who caught five salmon in one spot during a day's fishing on Loch Awe. From Loch Ederline the pike spread down into Loch Awe and they are now found in all the loch's suitable shallow and weedy habitats. Pike fishermen on Loch Awe were responsible for introducing roach into the loch when they used them for live-bait fishing. They released them into the Ford end of Loch Awe where they have bred and multiplied and are now a well-established species. Another non-native species, which was introduced into the wild in recent times at Loch Ederline was Canada geese, which were hatched out by the keeper at Ederline and then set free. They have now multiplied to considerable numbers and spread around the district but at least they are not as destructive as pike and they may even be a good addition to the local fauna.

Set on the hillside above Loch Ederline is the old mansion house of Auchinellan (Field of the Island) and the island it took its name from is probably the one at the Ford end of that loch where the old Ederline

The Celtic cross commemorating the Bruce family owners of Ederline Estate from 1872 till the end of the century.

lairds are buried. There are grave slabs of the old Campbell owners of that estate and a prominent Celtic cross commemorating its later Bruce family owners. Not far from the loch, on a rise below the present Auchinellan entrance, are the remains of an old house and other buildings, which suggests that that may have been the original Auchinellan. The present house, with its converted farm buildings and cottages, is now a small self-catering holiday complex.

Auchinellan in past centuries was owned by a Campbell family who were Rectors of Kilmartin Parish and during the time of Colkitto and his Royalist Catholic band's killing and burning rampage through Argyll in the 1640's, he apparently made an exception and spared Auchinellan because of this religious connection. This is somewhat surprising as the owner then would probably have been Donald Campbell who was appointed Kilmartin's first Presbyterian minister in 1639. It was perhaps because of this past religious connection that James Wright, the owner in the mid-1900's, had a small but beautiful stone oratory built there.

James Wright was generous in many ways, and any tinkers or beggars who called there were always given a hand out of money. That is until he discovered that some of them were going straight to the pub to spend it and so he started giving vouchers to spend on groceries instead.

He was very keen to ensure that the Auchinellan land would not be sold on for forestry when he died as was happening to so much other land at that time, and so he left the place in trust to a very young niece until she reached maturity. She then took over and now runs the place with her husband.

Auchinellan in the past appears to have been a small hamlet. It had 61 inhabitants in the 1841 census and I notice a mention of it in the 1880's in the JP Court records for Lochgilphead, when a Cuthbert Jobblin from Auchinellan and a person from Ford were both fined 5/- for having no names on their carts and driving the horses with a single rein.

There is a collection of dance tunes called the Auchinellan Collection that has tunes called Auchinellan Jig, Crown House, Ederline, Farmhouse Jig and The Ford Strathspey.

Between Auchinellan and Ford, and at some distance to the left, can be seen a three metre high standing stone. This must have been dragged there by the local people with much sweat and effort from a cliff or rock face, and erected there sometime during the late Stone Age. The question is why? Was it erected to commemorate some important event, in memory of some big and important chief or possibly it was lined up with its missing companion stone on some distant celestial body by the intelligentsia of the day? The theories are many but the answer it seems has been buried with the people of that time. Near to it and until the late 1800's there was another smaller stone, but this fell down and for some reason it was moved to Auchinellan and now appears to be lost.

The next place we come to is the small village of Ford, which took its name from the old ford across the river there. Originally its Gaelic name was Anagra meaning Ford of the Hazels. In a 1723 list of people charged with contravening the Excise Acts, which would mean that they had been distilling, smuggling, or selling contraband goods, there are three noted from the Ford of Annacraw. But with the arrival of English names this became The Ford, or as it was often then called and spelled The Foord, and then it simply became Ford.

It was always a somewhat scattered small village or hamlet and possibly existed because it was at the junction of several old roads. During the cattle-droving days it would have seen quite a lot of through traffic of cattle, some of them heading for the local market at Kilmichael, but many others to the southern markets of Dumbarton and Crieff because the buyers from England, where most of the cattle were going to in these days, would not risk coming up into the lawless Highlands and so most of the cattle had to be driven to the safer southern markets. The cattle heading to the southern markets through Ford would mostly have come over the hill road from Kintraw and Craignish, with many of them having been shipped across from Jura and Islay. Ford had its own stop-over stance for cattle and travellers by the riverside just below the present bridge. The cattle going east and south would then have gone by way of Kilneuair over the Leckan Muir road to Auchindrain and on up round the head of Loch Fyne.

Ford also had twice yearly horse fairs and markets held on the first Thursday of August and the first Thursday of September. In the days when the horse was the main form of transport and power, they would have been important affairs. The Statistical Account of 1840 says that lambs, sheep and wool were also sold but many other things would be sold and traded by local and itinerant tradesmen on its various stalls.

These fair days would be holidays for the local people and as they were, apart from New Year's Day, possibly the only ones that they would get, these fair days would be eagerly looked forward to.

In 1830 a young Irish horse-dealer called John MacAlaster arrived at Ford for the September Fair with money to buy horses, but he was assaulted and robbed of fifteen pounds in a change house, by an Irish-born criminal from Campbeltown called Archibald Sproul. The outcome of this was that Sproul was tried before a jury at Inveraray Court, found guilty, and sentenced to life transportation.

Tourism from the 1800's onwards became a new source of income for Ford and the loch-side. One of the early tourists was the poet John Keats. In 1818 when he was a young man he and a more elderly companion embarked on a walking tour of Scotland. One day they set out from Inveraray, walked up Glen Aray, probably taking the shorter drove-road from Tynafead to Ardbrecknish and then down Lochaweside to Ford. Their route down the loch-side would have been by the old road that mostly ran at a much higher level than the present one and gave good views of the loch, which Keats said he was much impressed by. His companion, however, suffered badly from blistered feet from what would be a gruelling walk of some thirty miles, and on arriving at the Ford Inn they were only able to get hard-boiled eggs and oatcakes to eat, which they were heartily sick of by then. Next day they walked across the road to Kintraw and on to Oban. They then went across to Mull, Iona and Staffa, and on returning, walked as far as Fort William before abandoning the walk.

The Ford Inn apparently improved because in the 1840's the Parish Statistical Account says that 'there is one inn and two change-houses in the parish, viz. the inn at Kilmartin, which is well kept, and two public houses at The Ford, which are more orderly and better provided than formerly'. These public houses cum change houses at Ford probably also hired out and changed horses for travellers but the Ford Inn, mentioned by Keats, ceased to be an inn and in 1907 became the home of John Boyd, the first head forester for the new state-owned Inverliever

Forest. It was then given the name of Crown House and the other inn or change house, which was at the main road junction and was firstly known as the Auchinellan Inn and later, possibly when it was rebuilt in 1860, had its name changed to Ford Hotel. In the days when Loch Awe had a great reputation for its fishing this became a very popular fishing hotel and kept a small fleet of fishing boats for hire complete with ghillies. It carried on as an hotel but it has now been downsized and is run as a boarding house.

Close by the junction is a prominent hillock known as Cnoc an Ath, which means hillock of the ford. This seems to be a glacial feature known as a kame and these were formed by a build-up of sand or debris in a water-melted chamber within an ice-sheet. There are a good number of them in the Ford area. The reason for this, it seems, is that some twelve thousand years ago, almost at the end of the Ice Age, there was a period when the weather turned colder for a few centuries and an ice-sheet advanced back down Loch Awe to beyond Ford. When it melted it left behind these strange hillocks. The Cnoc an Ath one had an ancient stone burial cist inserted in its top and its capstone still lies there.

Ford in 1914 showing the Hotel, Post Office and Church.

It quite likely had stones on top of this but if so these have all been removed for other purposes.

Still in the village a road branches off to the left past a housing development, and then continues on as the old road over the hills to Kintraw and the coast. Near the Ford end of that there are three lots of ancient cup markings on rocks at the following map references: 8656 0382, 867 039 and 8653 0393. These would have been pecked into the rock with a hand-held hammer-stone and probably finished off by grinding, but here, on the exposed rock, they are very badly eroded and shallow as a result of thousands of years of weathering, and rings or any other features that they may have had are long gone. But what was their purpose? Again it is no use asking the archaeologists, as this has baffled them and everyone else, ever since modern man first became curious about them. They do appear to largely face the sun and one time I got the notion that if they were the right shape, rubbed smooth and coated with say polished copper, they could have been used like a parabolic dish, to concentrate the heat of the sun on one spot and make fire. This would have been magical to the people and a sign of the Sun God's power. To test this theory I made cardboard arcs of different diameters and went to test the shape of some well-preserved cups. Amazingly, the first place that I went to, the cups were almost perfect arcs but other sites that I tested were not, which seemed to kill that idea stone dead.

At a Justices of the Peace Court held at Lochgilphead in the 1880's four people from Ford were each fined 2/6d for allowing their pigs to dig up the road at Ford, which does not seem to say much for the state of the road at Ford in these days.

Ford Church does not have a long history and the present church is the first one on the site. It was built around 1850 and paid for by Poltalloch Estate and Church funds. It is not a very impressive church but it does have a very good stained-glass window, which was gifted by Henry Bruce of Ederline Estate in memory of his wife who died in 1882.

The Ederline Estate land begins across the river with Loch Ederline as the boundary between it and Auchinellan. Another land boundary is formed by the small burn that runs off from the river at right angles through the village and up into the foothills of Dun Dubh. In the 1800's this was the boundary between Auchinellan and Poltalloch Estate and despite the voracious buying up of land by Poltalloch Estate during the Malcolm owner's empire-building days, which resulted in them owning almost all the land around that part of Argyll, they never did manage to acquire Auchinellan or the larger adjoining Ederline Estate. But the fact that Ford Village land was owned by three different landlords may have hindered any development or enlarging of the village and it is only in the past century that it has expanded, firstly by the Forestry Commission building of houses for workers, and more recently and faster, by private enterprise. Unfortunately it has now lost its school, shop, hotel and post office but still retains its church although services are only held there every third week.

Past the church, where the ground slopes down towards the river bottom, was for many years a forest nursery growing young forest trees. It was started in 1907 by the Office of Woods and Forests who had been given a government mandate to pioneer and create timber-producing forests in the country. By then Poltalloch Estate was hard up and selling land and Inverliever Estate had been bought from them for £25,000 and a programme was started to create a large conifer forest on its land. This nursery was the source of the young trees for planting out in the forest and it was in operation until after the Second World War, during which time it produced millions of trees. Almost all of these early planted areas have been felled for timber, replanted and felled again, but a number of the early planted trees are still growing at a place called MacKenzie's Grove, which is past Kilmaha and was named after a retiring Inverliever forester.

Above the old nursery and at the edge of the conifer forest there was once the old settlement of Echlie, which according to Alan Begg in his excellent booklet The Deserted Settlements of Kilmartin dates

The early forestry nursery plots at Ford visible below and to the right of the Church.

from at least the 1700's. A letter written from Echlie by a John Campbell in 1825 included the following paragraph, 'It is mournful news that
I have to state. On Monday 31st October, about 10 o'clock forenoon
my beloved and most dutiful father departed this life after seven weeks
severe confinement. He was struck by a pain in the back taking a creel
of peats to the kiln for the purpose of drying corn. Dr McKellar
thought it to be a fever which has been prevalent in the Highlands this
year'. This is a well-written letter from a time when most of the people
would not be very literate, and it is not surprising to learn that the writer
went on to become a schoolmaster in Lismore.

In the 1841 census there were 13 inhabitants living at Echlie made
up of two families plus two female farm servants. The two adult men
there were listed as farmers. Shortly after that Poltalloch began clearing
all the small farmers from that stretch of their estate as their short leases
ran out and replaced them with one farmer and a new large-scale sheep
farm at Torranmor. A Mr Somerville from Lochgilphead, writing
sometime later said that 45 families were cleared from a nine mile
stretch of west Lochaweside to make way for sheep, and that was the
stretch between Ford and Dalavich.

The next places past Ford are Torranbeag and Torranmor, or Little
Torran and Big Torran, and both are mentioned from at least as far

back as 1685. In the 1841 census Torranmor lived up to its larger image by having 56 inhabitants to Torranbeag's 25, but Torranbeag later became the more important place as it became the site of the pier and terminus of the Loch Awe tourist steamers. It is situated at the southwest end of Loch Awe by An Lodan (The Pool) or, as it is more usually known nowadays, Ford Bay. This is a large lagoon-like sheltered basin with a narrow entrance channel called Caol Chaorann (Rowan Strait) but usually referred to now as the Narrows.

Only stumps remain of the old steamer pier but in the tourist season it was once quite a busy place with two steamer arrivals and departures daily and horse-drawn coaches connecting with them. The first passenger steamer to sail on the Loch Awe route was the *Queen of the Lake*, which was a converted wooden cargo boat. She began running summer trips from Ford, to a pier in the Pass of Brander, in 1863. Coaches connected with her at either end, with the Oban to Ardrishaig coach meeting her at Ford, and an Oban coach connecting with her in the Pass of Brander. A round trip from Oban to Glasgow by way of Ford, Ardrishaig and Helensburgh would then have cost about a pound.

Later in 1876 the larger iron-built *Lochawe* took over the run. She was built on the Clyde but had then been dismantled and transported to the loch-side where she was reassembled. Both boats had originally been owned by David and Alexander Hutcheson but in 1879 the firm was taken over by David MacBrayne who was founder of the MacBrayne Shipping Company. After the arrival of the *Lochawe*, the *Queen of the Lake* appears to have been redundant and she was beached on the shore between the pier and mouth of the river and presumably, after any valuable material had been removed she was left to decay and break up. When the level of the loch is very low some pieces of her keel can still be seen.

A big boost was given to the Loch Awe tourist cruises in 1880 when the Oban railway line was opened. As it ran past the north-east end of the loch, a village named Lochawe, and a station and pier called Loch Awe were built and this became the new terminus for the steamer

GRAND NEW PLEASURE EXCURSION FOR TOURISTS, DAILY,

ON LOCH-AWE,

By the New Saloon Steamer, "QUEEN OF THE LAKE."

LOCH-AWE comprises scenery unsurpassed in Scotland for its variety, beauty, or grandeur. There are twenty-four islands in it, with the ruins of four Castles and two Monasteries on them.

The Coach leaves Oban at 7-30 A,M., for Loch-Awe, returning same evening. Fares for Coach and Steamer for the day, 12s—Fees extra.

A Coach leaves Dalmally at 9-30 A.M., in time to meet the Steamer at Cladich, returning same evening. Fares for Coach and Steamer for the day's excursion, 6s.

Parties can dine on board the Steamer.

ABOVE: A tour aboard S.S. "Queen of the Lake" the first passenger steamer to sail on Loch Awe.

BELOW: S.S. "Loch Awe" seen here at Ford pier was introduced to the loch in 1876.

17

sailings. The railway brought many more passengers and new excursion possibilities. Folk from Glasgow, or the Clyde area, could catch a train in the morning to Loch Awe station, a steamer down Loch Awe, which is claimed to be the longest loch in Britain, then a coach to Ardrishaig and a steamer back to the Clyde, or of course, vice-versa. Up until 1908, coach and horses ran from Oban to connect with the steamer but in 1901, a company called The Oban Ford and Loch Awe Motor Syndicate ordered a special Albion motor car to be built, so there was a motor connection on the route, which, assuming that it ran, must have made it one of the first motor bus services around. After the arrival of the railway, the steamer *Lochawe* was based at the village of Lochawe during the summer cruising season, but she still returned to Ford for the winter. The five large squared beams, which she was drawn up on sideways out of the water can still be seen on the Ederline side of the entrance to Ford Bay.

The Loch Awe tours proved popular and the *Lochawe* was soon

An early image of Loch Awe Station and book stall following the opening of the Callander and Oban line from Dalmally to Oban in 1880.

joined by the *Countess of Breadalbane*, which was owned by the Loch Awe Hotel Company. The two boats ran from the Loch Awe terminus to Ford at different times, and although they were primarily tourist boats, they were also duty bound to pick up or drop off local passengers or goods, at the many piers along the loch-side. To get a steamer to stop, a flag was simply hoisted on the pier. These steamers also had their on-board dining facilities and pipers, and any couples going on honeymoon got a red carpet reception.

There were stables beside the pier at Ford for the coach horses and the ones that had travelled from Ardrishaig would be changed before the return journey. Captain Donald Carmichael, a captain on the *Lochawe*, built for himself and his family the prominent cottage that overlooks Ford Bay. Both steamers ran until the First World War stopped such tourist trips and they were then laid up. After the war the *Lochawe* did not resume sailing and the *Countess* carried on alone. She was replaced by a new *Countess of Breadalbane* in 1936. This new boat

S.S. "Countess of Breadalbane", put onto the loch in 1882 and capable of carrying 100 passengers, at Ford pier in 1933.

was diesel-powered and at 106 tons, the largest to have operated on the loch. On her daily trip she left Loch Awe pier at 11.40 am, called in at Portsonachan and Taycreggan on the way to Ford, then returned at 3.00 pm. She also did some evening cruises. She was laid up during the Second World War and afterwards commenced running again in 1948, but folks' holiday ideas had changed and they wanted more than loch cruises so she ceased running in 1951.

This was not the end of the *Countess* by any means, as she was stripped of as much weight as possible, winched up to the road west of Lochawe village on a specially constructed ramp, loaded on to two large motor trailers and transported to Loch Fyne. There she was re-launched and towed back to the Clyde, where she was originally built, and after being fitted out again, went into service around the Firth of Clyde for many years. She was then sold, became the *Countess of Kempock* and for two seasons ran cruises from Mull to Staffa and Iona. Then sold again, she was transported to Loch Lomond and ran cruises there for many years under the name of

The first motor passenger vessel, T.S.M.V. "Countess of Breadalbane" introduced in 1936, boasted a promenade deck the full length of the ship with an observation lounge at the forward end.

T.S.M.V. "Countess of Breadalbane" is carefully managed onto a ramp over the railway line below St Conan's Kirk as she leaves Loch Awe in 1952.

Countess Fiona, until she was finally laid off and eventually scrapped.

An entry in the Parish Records of 1727 records how a Mary McLlayuinn appealed for her name to be cleared of the slander of witchcraft, which she said was being spread about by John McNicol who was change-keeper at Ford. He apparently had said that Archibald McCaik of Portinnisherrich and Margaret McCallum of Arinechtan had seen this Mary McLlayuinn of Auchinellan standing in the march burn between Torranbeag and Torranmor throwing a handful of water toward Torranmor and two towards Torranbeg a short time before cattle at both places became ill. Her name was apparently cleared and the records say that all parties were rebuked.

An old gravestone at Kilneuair Church is in memory of a Duncan McDonald of Torranbeg and his family and the inscription on it ends by saying 'whose family are residing in the above saide place this 500 years'. I don't know the date of the stone but there are descendants of this Duncan McDonald living in Canada and one of them recently paid a visit to both the gravestone and Torranbeag.

In the late 1700's, cultivation on the local farms still seems to have been rather crude, despite the 1790's Parish Statistical Account saying that 'ploughs were much more efficient, now that a professional plough-maker was employed'. The ploughs were still, however, being largely made of wood and required four horses to pull them with a second man walking backwards in front of the horses to guide them. But if we move forward 50 years to the next Statistical Account it says that the farmers now have 'a well-modelled and constructed iron plough, drawn by a pair of horses and easily managed by one man performs double the work, and doubly better done in half the time'. This despite its seemingly late arrival in the parish must have been the Small's plough designed by him in the 1760's with the curved type of mouldboard that is still being used on present day ploughs. But it should also be noted that by then the horses used were bigger and stronger.

In the mid-1800's both Torranmor and Torranbeag were largely cleared of their people by the Poltalloch Estate. A farmhouse and steadings were built at Torranmor and it became one of the new, mainly sheep farms, that were taking over in most of the local estates, and were usually leased out to incoming sheep farmers from the south. Tenants of this farm from at least the 1880's were Thomas Richmond and later his son Logie who farmed there up until the 1960's. Logie Richmond was a very innovative farmer and one of the first car owners in the area. It is said that when he needed a new car he went down to London, bought one and drove it back home.

In the early 1880's two Torran boys were out ferreting rabbits on the steep hillside above the bay. Their ferret had killed a rabbit and stayed down in the hole with it and they were digging to retrieve the ferret when they found three ancient metal objects. They took them home and it seems that they were given to Henry Bruce of Ederline, who took them to the Society of Antiquaries of Scotland, where they were exhibited and identified as being two large bronze spear-heads and a small socketed gouge from the Bronze Age. One spearhead and the gouge are in the National Museum in Edinburgh but what happened to the other spearhead is not known.

Strangely no one investigated the site further until 1962 when

Calum Crawford, Ian Cummings, Logan Richmond and John McKillop at Oban market in the 1970's.

Marion Campbell, the local historian and archaeologist, was mapping and recording the sites of old archaeological finds and she visited Logie Richmond, the farmer in Torran, to see if he could tell her where this site, marked down as Craig Beoch, was. Logie, she luckily discovered, was a younger brother of one of the two boys who had found the bronze objects. At 85 he was not able to go up the steep hillside but directed her to Alasdair Carmichael (a son of the Ford steamer captain) who lived at Torranbeag and to whom Logie had once shown the site of the discovery.

Alasdair, Marion and Mary Sandeman then climbed the steep forested hillside to the place beside Creag Beathach (Crag of the Wild Beast) and there, in a mass of large jumbled boulders, Alasdair pointed out what he thought was the spot beneath a large perched rock, but it did not look a promising place and they searched around for about an hour without discovering anything. I was told Alasdair had stopped and started to fill his pipe, to help discourage the midges, when he noticed a metal object lying below the original rock, and it turned out to be a bronze ring or bracelet. Further careful searching among the needle litter produced two socketed axes, a second ring, a fragment of bronze and a socketed knife, which again was resting on a stone under the original rock. The next day a third axe-head was found among the forest debris. Marion then obtained permission to do some more invasive searching of the site but her excavations yielded no other artefacts. She says in her notes that there could be more lying below the jumbled boulders because she thought the bronze objects were originally hidden in a rock shelter that had collapsed and slid downhill.

The boys, I think, must have been digging for their ferret to the side of these jumbled rocks. They said that they had dug six feet but Henry Bruce reckoned the depth as being a foot and a half. This discrepancy can be explained by the fact that the boys' six feet would be six feet into the rabbit's burrow and not six feet down.

These finds are now, along with the two original ones, in the Ed-

The Torran Hoard of Bronze Age artefacts. © Kilmartin Museum Trust.

inburgh National Museum and have been dubbed the 'Torran Hoard' but some very good replicas can be seen in the local Kilmartin House Museum. These bronze objects, which range from good condition to very old and worn, are also of different styles and it is thought that they could have been the stock of some bronze-age trader or metal-worker that was hidden for safe-keeping and never recovered, or could this spot, by the massive ridge of rock that overlooks the bay, have been some kind of sacred site and were these valuable bronze objects, gifts or sacrificial offerings to the people's gods?

An early building near there would have been the Tower of Caol Chaorann or Castle Torran, as it was called on a 1790's map, whose ruined remains are situated on a small rocky mound by the loch-side north of the entrance to Ford Bay. This tower certainly appears to have been a defensive building and probably dates from the unsettled times of late BC and early AD. This must have been a dangerous time to live in judging by the number of defensive buildings people built. Some of the stones from this tower were at one time used to build a jetty and a boathouse, now ruined, in the small bay below.

From a much earlier date than the 'tower' is the three metre plus standing stone at Torran. This has had a cross carved on its side in early Christian times to Christianise what would be regarded as a pagan memorial. The name Torran means small hill and this name would seem to refer to the hill to the east of the farm, which has on its summit the scattered ruins of a dun or small fort called Dun Toisich (Fort of the Chief). It probably dates from the Iron Age but who the Chief was and who built it is unknown. He certainly chose a site with an outstanding view for his dun and it must have looked quite impressive when its walls were standing. However the location, with its superb view of the surrounding countryside, would have been chosen as a defensive site to give good warning of any approaching hostile band.

A new Torran farmhouse and steadings were built a few decades ago and the old farmhouse and its attached steadings were converted into council-owned flats. Recently the farm moved again to a site higher up the hillside and along the old road that ran towards Inverliever because the land surrounding Torranmor Farm is being sold off as building sites by the owner and the farm buildings have been moved out of this new development. So Torranbeag and Torranmor have now become joined up by new housing.

A new development was begun by the loch-side at Torranbeag consisting of a restaurant, lounge bar, shop, backpacker hostel and function room by the owners of Torran Farm, Joachim and Sheila Brolly. The low-lying site at the water's edge was raised to the required height and ready for building in January 2007, when there was a spell of very wet weather and the loch level rose and rose until the site of the proposed complex, roads and car parks were all under a good two feet of water. This luckily happened before any building had started and it seems that, with a long narrow loch like Loch Awe, the head of the loch at Ford can rise higher than its outlet, which is controlled by a barrage in the Pass of Brander and that is where the high water levels used in planning would have been taken from. The Torran Bay Hostel opened in July 2012.

Travelling up the loch-side from Torran one passes Ford Gun Club's clay pigeon shooting site. This is an organisation that has been in existence for at least a hundred and thirty plus years. Where they shoot now is close to what used to be called Coal Harbour, which was where local coal was discharged from cargo boats in the days of steam transport on the loch. Such cargo mostly came by rail to Loch Awe Station and was then transported down the loch by steam barge.

It will be noticed that I, like other locals, refer to the Ford end of the loch as the bottom end and the other end the top end. This is not really true because the loch discharges out at the Pass of Brander end and Ford is therefore, correctly speaking, at the head of the loch. I don't know why the head of the loch should be called the bottom end, but I think that it must simply be because it is the south end. In the

Ford gun club in 1880. The brothers in light coloured tweeds were gamekeepers at Inverliever. The club continues to exist at date of publication.

next bay past the shooting site the stone foundations of an old crannog can be seen, and in the muddy bay before Inverliever Point, or Island as it gets called, there is a circle of foundation stones visible when the loch is low, but these are of fairly modern origin because they were the foundation stones of an estate duck-shooting hide.

There are a number of peninsulas around Loch Awe, which are called islands and the reason for this is that Loch Awe's level was lowered some seven feet in 1818 by dredging in the Pass of Brander, and places that were islands, or virtually so before then, no longer are. On top of a rise on the hillside opposite the bay at map reference 890 052 are the robbed remains of an old oval-shaped burial cairn with a seven feet long sunken burial cist. This is very unusual because burial cists were usually about half that length due to bodies normally being buried in a crouched position or cremated before burial.

CHAPTER TWO

INVERLIEVER, KILMAHA AND CRUACHAN

The next place that we come to is Inverliever (Mouth of the Liever) and it too consisted of a big and a little settlement in the past. Inverlievermor was situated among the new house builds to the left of the river and beside the old road. This road ran up the side of the Liever Burn, swung round to the left and across the hillside to Torranmor, and it would have once been the main loch-side road. It has now been made into an access road, which serves the new houses and follows the old route through to Torran passing a stone-built well called the Angel's Well on the way. The reason for that name is not known. The new farm steadings are also on this road. They were built in a large quarry that was opened to supply hard-core for the house roads and the new development at the loch-side. Two new houses have also been built beside the old gamekeeper's cottage and there are quite a number scattered around on what was Mr Brolly's ground.

The ruins of the old Inverlievermor settlement show the remains of a number of buildings, but only one still has its walls standing and one gable-end intact. This was a large building 50 feet in length with no sign of interior walls and only one doorway. It is suggested that this was originally a chapel that was later put to more mundane uses and it certainly is a puzzling ruin. Out from its still standing gable-end is a large upright boulder that is in line with other upright stones and so appears to have once been part of a wall. This boulder has been called the Sun Stone because on its side it has a

28

large sunken disc with a raised centre to it, and it was said that faint incised rays radiated out from the disc. These rays I suspect were scratched on the stone to make the 'sun' appear more convincing. There is doubt as to whether the disc is man-made or not, because despite it being said that there is an outer ring to the disc and faint cup marks on the stone, similar discs are said by geologists to be natural. A pit among the old building foundations too is somewhat puzzling, but it looks as if it could have been the result of quarrying limestone rock for lime burning in later times.

Inverliever was for several centuries owned by a branch of the powerful Campbell Clan, and Langland's map of 1801 shows a mansion house there and the estate still being the property of a C Campbell Esq. A story connected with Inverliever, tells how in 1495 a young child of four years old had been left the title and lands of Cawdor, which were situated to the east of Inverness. The then Earl of Argyll had got himself appointed her guardian and he wanted young Morella, or Marion, in Inveraray where she would be under his control, so he sent Campbell of Inverliever with an armed force of 60 men to collect her and bring her back to him. Things had gone according to plan and they had got the child and were well on their way back when they were overtaken by the child's Cawdor relatives with a large force bent on recovering the girl. Inverliever, however, managed to get his young charge and six men away unseen and to fool the pursuers he dressed up a sheaf of corn in the girl's clothes and then turned and engaged the pursuers.

The Campbells suffered badly in the fight that followed and lost many men including, it is said, six of Inverliever's sons but they held off the attackers long enough for the child to be got safely away before retreating. This encounter is said to be the occasion when the phrase 'it's a far cry to Loch Awe' was first used after someone had said that he wished that they had some more of the men from back there to help in the fight, and that was the reply he received. So the operation was successful and Morella was delivered safely to Inveraray where she grew up and later married a suitable Campbell husband. This gave the Campbells ownership and control of another sizable piece of land and property, and allowed the future Campbell owners to call themselves the Campbells of Cawdor.

In the list of rebels who had supported the Earl of Argyll's 1685 rebellion against the King and joined up with his army at Tarbert were three from Inverlievermor, three from Inverlieverbeg and four from Glenliver, which was an old settlement situated about two miles further up the glen. During the occupation after the rebellion the Inverliever people were apparently robbed of almost everything valuable, and later Campbell of Inverliever claimed £6,339 16/- 8d Scots from Lochnell, Inverawe and the Tutor of Appin who were the people that he held responsible for his and his tenant's losses, but I do not know whether he was successful or not. Glenliver is marked on Langland's map of 1801 but it must have been abandoned or cleared before the 1841 census. It states Inverlievermor had 19 inhabitants and Inverlieverbeg 11.

A famous soldier who had a connection with Inverliever was General Sir Colin Campbell of Crimean and Indian Mutiny fame. His father had come from Inverliever but his name was MacLiver. The MacGregors claim he is one of their clan and it seems that an ancestor must have adopted the name MacLiver during the times when the name MacGregor was outlawed. When Sir Colin was a young man his uncle, who was a Campbell, had bought a commission for him in the British Army, but it was under the name of Campbell and he was stuck with that. He went on to have an extraordinary career and saw action in many parts of the World. He was an aide to Wellington at Waterloo and then was the very popular commander in charge of the Highland Brigade, which was responsible for the 'Thin Red Line' that stood up against and defeated the Russian cavalry at Balaclava.

The Times correspondent of the day who witnessed that battle wrote, 'As the Russian cavalry on the left of their line crowned the hill across the valley they perceived the Highlanders drawn up at a distance of some half mile. They halted and squadron after squadron came up from the rear. The Russians drew breath for a moment and then in one grand line charged towards Balaklava. The ground flew beneath their horse's feet, gathering speed at every stride, they dashed on towards the thin red line tipped with a line of steel. The commander of the Highland Brigade, one of the greatest military leaders of all time, Sir Colin Campbell, gave his 93rd a final brief address as the Russians approached. 'There is no retreat from here men. You must die where you stand.' To which his right hand man, John Scott, replied: 'Ay, ay Sir Colin, an' needs be, we'll do that!' and these words were echoed down the line. The Sutherland Highlanders stood their ground, and, at 250 yards, opened fire on the Russian cavalry. Their fire met with resounding success as the cavalry began to split up and turn round in headlong retreat. Balaklava had been saved'. Sometime after this Sir Colin was sent to India to take command of the British forces during the Indian Mutiny and he was the person who led the British force that relieved the city of Lucknow after it had been besieged for four and a half months, and there it is said that he marched in at the head of his men with the pipers playing 'The Campbells are Coming'.

The local meal-mill was at one time located at Inverliever and powered by a water-wheel driven by water channelled from the river, and as was usual the estate tenants would all have had to take their grain there to be ground. At the present time a hydro-electric scheme has been built at Inverliever and is using the river's water taken from high up in the glen. The generating station, complete with solar roof panels, is beside the entrance to Inverliever and a spin off from it is that it is providing a plug-in point for electric cars.

In Victorian times Inverliever became a sporting estate. The

Inverliever Lodge, built by the Malcolms of Poltalloch circa 1840-1850 replacing an earlier house of the 1750's, was demolished as part of an army exercise in 1966 having been deemed too costly to repair.

mansion house along with its shooting, hunting and fishing rights was leased out by Poltalloch to wealthy families who wanted to be part of the then very popular fashion of owning or leasing a shooting lodge and sporting estate, with all the prestige and social standing that went with it. This sporting estate period also carried on for some time after the estate was sold for forestry as the land was only slowly being turned into forest. In late Victorian times it was the country house of John Wingfield Malcolm, who was a JP and MP in Kent and later in Argyll. He inherited Poltalloch Estate and was made Baron Malcolm of Poltalloch but he died not long afterwards and with no family of his own to inherit the title it was discontinued.

During the Second World War the mansion house was used as a hostel for women forestry workers who were helping in the drive to produce much needed timber for the mines. After the war had ended it housed returning servicemen who had been promised a career in forestry and were helping to provide the manpower for a big expansion in afforestation. The house afterwards lay empty for a period until in the 1960's it was sold for a nominal sum to a London school trust as an outdoor centre. It was found however that it would be too costly to repair and so it was demolished and chalet accommodation was built on the site. This accommodation was used for a good many years by a number of London schools whose teachers and pupils came up to it for a week's course of outdoor activities and schoolwork. However this Inverliever outdoor school has now unfortunately been forced to close due to lack of money. The buildings have been bought and are now used as living accommodation and for other purposes.

Fish farming on Lochaweside was started at Inverliever by a Mr Fairweather and his son in the early 1970's. Beside the loch they started raising young rainbow trout in a large pressurized plastic-bubble building, and then reared them up to market size in a series of stepped brick-built ponds, or raceways, with the water for the scheme pumped from the loch by electric power. Later this operation was taken over by a subsidiary of the Shell Petroleum Company who ran it until an outbreak of disease caused a halt to fish farming there. After this the site was bought by the Willis family and converted into a plant nursery with a large expanse of polytunnels growing heathers and other plants for the wholesale market. This heather-growing operation then greatly expanded at Inverliever and elsewhere, and under the trade name of Highland Heathers they operated four nurseries producing millions of plants annually for the wholesale market with Inverliever being the headquarters of the operation. Unfortunately in August 2012 Highland Heathers went into liquidation and all of its 43 employees were paid off.

The next place that we come to on the loch-side is Arihamish, which in 1685 was home to three rebel supporters of the outlawed Earl of Argyll. As a punishment for this they had their livestock confiscated. They were Dougald mc Ollvorie who lost 9 cows and 1 horse, John mc Ilvorie who lost 6 cows, 1 horse and 1 mare, and Lucas McIndeor who lost 5 cows and 1 mare. However by the 1841 census, it had only five residents and was no longer a farm (almost all its land was forested) but still had the farmhouse and two cottages. Later it was to become one of Poltalloch Estate's new sheep farms.

Past Arihamish the road leaves the loch-side and climbing up enters the forest and does not return to the loch-side for about another six miles. But before we leave the loch-side I would like to quote what the Rev Hugh Campbell has to say about Loch Awe and its fish in the 1790's Kilmartin Statistical Account, 'It abounds with trouts and salmon. There is a peculiar species of fish in it called 'black trouts', which are short and thick, black in the skin and red in the fish. The incumbent has seen one of them that weighed 16 lb and when cut up, two small trouts were taken out of it entire, one of them measuring 12 inches, the other 10. This fishing, however, has not hitherto been so very productive, as to make it an object of much public notice'. This however was to change and 50 years later the next Statistical Account says, 'Loch Awe is celebrated for salmon and trout fishing'.

Through the conifer forest below the road and beside a small burn I was shown a small ruined place that I was told was Slochd a Bodach (Hollow of the Old Man), but I have been unable to find any other reference to it. A short way through the forest from there is the abandoned settlement of Arinechtan (High Pasture of Nechtan). Nechtan appears to have been an old Pictish name that was held by both a king and a Scottish saint and the name is still around today but in a different form. It changed firstly to Nachtan, then to MacNachtan and finally to MacNaughton and the clan had a castle on Fraoch Eilean and lands towards the other end of Loch Awe.

Arinechtan is mentioned in 1685 when three rebels from there had their 25 head of cattle confiscated and in the 1841 census it had 16 inhabitants. There are the visible ruins of what had been quite a large building and a later corrugated iron and wood bungalow nearby, which I think had been built as a shepherd's house and survived until the mid-1900's.

In 1790 a dyke-builder called Alexander Crawford lived at Arinechtan and his name crops up in a number of local Justices of the Peace Court cases, which was where disputes and not too serious criminal cases were taken for judgement, firstly he was claiming money from a certain Dugald Blue who he had taken on as a partner to help build a march dyke between Arinechtan and Kilmaha, but it seems that Blue had abandoned the job and owed him money. In the same year Crawford was in court twice on one day. Firstly because Hugh Downie in Cruachan claimed £2-10/- that was owed to him for a horse and Crawford was ordered to pay. Then Crawford claimed 19/-9d from Thomas Hall, tacksman in Brenchoille, Lochfyneside, for work done in that township but the outcome is unknown. Three years later Crawford was again involved in a court case when Colin Campbell the laird at Cruachan claimed for damage done by him to the road at Kilmaha when he was building a dyke there. He was fined 2/-6d, which was to be used to repair the road. In 1790 the local JP's for that part of Mid Argyll were Dugald Campbell of Kilmartin, another Dugald Campbell from Ederline and Neil Campbell of Inverliever, which illustrates just how much Lochaweside and elsewhere was being run by the Campbells.

A short distance past Arinechtan is a car park and the starting off point for 'Duncan's Walk', which takes you to Dun Corrach where from that height a magnificent view of much of Loch Awe and the surrounding countryside can be seen. Duncan's Walk is named after Duncan MacDougal from Kilchrenan who was a long time forest worker in Inverinan and Inverliever forests. Past the Duncan's Walk car park we climb higher and then drive across a very steep hillside with a drop of hundreds of feet down to Loch Awe, and it was here I think in 1971, when the trees on the hillside had been felled, that a film company filmed scenes for *To Catch a Spy*, which is a Kirk Douglas spy thriller and has a sequence of a car plunging off the road and rolling down into the loch below. Actually the car did not reach the loch when first filmed but that was no problem as they simply filmed it rolling into the loch and joined the two bits together. A short distance on from here there is a tiny burn, which is the boundary between the Kilmartin and the Kilchrenan and Dalavich Parishes. It is also the boundary between the Mid Argyll and Lorn districts and it was probably the boundary between Arinechtan and Kilmaha.

Further on we come to a car park and viewpoint giving a great view of Loch Awe and the hills and the forest of Eredine on its eastern side. Below us on a hillside terrace, but hidden by the trees, are the twin houses of Kilmaha and lower still and close inshore in the loch is Kilmaha Island or Innis Stiuire (the Steer Island). This latter name is from the days of the steamboats when the boats used to set their course to the outside of the island.

There are ruins of a small rectangular building on the island but I think that a more interesting thing there is a scattered lot of somewhat flattish stones by the water's edge at the south-west corner of the island. I think these could be remains from a very early Christian beehive-cell type of building, which would be quite appropriate as Kilmaha is named after St Mochoe of Nendrum also known as the 'Silent One'. He lived in the Century before St Columba and died about the year 490. If a religious site was founded there by him it would be very early indeed. The fact that the stones are scattered can be explained by the fact that the loch level appears to have been at a low level as shown by the low-lying rock carvings at nearby Fiddler's Point, and the small and also low-lying Priest Island with its small stone priest's cell. Gradually through a build-up of debris in

Early Christian rock carving at Kilmaha of a Maltese ring-cross flanked by two robed figures with heads resembling birds.

the Pass of Brander the water level rose and that would allow storm waves to break up the beehive structure and scatter the stones. In 1818 the loch level was lowered by seven feet by the Breadalbane Estates who dredged the debris from the Pass of Brander outlet.

The place usually associated with St Mochoe is the nearby Fiddler's Point , which is at map reference 937 078. It was the site of an ancient graveyard and has the faint remains of two oval-shaped enclosures or buildings. The bedrock at the actual point has two monk-like cowled figures carved into it with an enclosed cross between them but very little remains of the old graveyard. Why the name Fiddler's Point? It is puzzling as it is a very isolated place and not where anyone would conceivably be playing the fiddle. The only explanation I can give is that the name may be connected with the rock carvings there and the enclosed cross that is sometimes called a mirror symbol because it re-sembles a hand-held mirror. It may be that someone once called this a fiddle, hence the name Fiddler's Point.

Tradition has it that the old graveyard there had at one time been the burial place of the Campbells of Inverliever. There were two very old upright stones with solid crosses carved in a similar style to the carving on the rock, but conifer trees that had apparently been planted during the early Inverliever Forest years blew down in the big 1968 gale and broke the head off one of the crosses, which somehow went missing before it was decided to move the crosses to Dalavich Church for safe-keeping, and if there were ever any carved grave-slabs these too have disappeared. One culprit could be Poltalloch Estate who moved or 'stole' any interesting carved stones from similar old graveyards on their estates to Poltalloch.

On the loch-side, between Fiddler's Point and the island, there was a small ruined lime-kiln, but that unfortunately was destroyed during forest operations. The limestone used to make the lime appears to have come from a surprisingly neat square-cut quarry at Fiddler's Point, and the fuel for burning the limestone would, if it was in operation before the railway reached the loch-side in 1880, have come from the trees on the hillside behind. The lime produced would almost certainly have been transported from there by boat. The ancient name of Kilmaha, along with a great many others on the loch-side, is at present being blatantly used on the internet to advertise all kinds of Argyll-based businesses.

I have been given the Militia List that was compiled for 1803/04 for the Parish of Dalavich. It records all the men who were liable for service: Durren 6, 5 farmers, plus a herd. Eredine 2, both fishers. Smithtown 1, herd. Kaimes 8, 3 farmers, 4 fishermen, 1 tailor. Portinnisherrich 4, 2 ferrymen, 1 smith, 1 shoemaker. Ardchonell 3, 1 servant, 1 herd, 1 workman. Kilmucha 3, all farmers. Cruachan 5, 1 farmer, 2 fishers, 1 shoemaker and 1 crofter. New York 3, 1 vinter (who must have been to do with hotel across the loch), 1 fisher, 1 workman. Barmadie 2, 1 given as esquire, 1 dealer in cattle. Barinlian 4, 1 dealer in cattle, 1 weaver and 1 tailor, 1 workman. Miln of

Avich 1 dyer. Drimdarroch 3, 2 weavers, 1 workman. Kilmun 3, 2 farmers, 1 labourer. Glen 2, 1 weaver, 1 workman. Duninerain 3, 1 farmer, 1 taylor, 1 labourer. Kilmun, Loch Avich, just has 'younger'. Narachan 1 cattle dealer. Duaig 1, farmer. Maolacha 3, 1 farmer, 1 workman, 1 herd.

A mile from Kilmaha on this public road, which is not dignified by being given a road number on road maps, has us descending the Long Brae, and here in 2007 a pair of ospreys surprisingly nested on an exposed tree with a broken top about 50 yards from the road and are still nesting there. At the foot of the Long Brae an old forest road leads downhill. If we follow this down and back to Cruachan Burn we come to a surviving group of some of the early trees planted by the Forestry Commission 90 years ago. Many are Sitka spruce and the largest of these has a girth of 16 feet. This group of trees is called MacKenzie's Grove and the reason for this is that at Ian Mackenzie' retiral, he was the Inverliever Chief Forester, some of the local forestry top brass were giving a boozy farewell to him there and they decided to call the large trees after him. They pledged that the trees would not be felled and so far this has been the case.

Cruachan is the name of the next place that we come to and this was also the war cry of the Campbell Clan. They were a clan who originated from Lochaweside and it is said by some people that their war cry of Cruachan refers to this place, but there seems to be no historical reason or associated story about the place that would account for this. I think that it is much more likely to have come from the mountain of that name, which is a very prominent feature from their old seat and stronghold of Innischonnel Castle across the loch. Cruachan is mentioned in 1685, spelt Crowchan, when five of its residents who had been out with the Earl's rebel army claimed indemnity from prosecution. They said that they were 'pressed' into supporting the Rebellion. In 1692 it had eight fencible men, ie men of military age, which was reckoned then as being from the age of

16 to 60. In the 1841 census it had 31 people living there. But it was later cleared of its people and only one house survived and was lived in until the 1940's. Cruachan was also in earlier days an estate. Langland's map of 1801 shows a mansion house there and the owner a C Campbell Esq who would appear to be the same person who owned Inverliever, and so this would be at that time a part of Inverliever Estate.

In the early 1900's there was a great deal of concern in Government and other bodies about the shortage of timber trees growing in the country and the Office of Woods and Forests was given the task of trying to rectify this. They bought Inverliever Estate in 1907 and set out to create a large conifer forest there. This was something that had never been done on such a large scale in the west of Scotland and much had to be learned. A considerable amount of pioneering work was done in Inverliever Forest's early days.

There were four main conifer forest trees grown in the country then but of these European larch suffered badly from canker, European silver fir was being attacked by a deadly aphid, and of the other two, Scot's pine required dry conditions and Norway spruce, which was the main tree planted in the forest in its early days, required good ground to grow properly, so it was a pleasant and welcome surprise when it was found that Sitka spruce from the west coast of North America loved the wet, peaty and rather poor soils in the west of Scotland. This is the reason that it is now the main forest tree planted around Lochaweside and in all the country's wetter regions.

Although Ford was the head forester's residence and the site of the forest office, Cruachan was for much of the time the working hub of the forest. A worker's hostel was built at Cruachan in the forest's early days. It housed forestry workers and usually some newly-trained foresters who were awaiting postings to other forests. This building was built of wood, sheathed with corrugated iron and was where a car park and a picnic site are now. Access to it was difficult as the road to Ford was only suitable for horse and cart and so people and goods were mostly transported by boat. In 1933 when I was a toddler part of this building was occupied by my family. My mother was the cook and housekeeper there and my father worked in the forest. On Hallowe'en night, when most of the folk were out guising and my father was staying overnight at Ford, the building caught fire probably due to an unattended candle in a bedroom. The fire was well alight before anyone knew about it and the remaining folk and my family had to get out fast. At least that was what I was told as I was only two at the time.

Almost everything was destroyed and the guisers had to stay in their fancy get-ups for some time. One of them, Jock MacLaren, had just been about to get married and had cashed in a large insurance policy so that he and his future wife could go and buy furniture and goods for their house. This money was in his room when he was out guising. The next day he telephoned his fiancée and told her that they would have to cancel the wedding because he did not even have proper clothes to wear. But she said they weren't doing that and they would get married as planned so with a lot of help from friends and others and the £25 that the folks were given by the Forestry Commission to buy essentials they were able to get married.

During the Second World War some Newfoundland lumberjacks came to work in the forest and they built themselves twin log cabins on the old hostel site. These were of upright logs and had the gaps stuffed with moss. However they did not stay very long and after they had left the cabins were lined and slightly improved. Then they were occupied by five girls and a supervisor from the Women's Land Army Timber Corp who came to work in the forest. One of them, Anna Henderson, later wrote a very glowing account of the interesting and enjoyable time they had spent at Cruachan. The five girls, she said, first met at MacBrayne's Depot in Glasgow and then travelled by bus to Lochgilphead where they met their supervisor Anne Reid. From Lochgilphead they travelled by forestry lorry to Ford on Loch Awe and then embarked on the Inverliever Forest's boat called the Coileach for a trip of some eight miles up the loch before disembarking at a jetty made of spruce logs. From there they had to walk up a muddy track through the trees dressed in their very unsuitable town clothes. Apparently one of the women even wore a Deana Durban hat. Their accommodation consisted of two crude log cabins joined together and devoid of any mod cons. Even the wood fuel for heating and cooking had to be sawn up by them. Rather dismayed by all this they decided that they would stay for a month and then ask for a transfer but all that was to change later.

On Monday morning they were each given a small saw and shown how to brash the lower branches off the trees to allow access for thinning the trees for their timber. At first their work was all in the forest, which they enjoyed. They lit fires to boil their billy cans of tea, and even found a pool in one of the streams where they could bathe. Later they went further afield, often travelling by boat, and they planted young trees on the hillsides, peeled the bark from felled trees, weeded young trees in the nursery, worked in the pit-prop yard across the loch and in the summer there was the bracken to be cut to stop it choking out the young trees. These jobs were of course all new to them but they soon got the hang of them and had an enjoyable time. The camaraderie, Anna Henderson said, was wonderful.

Their change of attitude had begun on their first day. Young Peggy McEachan, who worked in the forest, arrived and showed them how to work things and invited them up to her home at Barmaddy Farm. They became very good friends with both Peggy and her mother and it became like a second home. They discovered that there was a social scene with dances for various causes supporting the war effort being held in the surrounding villages, but these were all a long way from the very isolated Cruachan. They sent home for bicycles and on Friday

*Colonel and Mrs Young amid the dancers enjoying a Saturday night dance in
the Barn at Portsonachan Hotel about 1952.*

after work they would set out for one of these dances probably at Kilmartin or Portsonachan. To get to Kilmartin they had to cycle 12 miles
with the first part through the forest being on an atrocious unmade and
hilly road. On the return journey from the dance they often stopped
off at Ford Pier and spent the rest of the night in the forestry boat then
travelled back with it next day. This generally being a Saturday meant
that they could spend the day in bed and only lose half a day's pay. Very
popular dances were held at Portsonachan but to get there they had to
be rowed across the loch to Portinnisherrich, and then hire Alec
MacLeod's taxi to take them there. Once they travelled to Oban and
went to a dance there, but on returning to their hotel in war-time Oban
found that it contained a lot of strange-looking people and so they all
spent the night in one room for safety.

They reckoned their supervisor was a woman of great courage because she accepted a dare to spend the night in Innischonnel Castle on its island across the loch, which they had been told was haunted. She had set out in a boat and was equipped to spend the night but when she returned safely the next morning she would not tell them about her experience. The local folks believed she had been joined there by her boyfriend, which was probably true. The writer, Anne Henderson, went on to say that their adventures and camaraderie were fantastic but after one and a half years they all went their different ways. It had been a truly marvellous time but it could not last for ever. These log cabins were later occupied by other women workers, but at the end of the war they were left lying empty until somehow they caught fire and were burned down.

In 1968 a great gale, classed as a hurricane, hit the west of Scotland and in Inverliever Forest it wreaked tremendous havoc. Most of the trees were then quite large and vulnerable. Whole stretches of the forest were completely flattened and a great deal of the rest was partly blown down. It was not all disaster as most of the timber was still usable if it could be felled, extracted and got to the mills before it started to decay. The fact that most of the trees were uprooted and not broken helped too as they would stay alive for some time.

A deadline of three years to clear the timber was set and much manpower and machinery was brought in to do this. It was fortunate too that forestry work was then becoming mechanized with power-saws, Isaacson winches, skidders and timber-loading cranes doing the work that had previously been done by men and horses. As the Scottish mills could not cope with all the timber that was coming from the forests much of the Inverliever wood was sold at the road-sides to saw-milling firms from Northern Ireland. For three years the forest was a very busy place indeed, but the operation was successful and the blown timber was almost all cleared on time. A les-

A horse dragging logs to the loch side at Inverliever in 1940 for rafting across to Durran and conversion into pit props for the coal mines.

son was learned from that big gale and since then most of the forest trees around Loch Awe and elsewhere are not being allowed to grow so big. They are generally being clear-felled on a 40 or more year's rotation.

Close inshore below and either side of Cruachan are two old crannog sites. The one on the Kilmaha side now consists of a large man-made stone island and goes by the intriguing Gaelic name of Carn Mhic Chealair. The other one has had stone added to a natural rock outcrop to give foundations for a crannog building. I was told a somewhat improbable story about this one by Dan Stuart. He said that it was called Eilean a H-earras and the reason for this, he said, was that the person who owned it had moved to some distant place, got married and boasted to his wife that he owned an island on Loch Awe. Eventually he died and his wife decided to travel to Loch Awe and claim what was now her island, but when she arrived there she discovered that it was this tiny rocky islet with a few tufts of grass and one bush on it. And the name Eilean a H-earras translates as 'Island of the Dowry'.

In the forest between here and New York there are colonies of large, nest-building wood ants of, I think, the Formica aquilonia species. These are rare in the West Highlands and the only other ones I know of in the area are in Glen Nant and Fearnoch Forest. A hundred years ago the Inverliever ones were living in a pine wood near New York (the Lochaweside one), but it was felled and the ants have since then managed to adapt to living with spruce trees. They still survive despite periods of blanket forest and clear-felling.

The road returns to near the loch-side at the intriguingly named New York. The single house here took its name from the York Building Company, which was originally a London firm that was bought over by a group of London and other speculators solely for the purpose of buying up estates and property that had been confiscated by the Government after the 1715 Rebellion. They, of course, had hoped to make a great deal of money from the enterprise but the fact that they were strangers taking over local estates and businesses made them rather unpopular. Although they did manage and run the estates and businesses that they had bought it seems that they were not very successful as the company eventually went bankrupt.

I don't know who the New York land had belonged to but I think it was probably Hugh Campbell of Cruachan and Barmaddy. A Campbell website says that 'a Margaret Campbell married Dugald Campbell, her cousin and son of Hugh Campbell of Barmaddy and later Cruachan on Loch Awe. Hugh's charter of Barmaddy was dated the 5th July 1706. He married Helen, eldest daughter of Campbell of Glenan, a cadet (family branch) of Kilberry', and his father may have followed the early lead of his fellow Campbell, the Earl of Breadalbane, and supported the Jacobites in 1715.

An ancient ferry ran across Loch Awe at New York and that was part of an important old route that went by way of Loch Avich and the String of Lorn to the coast. It is said that it was a route used by funeral corteges and others travelling to the sacred Isle of Iona, and if that is so, it is likely that kings both dead and alive would have travelled that route. The ferry had been run from the Portinnisherrich side since early times, but in 1870, after Poltalloch Estate's factor requested its closure as it was no longer viable, there were protests from the Church and others, which resulted in a subsidy of £10 per year being paid to John MacIntyre of New York on condition that he ran a ferry service. He died in 1899 and his son, Sandy MacIntyre, took over running the ferry but in 1909 the Argyll County Council reported that the subsidy was no longer being paid and that the ferry did not run regularly. It seems the ferry service ceased to run about that time.

Sandy MacIntyre and his wife Betsy lived in New York in the house built by the York Building Company until he died sometime after the Second World War and his widow stayed there until about 1960. Apart from its thatched roof being replaced by a corrugated iron one the house appeared to have changed very little since it was built. It still had a clay floor and no mod cons right up until it ceased to be occupied. It then lay derelict and ruined for many years and during this time some of the local kids found the remains of an old sword hidden in one of its walls. It has now been replaced by a modern building, which still retains the old name of New York, and the old ferry road still runs past it to the ferry's old stone jetty, which would once have seen the passage of cattle, horses, horse-drawn vehicles, foot passengers and much more across the loch. Sandy MacIntyre was nearly always referred to as Sandy Hook, which was a sandy spit of land on the seaward approach to the other New York. I was told that this came about because of an incident on a loch steamer when a local person on board was indicating places of interest and pointed out New York. Where then, asked an American, was Sandy Hook? And knowing only one Sandy thereabouts and seeing him on the pier the local replied 'there's Sandy Hook' and the name stuck. When I was a boy this Sandy Hook had a pet raven that flew free and could talk but only in Gaelic.

Just past New York a road leads off to the left and up through the woods to what was Barmaddy Farm. Part of the way up that road an old forest spur road on the right had a boulder on its high side with a hand-print carved into it that was known as the 'Lady's Hand'. Unfortunately this stone appears to have been dug away during a road-widening operation and covered over. I believe, however, there is a similar hand-print somewhere around Kinchrackine near Dalmally, which we shall pass by in due course.

Barmaddy translates into the 'hill of the fox, or wolf'. In 1692 two fencible men were listed as living there. In the 1841 census there were 10 inhabitants in Barmaddy and in the sheep-farming boom days Barmaddy became a sheep farm. However it was part of the land bought for Inverliever Forest and the land was gradually planted up with trees. It eventually ceased to be a farm and the farmhouse is now let out as a bothy-type accommodation.

CHAPTER THREE

DALAVICH
AND LOCH AVICH

Not far past Barmaddy road-end is Dalavich Cottage, which is now a modern house. But for most of the 1900's it was a corrugated iron and wood cottage, which was home to two generations of the Clark family. I was told that it had been built by the first Mr Clark, which probably accounted for the fact that the building was not quite level and sloped down towards one end. The two Clarks that I knew living there were Angie and his sister Chrissie, and Angie in his spare time, ran an unofficial ferry service across the loch for a great many years.

Dalavich is now a small village but in the past it consisted of a few scattered houses and in the 1841 census it had only 11 inhabitants. It had a school and it was the site of the parish church, which was its main claim to fame. The date of the first church building there has been given as 1770 but it seems that it must have had an earlier church. The Rev Duncan Macfarlane says in the 1950's Statistical Account that 'the kirk-yard (at Kilchrenan) houses a memorial erected in1869 by the 8th Duke of Argyll to his famous ancestor, the Covenanting Marquis.

His contemporary, the Rev Robert Duncanson, then minister of Dalavich, was also an eager supporter of the Covenant and in 1649, when the Synod of Argyll decided to have the Psalms translated into Gaelic, he was appointed to superintend the translation of the first 50 Psalms. At the restoration (to Monarchy and the Episcopalian Church) in 1660 he was arrested and for a time imprisoned'. Dalavich Church had taken over from the two earlier ones of Innisherrich and Kilmun and so it served both sides of the loch. That was not a problem in those days when it was often easier and quicker to travel by water than land.

The parish of Dalavich was always relatively small and so for most of its life it has been joined with Kilchrenan. It stretched from Kilmaha to Druimdarroch, included the Loch Avich district as far as Maolachy, and on the far side of Loch Awe, Durran to Ardchonnel. By the 1901 census it had only 34 households and a population of 158 people and almost all the people were said to be bilingual in Gaelic and English apart from a few English-speaking incomers.

Memorial window honouring John MacPherson, long-serving Elder of Dalavich Church and teacher at Ardchonnel School from 1874 to 1902.

The Church itself is pretty austere but it has one stained-glass window in memory of a John MacPherson who was the schoolmaster at Ardchonnel and died in 1902. The graveyard does not have many very interesting gravestones in it but it does have one, which is described as 'a recumbent slab from 1757, now somewhat indistinct, to Dugald and Sarah McLerren, with an inscription and two ascending souls who appear to be rising Heavenwards on angel wings'. Quite a number of stones appear to have suffered badly from careless mowing.

Up until 1877 the local school building was attached to the church but then it moved to a new building at Barnaline. Across the road from the church is the old church manse now called Castle View. With the parish joined to Kilchrenan it did not usually house a qualified minister but was sometimes used to accommodate a missionary or others associated with the church. The manse is a corrugated iron and wood building, which dates from around 1900 when 'corrugated tin' buildings were popular. Ready-designed kit houses and other buildings could be purchased from firms who specialised in them. There was a similar one on the hillside above the village in which the Gillies family lived for many years. At about the same time too all the thatched cottages on the loch-side were given a roof of corrugated iron, which was occasionally put on over the existing thatch.

In 1670 the trial took place at Inveraray Tollbooth of Donald dow McGregour from Dalavich and Donald McIlmichael a vagabond without residence. They were charged with stealing a cow from John McIlverie of Dalavich. A strange twist to the trial emerged when it was said that Donald the Vagabond had been consorting with evil spirits and was made to confess that he had been meeting with witches and warlocks and consulting with the Devil. The outcome of the trial was that Donald the Vagabond was found guilty and hanged at the Gallows Farlane, which was near to where the present Inveraray Pier is. I believe Donald McIlmichael was later found guilty and also hanged. Fifteen years later two men from Dalavich joined the Earl of Argyll's unsuccessful rebellion against the King and are listed as rebels. I don't know what punishment they received.

I was told by Dan Stuart about the annual New Year's Day shinty matches that were held at Dalavich back in the days before the countryside was cleared of most of its people. These matches were between north loch-side and south loch-side and the boundary was the River Avich. Probably both sides of the loch took part in matches that, he said, could have anything up to a hundred players on each side with players joining in or dropping out as they wished and the pitch stretching over much of the level ground at Dalavich. There would have been some sort of goal at each end, few rules, no referee, plenty of bootleg whisky to sustain the players, and the game could continue until the early darkness stopped play. Why were these matches played on a cold, dark, short day in mid-winter? Simply because New Year's Day was about the only holiday that workers were allowed in those days. Sunday, apart from church attendance and necessary work such as attending to livestock, was of course free but no one would dare play shinty on a Sunday.

After the Second World War a big afforestation drive began in the country and a village of forty plus houses and a new wooden school were built at Dalavich to house new forest workers and their families and provide schooling. The first houses were wooden kit-houses that were shipped over from Sweden but later ones were constructed of brick. These houses were mostly let out to young married couples from Glasgow and the surrounding area, the idea being that their families would provide the enlarged workforce that it was envisaged would be needed in the future.

This relocating of city people into an isolated place like Dalavich, which had very few amenities, did cause problems and resulted in a very unstable community and workforce for a while, but gradually people settled and a community developed there. Unfortunately the forward planners had got it all wrong as to the number of workers required in the future. With the mechanisation of the forests and the switching of most forest work from direct labour to contractors the number of on-site workers employed plummeted and most of the houses were empty by the 1980's.

These were let out as holiday houses for a time but have now been sold off and are almost all occupied by folk outwith forestry. The school too has closed and the emphasis is now on outdoor recreation and holiday accommodation. Forty chalet-type wooden log-cabins for holiday letting and a social centre were built beside the village and planning permission for more holiday chalets has been granted and these are being built.

Past Dalavich and its chalets we come to Barnaline, which seems to translate into broad or beautiful hill. In 1685 four men from there joined up with the Earl of Argyll's unsuccessful rebellion against the King but after it failed they appear to have given themselves up and been pardoned under the then Act of Indemnity. Seven years later, however, in 1692 only two fencible men could be found at Barnaline as is shown by the list that was compiled at that time in order, it was said, 'for putting the Countrey in a posture of Defence against an invasion of French and Irish Papists'. In 1779 however it had an amazing 37 men but it was the Minister's property which might account for the increase.

In 1794 an Archibald Munro is said to have moved from Stuckghoy in Glen Shira to Barnaline. As this was a year after the Rev William Campbell died at Barnaline it appears that it had belonged to him, and as the present Barnaline Lodge is an old house with adze-worked beams, this house was probably involved. These Munros lived at Barnaline until 1901 when the then owner died and the place passed to a family member who had emigrated to Australia. The estate was entailed but the new owner succeeded in having it disentailed and sold it in 1902.

In the 1841 census Barnaline had 37 inhabitants and the Mill of Avich beside it another six. There were two water-driven mills beside the River Avich with one the local meal-mill and the other a waulk mill, which was used for finishing off the locally woven tweed. The 1790's Statistical Account has 22 weavers listed as working in the parish of Kilchrenan and Dalavich. In 1789 Duncan MacKenzie, a miller at Avich, claimed in the local JP Court that his wife had been overcharged when she had four and a half pounds of wool dyed by John Mac-Corquodale who was a weaver at Kilmun. However the court did not appear to think that this was their business. These mills would have been driven by a lade feeding an overshot water-wheel that was driven by the weight of the water in the wheel's buckets.

A later power plant below the Avich Falls used a water-turbine to drive a small hydro-electric plant, which in the 1920's and 1930's supplied electricity to Barnaline House through underground cables. The iron pipes that carried the water can still be seen running down by the side of the Avich Falls and some remains of the plant are still in the generator-house ruins by the riverside.

Another part of Barnaline was Barnaline Farm, which was situated some distance above the road and back towards Dalavich. It has now been almost completely demolished apart from one farm building that is now used as an interpretation centre for the surrounding oakwoods and forest. These oakwoods are accessed by a forest trail and have now been granted SSSI status (Site of Special Scientific Interest).

In the 1700's and well into the 1800's these woods would have been coppiced and harvested on a 20 plus years' rotation to provide wood for making the charcoal fuel used in iron-smelting at Bonawe Furnace near Taynuilt. During the summer months there is said to have been about 600 people employed around the countryside creating charcoal for the Bonawe iron-smelting business. It took about seven tons of wood to make one ton of charcoal. The 1790's Statistical Account for the Parish states 'enclosing, cutting, barking or peeling, and coaling the extensive woods in this parish employ many hands. The wages of the people employed are, men from 1s to 1s 6d and women from 6d to 9d per day'. The barking or peeling mentioned would probably be the women's job and this was carried out because the oak bark was then a valuable commodity and was being sold for tanning leather.

Barnaline House is now run as a care home for elderly people and a new house called Inveravich has been built nearby. One of the old mill-houses is still occupied and the old school building, which dates from 1877, is now renovated and lived in. Across the river from there is Druimdarroch (Ridge of the Oak). It is marked on Langland's 1801 map and there is a gravestone in Dalavich churchyard dated 1802. In the 1841 census it had 15 inhabitants but now only one house remains and that is let out as a holiday home. In the 1600's Druimdarroch, Kilmun and Dalavich were all part of the Innischonnel Castle lands and were feued out to the MacLachlan captain of that castle.

After leaving Druimdarroch we divert off the Kilchrenan road and take the narrower, winding and hilly road for Loch Avich. This was once part of an ancient route to and from the west that went across the Loch Awe ferry and on to Lochfyneside and beyond. Near the start of this road is a small wooden building that contains the automated Lochavich code telephone exchange. The first telephones in the area are said to have been introduced in 1922 with the connecting line routed through Kilchrenan. Before that a telegraph system must have operated with an underwater cable across Loch Awe to Ardchonnel School,

John MacLeod, teacher at Ardchonnel School from 1902 to 1925, pictured outside the old school in 1920, with his son Alec driving a Rover 12.

which housed the Post Office. I remember Alec MacLeod, whose father had been the schoolmaster there, saying that as a boy he often had to row across the loch to deliver telegrams. That would have been before the First World War and later, when I attended that school, the end of the old cable could still be seen at the water's edge.

Some way along the Loch Avich road on the right hand side at map reference 966 142 and marked on some Ordnance Survey maps as 'Larach na Lobairte' there is a circular level area of 50 plus feet diameter with some stone edging that appears to be a large hut-circle. This probably would have been the foundation for a large, round, wooden building. I was once told that it was an ancient burial ground but as the bedrock around there is near the surface of the ground I do not think it is likely. In the dry bracken ground beside this old site can be seen the marks of old cultivation with the rigs spaced at about nine feet apart, a distance that would allow two rigs at a time to be broadcast sown with corn. As these rigs also continue inside the old hut circle this must mean that the work was done by hand and most likely by a cas chrom, which was an old type of angled foot-plough or spade that was worked by one man. Further along this hilly road one of the hills, I was told, was called Murderer's Brae because at some time in the distant past, a young well-to-do fellow from Loch Avich, had got a servant girl pregnant and was so fearful of the consequences when it was found out, that he lured her to this spot, shot her and then hid the body. But I don't know what happened to him when the crime was discovered.

While digging ditches in a hollow below this road I dug through an ancient campfire that was a good two feet down in the peat and had egg-sized cooking-stones among its ashes. Such cooking-stones, I understand, were used to boil or cook in a container that could not be put on a fire. The stones here were scattered through the area of the fire unlike those in another fire I dug up elsewhere. There the stones were arranged in a neat circle around the edge. But I am puzzled as to why both fires were in the wettest parts of peat bogs. The best explanation I can come up with is that the fires had been sited in these wet parts by some hunter gatherers during a very dry period. Elsewhere the dry peat or woodland floor would have burnt too easily. Incidentally when I spent many years digging ditches with a digger in the forests around Lochaweside and elsewhere I found that the biggest accumulations of buried ash and charcoal were often in very wet places. This is curious and I can only suggest that in early times, possibly BC, people were clearing and burning woodland and again wanted to avoid burning the dry, combustible woodland floor.

Our road soon descends down to the end of Loch Avich, which in the past was claimed to be the Loch Luina of ancient Celtic and Ossian tales. The loch according to the Rev William Campbell in the 1790's was 'the resort of gulls, cranes, water-eagles and wild-ducks', but cranes died out in Britain in the 1500's so possibly he meant herons, which can have the same name in Gaelic. His water-eagles, I suppose, would have been ospreys. He also says that 'this lake discharges itself into Loch Awe by the stream or water of Avich buried in wood; having six fine falls with large circular ponds at the foot of each, and possessing the peculiarity of never freezing; even in the year 1740, not a particle of ice was observed on it, though the lake, from whence it issues, was entirely frozen over'.

From the end of Loch Avich, Glen Meisean runs through the now deserted and forested hills, to Inverinan. It carries one of the forestry's 'Strategic Timber Routes', which are designed to take timber lorries off unsuitable public roads and the narrow winding Loch Avich road is certainly not suitable for them. It is quite likely that on a trip around Loch Awe one will see a timber harvester felling and cutting the trees and a forwarder transporting them to a loading point for lorries as this is now the usual way of doing that work.

These harvesters fell the trees, sned the branches off them and using a computerised system cut the trees into the required timber lengths, while at the same time laying down a brushwood road from the tree's branches and points on which it and the forwarder run. The forwarder then picks up and transports the logs to a forest road or timber-loading point and leaves them stacked up in their different sizes and types ready for the timber lorries to pick up. This is all very far removed from the days of crosscut saws, axes and horses and a main reason why forestry villages and large work forces are no longer required.

A downturn to modern day forestry is that with better transport and roads, the forest workforce now tends to live in the nearby small towns and travel into the forests to work. Very few of the people living in the forests now work in them. In the past there were two small settlements near the Loch Avich end of Glen Meisean. The first of these was Glenisha, which must have been abandoned before

Drissaig Cottage, with Shore Cottage closer to Loch Avich, have been home to three generations of the McPhie family. Tom was Manager on Drissaig Farm from 1936 to 1967, his wife, Ali, was Postmistress operating from the porch at Drissaig Cottage while Moira MacDonald, the Postlady, delivered mail throughout the glen on her bicycle as far as Finaglen which was last occupied by the McGinty family who later moved to Kilmelford. Shore Cottage, built of corrugated iron sheeting, was demolished in 1972/73.

the 1841 census, and a mile or so further up the glen was Craignamoraig, which was probably the Craigdarnvaig that was listed in that census and had four inhabitants. The house I knew of as Craig was occupied right up until after the Second World War when the MacInnes family moved to Inverinan..

Loch Avich, which we now drive alongside, is mentioned in the 600's by Adomnan, the Abbot of Iona. He spells it as Loch Abhaich (bh in Gaelic is pronounced like the English v), and it seems to have taken its name from the river. The first part of the loch-side land is part of Drissaig Estate now owned by Loch Avich Estates Ltd and it stretches back into the hills a considerable distance. At 3285 acres it is by far the largest area

Johnie McPhie, son of Tom and Ali, posting a card in the postbox at the gate to Drissaig Cottage where his mother was Postmistress. Johnie took over management of Drissaig Estate from his father in 1967 and, ably assisted by his wife Mairi, filled that position until his sudden death in 1988.

of un-forested land around there. The mansion house with its cottage and old walled garden is set back from the road. This 'Big House', as it would likely have been called, seems to have an older and a newer part. The old part is probably what is marked on Langland's 1801 map with the name A Calman Esq as owner, whilst the newer part was likely to have been built during the Victorian era. There must have been a more ancient Drissaig as that is listed in 1692 as having two fencible men but it is not mentioned in the 1841 census. Later on in the 1900's there was a corrugated iron Post Office and a house beside the road, which I remember seeing being demolished about 50 years or more ago.

The next place that we come to can possibly claim a longer pedigree but not under its present name of Loch Avich House. Its ancient name appears to have been Drumvereran and according to the History of Kilchrenan and Dalavich it is mentioned in the church parish records of 1414 as 'the pennyland of Drumvereran'. It was spelt that way in 1692 when two fencible men were listed there but by the 1895 Ordnance Survey map the name appears to have changed to Duainrin. Soon after that the site seems to have been cleared and Loch Avich House was built. The place currently has this house and one cottage.

Opposite Loch Avich House an old track runs up the hillside and on past Lochs na Streinge and Scamadale. This is the old String of Lorne route to the west coast and it was beside this track that a battle took place in 1294 between the Campbells of Loch Awe led by their chief Cailean Mor, Colin the Great, and the MacDougals who owned most of the territory to the west. The cause of the trouble seems to have been a dispute about where the boundary between their lands was and to try and settle this they agreed to meet at a certain point on the String route. This was probably at the watershed between Loch Awe and the coast but it seems that the MacDougals were late at the rendezvous and the Campbells had carried on past the agreed point. This caused an argument, which eventually developed into a fight and pitched battle. The Campbells had the superior numbers and appeared to be winning the fight until a MacDougal archer shot and killed their chief, Cailean Mor. The Campbells then retired with their chief's body and carried it to Kilchrenan where it was buried. A cairn called Carn Chailein, which is marked on maps not far past Loch na Streinge is said to mark the fatal spot.

A mile or so past Loch Avich House and where a newly built

log-house replaces a much older one is Kilmun, The Holy Place or Cell of St Munn. There are a number of places named Kilmun around the West of Scotland. There appears to have been two holy men called St Munn - an Irish born one and a Scots born one. But the one who left his mark so much in Argyll would seem to have been the Scots' Saint who died in 635 and is credited with founding churches on Eilean Munde island in Loch Leven and at Kilmun on the Holy Loch. This is where most of the local Campbell chiefs from knights to dukes were buried but whether he actually founded all of the old church sites that bear his name is very doubtful.

Across Loch Avich and situated some distance up a glen are the ruins of Coriebuie (Yellow Corrie). It is now isolated in conifer forest but in the past it was reached by a track from Barnaline Farm. It was mentioned in the 1692 list of fencible men as having one such person. In an 1801 map it appears to have had two houses and in the 1841 census it had six adults living there. These were Margaret McIntyre, age 60, and five Carswells, who were Archibald, 70, John, 30, Peter, 30, Mary, 25 and Robert, 20. Having their ages ending in nought or five would have been very unlikely to be correct but it was the norm in those days to record people aged between 20 and 25 as '20' and between 25 and 29 as '25' etc. Another thing that struck me from the old census returns was the surprising number of people who moved around the countryside. This is backed up by the fact that the children were often born in different parishes, which may be connected to the yearly or six monthly contracts that farm workers were employed by. The contracts generally began and ended at the May or November terms.

A short distance past Kilmun is Narachan, which is mentioned from 1692 onwards and consists of one house and that is still the case. Off a point in the loch there is the site of an ancient crannog and not much further along the loch is the ruined Loch Avich Castle or Caisteal na Nighinn Ruaibhe, which translates into Castle of the Red-haired Girl. It is hidden among the trees on the small wooded island of Innis Luana. Not much is known about the castle's history but it is described officially as having been a hall-house probably of three storeys measuring about 50 feet by 35 and built of random rubble with some dressed stonework. An outer protective wall can be traced as can another building to the west of about 50 feet by 30 feet, which is now very much ruined.

Tradition says that the castle came into Campbell hands in the 13th Century through the marriage of a Campbell of Craignish to Bridget, daughter of a Loch Avich chieftain. A charter from 1414 says that 'Duncan Campbell of Lochaw with the consent of his son and heir Celestine granted to his kinsman Reginald Malcolmson of Cragynis (Craignish) certain lands including the four penny lands of Lochaffay (Lochavich) … lying in the Lordship of Lochaw for pay-ment of the usual services and a ship of twelve oars, and with pro-vision that if Reginald or his heirs should build the Castle of Lochaffay they should be constables thereof for the overlord and his heirs'. That sounds as if this could have been a new castle to re-place the older more ruined building that is there.

This Celestine, son and heir, is said to have been studying in England when he became very ill. His father, Sir Duncan, then went to try and help but his son died and the father then had the task of bringing the body back home. By the time that he reached the Holy Loch it seems the body was decomposing fast and they buried it with the permission of the local Lamont chief in or at the local church at Kilmun. Later in 1442 Sir Duncan had the Kilmun Church made into a Collegiate Church that was charged with the duty of praying for his son Celestine and his own two dead wives. He was also buried there when he died and Kilmun then became the traditional burying place for the Campbell Chiefs right up until the 10th Duke in 1949.

There are two stories told to explain the castle's unusual name. These are likely to have been made up by the old-time travelling story-tellers and as there may be a small amount of truth in them I will tell them. It is said that the Chief who owned the castle wanted a secret underwater causeway built to it and he employed a father and son who were experts in work such as this. This causeway would have been made with secret turns and traps to stop any but those who knew its secrets from using it. The Chief did not want to risk having the builders, reveal its secrets to anyone so he planned to kill them when they completed the work. However the Chief's red-haired daughter, or as another version says a red-haired servant girl, knew of this and as she had fallen in love with the young builder, she warned them of the Chief's plans and they fled. The chief was so mad at the girl that he had her thrown from the ramparts of the castle to her death.

The other version has it that the father and son were in charge of the castle's building and the Chief intended to have them killed to avoid having to pay their fee for the work. Again the Chief's red-haired daughter, or servant girl, had warned them of this but it was too late to escape. The father then told the Chief that there was a problem stone in the castle and that it must be removed as it weakened the whole building, but to remove it he required a special hammer that was at his home in Edinburgh. The Chief wanted to send a messenger for it but the father said that his wife would not hand it over. They eventually agreed that the Chief's young son would take a letter from the builder with instructions about handing it over. In the letter he said that he was sending a small hammer and that she was to keep this until the large hammer was returned. This she understood and she immediately imprisoned the Chief's son and then sent a letter back to the Chief telling him so. With his son a prisoner in Edinburgh the Chief had no choice but to pay the builder his money and release him and his son. However in revenge the Chief had the girl thrown to her death from the ramparts of the castle and it is said that on some nights when the moon is full lights are still to be seen in the castle and the girl's scream heard.

The point of land opposite the castle is called Dorlin Point and as

Dorlin Point opposite the site of Caisteal na Nigheann Ruaibhe on Loch Avich.

doirlinn in Gaelic usually means a spit of sand or gravel joining an island to the shore it sounds as if there was some connection between the shore and castle whether a secret one or not. In later years there was a house called Dorlin there just to the west of the modern picnic site, and in the 1841 census it is listed as having five inhabitants but very little trace of it remains. The only occupied place at this end of the loch now is Duaig some distance further on and it would have been a sheep farm back in the days of blackface sheep farming and before all its land was given over to forest. Across the loch by the edge of the conifer forest the remains of Dalachulish (Field of the Narrows) can be seen. It is mentioned in 1692 with one fencible man and it is on Langland's 1801 map but it must have been abandoned before the 1841 census. Past the end of the loch is the ruined cottage of Achnasaal, which has its concrete walls still standing. The name possibly translates into 'field of the heel'. The place had two fencible men in 1692 and the 1841 census had five people who were probably living in this cottage, which appeared to be still occupied in 1895.

CHAPTER FOUR

INVERINAN, FERNOCH, KILCHRENAN AND BARRACHANDER

From there we retrace our route back down to the Loch Avich road junction and then climb up a very steep hill on the Kilchrenan road, however if we were we travelling this way in earlier days we could have avoided these steep hills by taking a bypass road that ran behind Kilmun and then joined up with the Kilchrenan road. This old settlement of Kilmun goes back a long way and possibly was founded by St Munn.

Above the old farmhouse, at map reference 971 145, there is a mainly natural platform on the hillside measuring some 30 plus yards across with traces of stone walling around its edges. In the centre of this is the remains of a building measuring 30 feet by 18 feet and facing north-west by south-east with possibly the remains of a smaller build-ing on the north-east side. This place is said to have been the site of an old chapel and graveyard but there are no identifiable gravestones to be seen. By the side of a forest road that passes below is an en-closed spring that supplies the farmhouse with its water. It is not stretching the truth too far to suggest that the founder of that holy site may have drunk from this spring and the religious settlement have been established there because of it.

Kilmun was also a secular settlement and it had seven fencible men living there in 1692, and in the 1841 census it had 40 inhabitants. It later became one large farm and then, after the afforestation of most of its land, a croft. At the present time it consists of this farmhouse and some converted steadings, which are let out as holiday accommodation.

As a very young child I lived there for six months after the Cruachan Hostel where we lived had been burned down. My father had then taken over the tenancy of Kilmun Croft, which had previously been part of Inverinan Estate. However sometime earlier he had been head gamekeeper and a farm manager at Inverinan Estate and it seems that he and Mr Wallis, the owner, had parted on very acrimonious terms. When the estate was sold to the Forestry Commission shortly afterwards Mr Wallis had spitefully put a clause in the sale saying that my father could not live or work on the estate. So, when this was discovered, my father was offered a house, croft and job on the newly acquired Eredine Estate on the opposite side of the loch and we moved there.

After passing Kilmun the road climbs still higher and continues through what is now Inverinan Forest. Most of the old Inverinan Estate land that was bought in 1934 has now been planted with trees. The stretch below the road was planted and well established before it was destroyed in a fire during the Second World War. It was then replanted, grew to harvesting size and was felled, then replanted again with Sitka spruce, which is now at that very difficult to access thicket stage. Somewhere in there at map reference 982 155 are all that now remains of Slocabhothan (Hollow of the Bothy). I couldn't find any historical reference to it but tradition has it that it was a small settlement that was abandoned when its people were struck down by plague. This may have been the 1830's outbreak of cholera that killed many people in Argyll.

After driving through a stretch of mainly coniferous forest we descend to more open land at Inverinan (Mouth of the Fionain river) and the settlement of Inverinan Mor. On the right hand side is the old estate mansion house with three cottages by the loch-side and on the other side of the road are two new houses and a farmhouse with steadings that date from the 1800's when farming was centralised in these large mainly sheep farms. Incidentally I was born in this farmhouse at a time when Inverinan was also a sporting estate and my father was the head keeper there. That was before the estate was sold to the Forestry Commission and it then belonged to Mr Wallis who had bought it from the Breadalbane Estates. Going much further back I think that the Campbell's of Breadalbane would probably have obtained it from the MacCorquodales who were styled the Barons of Phantilands and at one time seemed to own all the land between the Avich and the Pass of Brander.

Across the Abhainn Fionain from Inverinan Mor is Inverinan Begg now known simply as Inverinan. It is a small hamlet of 10 houses that were mostly built to house the forestry workers and nearby was the nursery that produced the young trees for the forest. The five pennylands of Innerynyn are mentioned in 1492. A pennyland was a measure of the value of the land for farming and not any set amount of land. In the 1692 list of fencible men Inverinan Mor had seven and Inverinan Begg had four but by the 1841 census Inverinan Mor had 11 inhabitants and Inveranby, as it was then written, 28. There was a water-mill beside the Abhainn Fionain somewhere below the present road but I don't know what kind of mill it was. If it was a meal-mill it seems to have been rather close to the Avich one on one side and the Fernoch one on the other.

In the bay at the far end of Inverinan is what looks like a small round stony island, which was a man-made foundation for a crannog. Many crannogs such as this would originally have had their buildings built on piles that were driven into the bed of the loch. Why then have they nearly all finished up as massive piles of stones? The answer, it seems, is that the sites were generally used for hundreds of years but not continually, and after one crannog building collapsed and another was built on the same site the old flooring and timber layer made it very difficult to drive piles down. So they were stabilized by piling lots of stones around their base. This means that in most crannog mounds there are the remains of a number of old crannog buildings complete with all their associated materials and artefacts generally well preserved below the stones. This makes them an amazingly good potential source for excavation. This crannog is known as Carn Dubh (Black Cairn) and a wooden bungalow along the road from there is named after it. This formed part of a wooden hut hostel that was erected after the Second World War to house forestry workers. For a time it held displaced persons from Eastern Europe and two of them married local girls and stayed on working in forestry, one of them until he retired.

From there we drive on through the forest past Coille nan Gobhar (Wood of the Goat) and on to Lower Fernoch Farm. Because of afforestation the farm is not as extensive as it once was but it still consists of 4,157 acres of mainly rough grazing. It is owned and farmed by the Leitch family, and the earliest member I remember was Jock Leitch, who was pipe-major of the Oban Home Guard pipe band in the Second World War. There is also an Upper Fernoch that consists of one lone cottage but it was not always that way because in 1692 it was home to six fencible men whilst Lower Fernoch had four. In the 1841 census Upper Fernoch had 22 inhabitants whilst Lower Fernoch had three.

Travelling on we come to a good viewpoint of upper Loch Awe before entering more woodland consisting of mostly hardwoods. We come to the Berchan Burn, which once drove Fernoch Mill or the Mill of Loch Awe as it was also known. This was a water-powered meal-mill and its ruins can be seen a short distance up the right-hand side of the burn. It was driven by a water-wheel powered by water that must have been diverted from higher up the burn. Nearby is the first of the current Coillaig houses and a short distance past there is the covered outfall or tailrace from the underground Nant power station, which can be seen running down into Loch Awe. The Nant hydro-electric scheme was built in the early sixties by the North of Scotland Hydro-Electric Board whose motto is 'Power from the Glen'. In this case the water comes from Loch Nant, which was enlarged by having two dams built to retain more water. The scheme also taps into water from the upper reaches of the Fionain and some small burns by means of a five mile long pipe-line and tunnel system running high up across the hillside. This is a relatively small hydro scheme with one generating turbine producing 15 megawatts of electricity.

The entrance road to the power station is a short distance ahead and the road runs alongside the old Druim an Rathaid (Ridge of the Road). There is a relatively modern house here with what seems to be a commercial plant growing operation nearby in three large polytunnels. There must, however, have been many more houses around here as the place is listed in 1692 as Kellagg with seven fencible men, and in 1841 it had 83 inhabitants making it the second largest settlement in the parish. From Coillaig an old road leads up the hill to Achnamady (the Field of the Fox or Wolf). At Achnamady the road branches with one branch of the old road and drove route going by Loch Nant and across the Midmuir to join the String of Lorne route, and the other branch turning right and going to Kilchrenan. Achnamady in 1692 had three fencible men and in the 1841 census it had 18 inhabitants.

In the field opposite the power station entrance there are the remains of an ancient burial cairn on top of a rise with a clear view towards Ben Cruachan. It has the remains of what appears to have been two burial cists or chambers in it and a standing stone in its south end. This standing stone is not likely to be authentic as it has three man-made slots in its edge which suggests that it had another use. Running down the slope from the cairn is a line of large boulders that are a good example of the field clearance work that was done in the 1800's. These have all been removed from the field and slyped (sledged) or rolled into this long line and some of them show the remains of the holes that were drilled into them by jumper drill-bit and hammer to allow a charge of gunpowder to blast them down to a more manageable size. By the roadside near here is Craigloiste, which takes its name from the rocky crags behind. This is a relatively

The Postman, James A. Sinclair, being handed a letter at Craigloiste in 1923.

modern development that was, I think, built to house people servicing the Nant hydro-electric scheme.

A short drive takes us to Lower Auchachenna croft and slightly further on is Upper Auchachenna and its farmhouse. The old farmhouse there was burned down with one fatality in 1973 and a new farmhouse has been built. In 1692 an Auchinna is listed with five fencible men and later this consisted of lower and upper with, in 1841, Lower Auchahinney having seven inhabitants and Upper Auchahinney 10.

Just before the junction of our unclassified road with the B845 Taynuilt to Taycreggan road is the hamlet of Annat, and at the start of this a road leads down to the loch-side and a house called Struan, which was originally the church manse and was built in 1802. Annat is an old name for a mother church or one containing relics of its founder and it may be a very old settlement. The local church must have been there but no records of these days remain and the earliest reference to it I can find is in 1692 when three fencible men were listed as living there. In the 1841 census it had 58 people but in modern times it tends to be considered a part of the larger Kilchrenan. After the disruption and church split of 1843 Annat had the Free Church built there and this continued as a separate church until sometime after 1929 when these two churches officially joined together again.

At the Annat road junction we take the road to the right, which went down to the old loch crossing at Taycreggan. Now this road only serves the local houses and hotel but in the past it and the ferry were the main route to Inveraray and the south. On our left as we turn down this way is the road to Barbreck, which now consists of a farm and cottages. The farm is a privately owned one of 2,210 acres, which includes the old Ballimore land and stretches in an elongated form, by way of Loch Tromlee, to the Pass of Brander. Barbreck is a very old settlement and was, according to the History of Kilchrenan and Dalavich, mentioned in Church records of 1510. In 1865 it had six rebels four of whom appear to have claimed that they were forced into joining up with the rebels and were pardoned. In

Competitors line up to test their skill at "Tilting the Bucket" at the Kilchrenan Games in 1926.

1892 the place had eight fencible men and by the 1841 census it had an amazing 126 inhabitants making it the largest settlement around. Below us on the level ground near the loch-side is the field where the local Lochaweside Games were held from the early years of the 1900's up until the Second World War.

We now leave Kilchrenan and Dalavich Parish because Barbreck and parts north and east of there are in the Parish of Glenorchy and Inishail. Inishail was once a parish in its own right with its Church on Inishail Island serving both sides of the loch.

I have the Militia List for 1803-04 and will list some of it: Auchlian 9, 2 servants, 4 weaver, 3 shepherd. Bocaird 1, 1herd. Bovuy 5, 1 farmer, 4 labourer. Cladich 3, 1 changekeeper, 1 apprentice, 1 smith. Drumurk 5, 2 weavers, 2 labourer, 1 taylor. Barundren 3, 2 taylors, 1 labourer. Keppuchan 2, 1 farmer, 1 labourer. Innishail 1, 1 carpenter. Barbreck 9, 2 farmer, shoemaker, 1 wright, 1 taylor, 1 surgeon, 1 servant, 2 not specified. Auchnacarran 9, 2 farmers, 2 labourers, 1 taylor, 1 crofter, 1 weaver, two not specified. Hayfield 4, 1 servant, 1 gardener, 1 herd, 1 labourer. Balmore 1, 1 farmer. Balbeg 4, 3 farmers, 1 shoemaker. Ichterachim 15, 1 agent, 1 wood manager, 1,woodcutter, 3 carters, 3 labourer, 5 workmen, 1 fisher. These would seem to be wood charcoal makers.

Alongside the Taycreggan road there are a number of up-market properties including the boarding house of Cuil na Sithe, which probably means nook of the fairies and was built as the new Barbreck mansion house and originally called Barbreck House. Some distance behind these are the remains of an old fortified dun called Dun Bhugan. The once small inn at Taycreggan (House of the Small Crag) with its prime loch-side site has now been extended into quite a large and modern hotel. Around 1850 under the name of Lochawe Inn, North Port Sonachan, it was advertised as having 'accommodation of the first quality afforded to Tourists and Commercial Gentlemen. Beds, Breakfasts, and Dinners. Foreign and British Spirits. Ales and Porters. Excellent Stabling and Lock-up Coach-house, Fishing Boats, Job and Post Horses, with careful Drivers'.

The old stone ferry jetty is still there and is a reminder that at one time this place was a busy ferry crossing. Only the large bolts and anchors in the rock remain of the old wooden steamer pier. These are relics from the days when this was a port of call for the Loch Awe tourist steamers and the connecting point for onward travel by waiting horse-drawn coaches. The way that the stones on the surface of the old ferry jetty are set on edge to give animals feet and hooves a grip is a sure indication that the jetty was used to transport cattle and horses as well as people.

Many people travelled the old ferry route including Dr Johnson and Boswell, and an urgent messenger carrying news of Prince Charlie's landing in Moidart in 1745 to Inveraray and the Duke of Argyll. However as the ferry boats were based at Portsonachan I shall wait until we are returning down that side of the loch before I give more details of the ferry.

North of Taycreggan there is the remains of another dun, Dun na Cuaiche, and three burial cairns. The number of duns, cairns and crannogs in the Kilchrennan area suggests that in prehistoric times there must have been a substantial population around there. Two of these cairns are called Cairn Ban, which is a common name for cairns and is probably due to the whitish encrusting lichen that often grows on their exposed stones.

As Taycreggan is now a dead-end we must retrace our route back to the Annat road junction and Kilchrenan, which means the Cell or Church of Crenan. Crenan was an Irish Holy Man from Donegal who was reputed to be a nephew of St Columba but as he had changed his name that is not entirely certain. However he did come from the same parish as St Columba - a parish that now goes by the name of Kilmacrenan. Whether the first Church that was founded was at Kilchrenan or Annat is not known but the local church is said to have been at Kilchrenan for at least six hundred years with the present one being built around 1770 and renovated in 1908.

The churchyard has a great many old grave-slabs but they are largely covered by turf and moss and what can be seen does not show much detail, but as they are mostly of soft slate they could be badly eroded. One slab showing a large two-handed sword carved in relief has been built into the church wall, and it is said to be that of the Campbell Chief, Cailean Mor, who was killed in the battle fought on the String of Lorne in 1294. However that is somewhat doubtful although it must be the stone of a Knight or someone of high standing. A more modern memorial to the Campbell chief is beside this in the form of a raised granite slab. Again with a two-handed sword carved in relief and with a scallop-shell on its handle. This was a symbol adopted by people who had made a pilgrimage to Santiago de Compostella in Spain where the Apostle St James is reputed to be buried. The inscription reads 'Cailean Mor Slain on the Sreang of Lorne A D 1294 Erected by George Douglas Campbell 8th Duke of Argyll 28th Baron of Lochow 1866'.

The MacCorquodale Chiefs of Phantilands are also said to be buried near there and another old stone showing a sword is believed to be one of theirs. Nearby is an intriguing boulder gravestone with a hollow in it that would once have been used as a saddle quern for grinding meal. It simply has the initials C Mc D cut into it but someone has obligingly added a wooden cross with 'Charlie's Stone' on it. But I don't know who he was.

One other stone that is built into the church wall says 'Interred here Duncan Campbell of Sonachan in 1691 and Alexander his son in 1738 Also in memory of Duncan Campbell of Sonachan and two of his sons killed at Altnalephen about 1633 and of Donald Campbell of Sonachan killed at Bridge of Stirling about 1666'. The sons killed at Altnalephen were those killed in the dispute over the Portsonachan Ferry Rights.

Inside the church there is a large memorial tablet on the wall in memory of Robert McIntyre, Surgeon, who had been born at lower Fernoch in 1773 and I believe made a fortune in India. He died in Toulouse, France, in 1815 but had left legacies to the parish for the education of poor children and for the relief of the sick and insane.

Kilchrenan in the past seems to have been a hamlet rather than a village and in 1692 it had only four fencible men in the place. In the 1841 census it had 99 inhabitants of whom 15 were in the manse. What appears to have been 'Old Kilchrenan' is the area below the church and between the road and burn where there are a number of ruined buildings. Among them a water-mill that still has its stone-built raceway and ruined mill building. The interior of this building was used as a sheep-fank and sheep dipping place before becoming a local rubbish dump. There are also the remains of a lime-kiln nearby.

Back in the days of cattle-droving Kilchrenan was at the junction of two busy droving routes, one coming by way of Glen Nant from the Oban coast and from Mull and beyond, and the other, that linked up with it just past the church, came by way of the Midmuir route and the lands to the south of Oban. Kilchrenan also had a yearly cattle market and fair where there would no doubt have been many other attractions in the form of stalls and goods for sale. According to the History of Kilchrenan and Dalavich it also had its Fair King and Fair Queen.

Kilchrenan had and still has a church, a school, a Post Office and pub, and in the past it appears to have had two water-driven mills and a smiddy. Considering there was also a smiddy at nearby Annt there must have been plenty of work for both smiddys due, no doubt, to the amount of traffic crossing on the Loch Awe ferry. The Kilchrenan smiddy had its own very rude song written about it, which was condemned and banned by the minister in the Kilchrenan Church.

In 1836 Sarah Brown a crofter's wife from Sephan, Kilchrenan, was tried at Inveraray Sheriff Court on a charge of attacking and seriously wounding Catherine Turner with a shearing hook or sickle. According to Sarah Brown she was at the peat moss cutting sprits, or rushes (likely for thatching), when she was told by Catherine Turner to stop and retaliated by attacking her. The sentence was a £3 fine or imprisonment.

Kilchrenan's old inn and pub was the Tigh Bhan, which later changed to its English name of White House, and has two stories told about it. The first concerns a cask of illicit whisky that was confiscated by the Excise men. They put it in an upper room of the Inn and left one of their number sitting on it to guard it until its removal could be arranged. The locals, however, had other ideas and by boring a hole through the ceiling of the room below, and into the cask they managed to drain away all the whisky into other containers and left the Excise men with an empty barrel. Loch Awe-made whisky, it seems, had a very good reputation.

The other story concerns a MacCorquodale funeral in 1714 attended by a large number of people, including it is said, Rob Roy himself. The funeral party left Inveraray very early equipped with much whisky to sustain them on the road to Portsonachan and its ferry. Across the ferry they were met by the Lorn MacCorquodales and they all proceeded to the churchyard. After the burial at Kilchrenan Church the local MacCorquodales invited everybody back to the Tigh Bhan for a drink but an argument arose as to the right of an Inveraray MacCorquodale to be buried in the same plot as the MacCorquodale Barons of Tromlee. A fight broke out and the Tigh Bhan was practically wrecked, the furniture smashed and the Inveraray men had to fight their way back to the Portsonachan Ferry. After this incident it seems the Inveraray MacCorquodales were no longer buried at Kilchrenan.

Incidentally Moray MacKay the author of that excellent local

76

history booklet The History of Kilchrenan and Dalavich from where I obtained this information lived in that very building, which is again called Tigh Bhan and is now a dwelling house. It is reconstructed from the then derelict building of the 1960's that had been called the White House.

At Kilchrenan an unclassified road leads off to Ardanaiseig and Tervine but we'll explore that later and continue along the B845. The first old settlement that we pass is Achnacraobh (Field of the Tree). This is listed in the 1692 list of fencible men as Achnacreist and had seven such men. In the 1841 census it had 32 inhabitants but it now has only one house. West of there on a rocky ridge is Caisteal Suidhe Cheannaidh (Castle of the Seat of Kenneth). According to the Royal Commission on the Ancient and Historical Monuments of Scotland it is a dun, or small fort, and they say that it measures 12 metres by 13 and has walls up to almost five metres thick. It is recorded that before its walls were robbed of stones for dyke building it stood six metres (20 ft) high. Such duns were usually built during the early Iron Age but there is unfortunately no recorded Scottish history from these times. But it must have been a period of unrest with warring bands and movement of displaced people around the country, which probably resulted in the building of these defensive duns and the crannogs in the lochs. Excavations were carried out in the dun in 1890 but in those days they were very crude and it was mainly a case of digging for artefacts. Several hearths were discovered and the bones of horses and deer.

Back on the B845 we have on the right an upgraded tarmac road leading to Ballimore, which is set in a green glen on the far side of Loch Tromlee. It was once a farm but its land is now part of Barbreck Farm. An 1801 map also shows a Ballibeg nearby and a mansion house is drawn at Ballimore. In the 1841 census Ballimore had 11 inhabitants and Ballibeg 17 but on an 1895 map only Ballimore is marked. Near Ballimore there is an old lime-kiln and like most such kilns it is built into the hillside to allow easy loading of the fuel and broken limestone rock, which would have been put in in layers before the kiln was lit. The old Ballimore house is now a ruin but a new house, cottage and barn conversions have been built there and are run as an upmarket eco-friendly bed and breakfast and self-catering business. From there the old road carries on in a more basic state across the moor to Tervine and the Pass of Brander.

Loch Tromlee is now home to large numbers of pike. Again these were fish introduced from the south and from Loch Tromlee they soon spread down into Loch Awe. Loch Tromlee in late medieval times had the MacCorquodale Barons of Phantilands stronghold on its small island. During Alasdair 'Colkitto' MacDonald's campaign of destruction through Argyll in 1646 he went to call on the Baron, who he seemed to regard as an ally, but not wishing to offend his powerful Campbell neighbours he purported to be 'not at home' and the ruse worked until one of his men stupidly fired a shot and killed one of Colkitto's men. After that unfriendly welcome Colkitto attacked the place, killed most of the men and destroyed the castle. However, somehow the baron escaped and it seems likely that he must have fled before the attack. It appears that the castle was never rebuilt and it's not known what happened to the not so bold baron, although a legend exists that he was killed in Kintyre. The ruins of the castle are still visible on its small island but it was never a very great castle and it is officially described as having been a fortified dwelling house. I believe that may have been the original Tigh Bhan.

Ahead of us on the B845 are a number of houses by a disused limestone quarry and the 1950's Statistical Account says that during the big expansion of agriculture and land reclamation that took place after the Second World War an old lime-kiln beside the road, about two miles beyond the village of Kilchrenan, was taken over by the Argyll Limestone Company and converted into a lime producing factory. It was equipped with a modern stone crusher and it had an average annual output of about 6,000 tons of lime and employed eight men. The rock in the vicinity it was said to contain 85% pure lime, and lime then was in constant demand by farmers for land dressing. With a later downturn in farming and farm subsidies the quarry ceased working and for a time the quarry buildings were used as a motor repair garage. Then they became a small factory producing glass-fibre tanks for water and sewerage but they are now derelict.

About half a mile further along the road is the farm of Barachander. This is a hill farm of 2,186 acres with most of its land to the left of the public road and stretching to the River Nant and loch of that name. The History of Kilchrenan and Dalavich says that Barachander was razed to the ground by Colkitto in the 1600's and I cannot find any other reference to it until 1890 although there are two old ruins just before the farm. Dated 1890, there is a tombstone in Kilchrenan Churchyard for a John Snodgrass who died at Barachander aged 79, and possibly the settlement was not rebuilt until it became a blackface sheep farm during the sheep-farming boom years. This John Snodgrass could have taken over the lease as its first sheep farmer.

CHAPTER FIVE

ARDANAISEIG, ACHNACARRON, LARACH BHAN, TERVINE AND THE ISLANDS

I regard Barachander as the end of the Lochaweside lands and so we return back to Kilchrenan's Trading Post and public house and take the Ardanaiseig road past the Moon Loch with its old crannog, and there on top of a rise by some old pines and a sweet-chestnut tree is the well-preserved ruin of a house, which still has one gable-end and chimney standing. At the end of the house is a walled garden, which still has an apple tree in it, blown down, but flourishing and also a surviving root of rhubarb. Across the road from there, among the old green and once cultivated fields, are the remains of two more houses. A further ruin is now in the forested land and some distance south of these was, I believe, the old farmstead of Achnaclaish.

Past the Moon Loch and on almost the highest point of a small ridge next to the road, and pinpointed by the fact that the roadside fence diverts around it, is a very large flat-topped boulder with, it is said, at least 30 ancient cup marks on its flat top. They are badly eroded, however, and it strikes me that most of the cup marks that I have seen on boulders have been shallow, but the ones on ground rock-sheets are usually deeper and in much better condition. It is quite likely that this is because they have been protected for most of their life by a covering of turf and moss.

Past the cup-marked boulder is the road leading down to Achnacarron. It is quite a long way down and it is not surprising that during that mansion house's heyday, in the early part of last Century, boats were used as the main means of transport and they provided a connection with the trains at Loch Awe Station. Two boats were kept for this and one of them was a fast sleek 45 foot steamboat called Bumble Bee, which was built with a clipper bow and a rakish design. The other boat was a small petrol-engine launch. The original house had been burned down in about 1905 but it was rebuilt to a grander style by the new owners, and it was they who had the fast Bumble Bee steamer. When they died it was sold twice and then became a hotel but this was also burned down in the 1950's and was not rebuilt. The farm and a cottage have survived since that time and there is now a converted boathouse chalet by the loch-side. The place was spelt Achinagarnan in 1685 when it had three rebels, and in 1695 it had seven fencible men and in the 1841 census it had 48 inhabitants.

Nearby is the Carn an Roin crannog and further on by the Ceann Mara point at Larach Bhan is another ancient crannog. Larach Bhan, which translates into white ruin or building was inherited by the dashing, raffish and larger than life character W E Campbell Muir. Under his ownership it burned down in 1910 a few years after Achnacarron had, and another of his estate houses, Hayfield, burned down shortly after that. This is all rather suspicious. Campbell Muir lived at the estate's main mansion house of Inistrynich on the other side of Loch Awe, and from there it was claimed by some that he swam across the loch, set fire to Hayfield House and then swam back again. It would certainly have been a very long swim, although it seems that he was a very good swimmer, but why swim when he could quite easily have rowed across and back during the night? His fast lifestyle left him continually short of money and this state of affairs was possibly helped by his eloping with a young heiress whom he married in a simple do it yourself ceremony in an Oban garage with two chauffeurs as witnesses. Such a marriage was legal in Scotland at that time.

Campbell Muir's grandfather, who had originally bought the loch-side estate in 1863, was a keen fisherman and he held the British trout record for almost a hundred years with a fish that he had caught in the River Awe in 1866. He had been fly-fishing for salmon in the river, just down from the loch, when he hooked this massive fish and after a long struggle lasting over two hours he managed to land it and found it to be a trout of 39 1/2 pounds. He had the fish stuffed and mounted but unfortunately it was burned in the first fire that destroyed Achnacarron. This fish was recognised as being the official British and World record brown trout until in the 1950's new stricter qualifications were introduced, and because this fish had been inadvertently hooked on the outside of its jaw it was disqualified as having been foul-hooked.

These large ferox-type of trout had been fished for in Loch Awe for a long time usually by trolling a herring or other bait very deep down in the loch, but nothing more approaching that size has been caught until recent years when specimen fishermen began to seriously fish for them. In 1996 a Loch Awe trout took the record back with a weight of 25 lb 5 1/2 oz. and the record has remained with Loch Awe trout since then. In 2000 Ken Oliver from Barrhead caught a fish of 30 lb 8 oz and this fish was mounted and auctioned at Christies in London for the record sum of £5,800. Then in 2004 a bigger fish of 31 lb 12 oz was caught by Brian Rutland from Cumbria but this fish was hurriedly weighed and returned to the water and so is apparently not acceptable for the record. These large fish are usually females because they grow to a larger size than the males. However, in 2001 a Stephen Pounder caught a 25 lb 14 oz cock fish, which would appear to be a record for a male brown trout. But big as these trout were they would have seemed rather small compared to a massive salmon whose remains were found washed up on one of the islands. It was reckoned that in life this salmon must have weighed about 89 lb.

Larach Bhan House was rebuilt and still stands with a cottage nearby. Larach Bhan and Hayfield were once part of the MacArthur

"The Bus", built in 1896 by Scotts Shipbuilding and Engineering Company and first owned by the Scott's of Eredine, was the first motor powered boat on Loch Awe and is seen here at the newly reconstructed pier at Larach Bhan in 1936 when it re-entered the water for the first time since the First World War following a complete re-fit under the ownership of the Rose family.

Clan's Tirievadich loch-side lands. Their land would also have included Achnacarron, Inistrynich and other properties on that side of the loch as well as the island of Inishail. Since Bruce's time the MacArthurs had owned these Lochaweside lands with much of them having been taken from the defeated MacDougals and Mac-Naughtons. They were also Captains of Dunstaffnage Castle and their chief, it was said, was 'chief of a thousand men'. They were considered to be a very old clan and there was a saying that 'there is nothing older, unless the hills, MacArthur and the Devil'. They have also claimed that they are descended from King Arthur but that, I think, can safely be said to be a myth. In 1427 they were involved in a dispute over some land elsewhere and this resulted in them being branded one of the 'troublesome clans' whose chiefs were summoned to attend a parliament of James I at Inverness. There Ian MacArthur, the chief, was seized, imprisoned and then beheaded and much of the MacArthurs' land was then confiscated and in later years they appear to have held their land under a charter from the Earl of Argyll. Hayfield is marked on Langland's 1801 map as having a mansion house and the owner being W MacNeill Esq, but this house was burned down in the early 1900's and Hayfield presently consists of a farmhouse with steadings and one cottage. These farm steadings are built in the form of a square with stone arches and look very impressive.

The land to the left of the road from Achnacarron to Ardanaiseig is now forested. It had been part of the Ardanaiseig Estate and it is now called Ardanaiseig Forest and belongs to a pension fund. Ardanaiseig House was built around 1834 by a descendant of the Inverawe Campbells as a replacement estate house for Tervine. It was initially called New Inverawe but when it was later sold to an English iron and coal magnate called John Ainsworth a condition of the sale was that it would no longer be called New Inverawe and so he called it Ardanaiseig (Point of the Ferry). This ferry would seem to have been the one based on Inishail that ran to both shores. John Ainsworth then became Liberal Member of Parliament for Argyll and was made a Baronet. Sometime after his death his son sold the property to Major Duncan MacCallum who was another MP for Argyll but this time a Conservative. After he died his widow broke up the estate of Ardanaiseig and sold off Tervine and Ballimore and then later Ardanaiseig and its policies. Ardanaiseig became an up-market country-house hotel, which is what it still is and it is advertised as a romantic holiday retreat. Its extensive gardens are open to the public.

From Ardanaiseig Point a number of islands can be seen. The furthest south of these is a group of three called the Black Islands. These were probably described as black because of the dark coloured pine trees that grew there. One of the islands still has a few very fine specimens of pine trees growing on it. The land at this end of

Loch Awe once had native pine trees on it and their remains can still be seen in the peat bogs, but further south the native trees all appear to have been broadleaved apart from some sparse yew and small juniper trees. Back in the early millennia BC the shores and hillsides around the loch would have been largely wooded but why and how the countryside became so denuded of trees, as it was in the early twentieth Century, is somewhat puzzling. In the latter couple of centuries sheep and sheep farming were undoubtedly the main cause of much of the woodland's demise, but earlier back into prehistory there must have been a good many other causes such as the apparently wetter climate in the last millennium BC that would not be conducive to tree regeneration. One thing is certain, early man did not simply physically chop the woods down. The trees would have grown up again much faster than he could do so. There are traditional stories told about loch-side woods being burned to get rid of wolves. I think fire would have been an important tool of Stone and Bronze Age man, which was used to clear woodland to improve pasture for grazing and hunting and to change the makeup of the forest-land to encourage berry and other food producing plants. So gradually over thousands of years the tree cover must have declined.

Close by the Black Islands is the fairly large island of Inishail now becoming overgrown with trees and bushes, but in the past it was very green and fertile and lived up to its alternative name of the 'Green Island'. There are many crannog foundation remains around this part of the loch probably because it is relatively shallow. If the winters in the crannog building days had been cold enough to completely freeze the shallower parts of the loch then I am sure that the crannogs would have been built with the piles and foundation building being done through the ice and all the materials transported on top of it. This would have made the whole operation much simpler. From early Christian times Inishail was considered to be a very holy place and was connected to Inchaffray Abbey in Perthshire. The

History of Kilchrenan and Dalavich states that a charter of 1275 mentions 'ecclesia Sancte Findoce de Inchealt', and this would seem to be when the island site was gifted to Inchaffrey Abbey by its Mac-Naughton owners.

At some early period there is said to have been a Cistercian Nunnery on the island whose nuns were famed for their piety and compassion, so much so that the island became a place of pilgrimage. Eventually the nuns left and a monastery was built there and the remains of the monk's fish ponds can still be seen. At some early stage a chapel called The Chapel of Findoc was built on the island and this became the place of worship for Inishail Parish which covered both sides of the loch. This Chapel remained in the possession of Inchaffray Abbey until the Reformation of the 1500's when it was taken over by the Presbyterian Church. It continued to be the local church until a new one was built, using some of the old church's stone, by the loch-side near Inistrynich in about1736. A ferry was based on Inishail and it operated to both sides of the loch with jetties at Ardanaiseig Point and just east of Inistrynich Island. There was a small farm on the island and there is said to have been a water-mill there but given how low-lying the island is and the fact that it would have had to rely solely on the limited rainfall there that hardly seems practical.

The parish graveyard was on the island from early days and it was the burial place of MacNaughtons, MacArthurs and Campbells. It contains a few interesting old carved medieval stones and is still used for some burials today. The 12th Duke of Argyll, who had unfortunately died during a hospital operation, was buried there in 2001. Prior to that the previous Duke's ashes were also buried there and it seems to have taken over from Kilmun as the Campbell Chief's burial place.

From the 5th Duke's instructions to his Chamberlain in 1771 it said that Thomas Turner was to be appointed keeper of the Rabbit

Within the ruins of the Parish Church on Innishail, an early Christian Cross was moved from the graveyard and erected on a plinth.

Warren of Inishayle. A house was to be built for him. He was allowed to keep a cow and calf, was paid £5-00 and had to live there and keep the ferns on one half of the island cut, sow some whine (whin) seed, and get some rabbits from Dunolly and Kintyre and write to the Bailie of Roseneath to send some as well.

An instruction on the margin said house was built, six rabbits were obtained from Kintyre, however, none came from Dunolly or the Clyde. The rabbits multiplied and seemed to be a success. They were later joined by a herd of fallow deer but they both appear to be long gone. The rabbits were possibly killed out when a conifer wood was planted on the island but this is also gone because it was felled for timber during the Second World War. Also in the 1700's it is said that an illegal distillery operated on one of the islands near here producing, it is said, a very potent whisky.

I have the Militia List of 1803 - 04 which gives the names and occupations of all the people living in this area who were liable for Service in the military: Parish of Innishail. Auchlian 9 four of them were weavers. 3 shepherds 2 servants. Bocaird 1 herd. Bovuv 5 1 farmer, 4 labourers. Cladich 3, 1, change keeper, 1 smith, 1 apprentice. Drumuerk 5, 2 weavers, 1 tailor, 2 labourers. Barundren 3, 2 tailors, 1 labourer. Keppuchan 2, 1 farmer, 1 labourer. Innishail 1, carpenter. Barbreck 9, 2 farmers, 1 shoemakers, 1 wright, 1 taylor, 1 surgeon, and 2 sons, 1 servant. Auchnacarran 9, 1 taylor, 2 farmers, 1 weaver, 2 labourers, 1 crofter, 2 nondefined. Hayfield 4, 1 servant, 1 gardener, 1 herd, 1 labourer. Balmore 1 farmer. Balbeg 4, 3 farmers, 1 shoemaker. Ichterachim, they were quite a squad, 15 in all, 1 agent, 1 wood manager, 1woodcutter, 3 carters, 1 fisher, 3 carters, and 5 workmen. They would seem to have been part of a squad making charcoal.

Back at the Ardanaiseig junction there was once a place called Creildarach nearby. It is marked there in 1801 but it is not in the 1841 census so it was possibly demolished when Ardanaiseig and its lodge house were built. A road from Ardanaiseig Lodge leads to Tervine Farm passing by some cottages on the way. The cottages are a mixture of old and new-build ones. Tervine farmhouse was originally the estate mansion house until New Inverawe, or as it is now called Ardanaiseig, was built.

The name Tervine means Land of Meal and it does seem to have been the site of a water meal-mill. A dam is still marked on Ordnance Survey maps. Much of the surrounding land has been cultivated in the past and it seems that any ground that was capable of producing crops had been used. Although it would not be cultivated continuously, as hillsides are not usually very fertile, and manure could not be spared from the in-by land to fertilize them. It would therefore be a case of cropping the outfield ground for about three years and then leaving it for a number of years to recover before it was cropped again.

According to the History of Kilchrenan and Dalavich Tervine is mentioned in the church parish records of 1375 spelt Terwhedych.

Later it was spelt Tiravain and in the 1841 census it had 20 inhabitants with Tiravain House having two. Tervine Farm is still a working
farm and on the loch shore nearby there has been an off-shore fish-
farming operation for many years, which is owned by Kames Fish
Farms. The fish farm rears rainbow trout in large netted cages in
the deep water at the beginning of the Pass of Brander.

Tervine is literally the end of the road and to carry on by car we
have to return to Kilchrenan, take the road past Glen Nant to
Taynuilt and then the A85 back to the Pass of Brander. But for the
purpose of the narrative we are carrying on by foot, which is something that should only be done by the experienced walker, because
one cannot follow the shoreline, as the Creag an Aoineidh precipice
and its associated scree slope, drop down almost perpendicular to
the deep waters of the Pass. The only way on foot is up and over
the top and it is a long hard climb of some five miles to the road at
the Bridge of Awe. A good view across to Cruachan Dam is obtained as we pass by Lochan na Cuaig (Cuckoo Lochan) with its burn
that tumbles down the precipice below.

McFadyen's Cave is marked on some maps to the side of this
sometimes impressive fall. This name comes from a tale that was
told in a 1400's poem by Blind Harry who was a renowned storyteller
of brave deeds and battles past. In it he describes how Robert the
Bruce and Sir Neil Campbell of Lochow fought a battle in the Pass
of Brander against a force led by a certain McFadyen who was a mer-
cenary in the pay of the English King, Edward I. In the poem Bruce
and his men were victorious but McFadyen and some of his officers
escaped across the river, climbed up and made a last stand high up
in this cave. Sir Neil and his men climbed up, killed them, cut off
their heads, dipped them in tar and displayed them on stakes along
the ridge above. This is a good story but all complete fiction.

An important battle did however take place in the Pass of Brander in 1309 and if we had been on top of Creag na Aoineidh on that

day we would have had a grandstand view of it taking place on the opposite hillside. This came about when the army of Robert the Bruce, with Sir Neil and Sir James Douglas' men met a large force of MacDougals and their allies, who were barring their way through the Pass of Brander. The MacDougals had set up an ambush on the mountainside above with a large force ready to roll down rocks and fall on Bruce's force when it advanced to attack. But Bruce knew all about ambushes and sent a lightly armed force, led by Douglas and Neil, even higher up the mountainside to attack the ambushers from above before he attacked the main body from the front. The Mac-Dougals were routed and many were massacred. It is said that the River Awe ran red with the fleeing MacDougals' blood. A poem called The Bruce written in about 1487 by John Barbour, the Archdeacon of Aberdeen, says that

> 'Ane wattir held thair way
> That ran down by the hillis side
> And was rycht styth bath deip and wyde
> That men in na place mycht it pas
> Bot at ane brig beneth thaim was.'

It does seem that there was some kind of wooden bridge across the river and that the MacDougals tried to destroy it, but were unable to do so before Bruce and his men captured it. They then followed on the MacDougals' heels and took their castle of Dunstaffnage where they installed a garrison.

After a long hard trek over the high ground we descend down towards the Awe Barrage and ahead of us on a flat area near the river are a number of small cairns said to be the burial places of the men killed in that battle. The Awe Barrage, or dam, actually lengthens that part of the loch and controls the outflow so that the water can be used to power a hydro-electric scheme. The power station is situated near the sea at Inverawe and is fed by a large underground tunnel that runs from the dam to there. But as it is only some hundred feet lower than the loch the water does not have a great deal of power and has to depend on volume rather than water pressure, which is why it requires a tunnel of 25 feet diameter to supply it. Water has also to be released down the river for the salmon and sea-trout and they have their own lift to get them up and down between the river and the loch. When the lift is in operation both water and fish go up or down as required. The hydro scheme was built during the hydro-building years after the Second World War and before nuclear power, cheap oil and gas became available. Such schemes could be said to have been the first large-scale providers of 'green power'. A short distance up from the dam, on this south-west side, is the ruins of two old houses but I have no information about them.

Assuming that it is allowed, which it is not, we now cross by the barrage and below us is a large pool in the river, which is a favourite fishing spot and a good place to see salmon leaping as they wait to go up by lift through the barrage. It was also around here that Campbell Muir hooked the mighty trout in 1866, which took him over two hours to land. We then continue on the A85 beside the water with the railway line running on the very steep hillside above. The Pass of Brander presented quite a problem to the builders of that line and the later modern road.

CHAPTER SIX

LOCHAWE
TO DRISSAIG

Next we come to the Cruachan Hydro-Scheme Visitor Centre and the car park is a good place to stop. Looking back we can see that the road that we have driven over is partly built out over the loch on concrete piles. This was because the railway line above did not allow it to be widened back into the hillside and so it had to be built out over the deep water. This was quite an engineering feat and was done during the road-widening operations in the 1960's. The visitor centre and car park are built on rock spoil that was excavated from the tunnels and power station chamber during the hydro scheme construction.

The Roadman's Cottage at Falls of Cruachan, home to Willie MacNiven, who maintained the section of road to Lochawe, was demolished to make way for the entrance to the Cruachan tunnel and offices. Descendants of Mr MacNiven still reside in the area.

Cruachan Dam, to which water is pumped from Loch Awe during periods of low electricity usage, for instant availability at times of peak demand.

Somewhere down in the loch there should be a large dump truck that was lost when someone reversed too close to the edge while tipping. Fortunately the driver managed to jump clear. It was never recovered because as an Irish workmate said 'it is a wild drop there to the bottom'. A red mini car is also down there somewhere. Some of the affluent hydro workers bought this new mini on a night out in Oban and on the way back to camp they were in a collision with another car and did not stop. They then realized that the police would be looking for a red mini so they drove the car to the edge of the water, loaded some stones into it and pushed it over. After which they realized that the police could find out that they had bought a red mini in Oban so next day, one of them went into Glasgow and bought a new red mini to replace it. Money was plentiful for the hydro-scheme workers but they worked long and hard hours often in conditions that would not be allowed today.

Power from the Glen is the logo of the North of Scotland Hydro-

Electric Board but power from the mountain would be a more accurate description of the Cruachan Scheme. An 150 foot high dam in a corrie 1,200 feet up on the mountainside creates a reservoir that powers the scheme. From the reservoir the water drops down two 55° angled penstock shafts to two giant turbines in a machine hall deep within the mountain. These turbines have a dual role because as well as generating electricity they can work in reverse as giant pumps. During the night, when demand for electricity is low, they use spare nuclear-generated power to pump water up from Loch Awe and into the dam. Because this power comes from the south of Scotland the Cruachan Power Station became part of the South of Scotland Electricity Company. These turbines can be powered up to full power in less than two minutes, and as each generates over 100 megawatts of electricity, this can be an important part of the board's generating capacity, and so the station is a very good power reserve in times of high demand. It is also a good tourist attraction with approximately 60,000 people taking the electric buses into the mountain to view the power station every year. This power station is actually at a slightly lower level than Loch Awe to let the loch's water flow into the turbines when they are working as pumps. One offshoot of pumping water from Loch Awe is that the dam reservoir now has char in it as well as the original brown trout which were living in the corrie's burn.

Deep within the mountain and connecting with this generating machine hall is a maze of tunnels and chambers serving many purposes. These and the machine hall, which is about the size of a football pitch 120 feet high and excavated out of solid granite, were the work of Edmund Nuttalls who was the main contractor on the scheme working with Thyssens, Wimpy and William Tawse. One large tunnel used for ventilation, cables and access goes straight up to the surface. This tunnel was excavated from the bottom up using an Alimak machine from Sweden, which used vertical rails bolted to the tunnel side and a working platform and cage that travelled up the rails to allow the overhead work of drilling and setting of explosives. The rail was removed before the explosives were detonated.

This scheme also makes use of what water can be obtained from the mountain's sides, and although this only amounts to 10% of the total capacity, it has tunnels branching out from both sides of the dam to catch the small burns descending from above. A tunnel from the back of the dam also goes right through the mountain and then branches out to catch the upper reaches of the Mhoille Burn and others that descend to Loch Etive. This part of the scheme was the work of the German firm Thyssens.

Most of the scheme's workmen were housed in two large hutted camps that were built at the foot of the Mhoille Glen, and as was to be expected, many of the men were a pretty rough lot and so to keep law and order they brought in a tough policeman to Dalmally in the shape of Donnie Graham. He earned the reputation of being able to settle trouble single-handedly. With the large amounts of money being earned there was some serious gambling taking place at the camps and professional gamblers were attracted there. One gambler called Docherty, who regularly made a big haul after pay day, met a sticky end after one session as his body was found wrapped around the prop-shaft of a bus. How it got there is not known but it was suggested that he had been killed and his body stuffed through an inspection trap in the floor possibly with the idea that the body would drop off somewhere on the road and his death be considered to have been the result of a traffic accident. As far as I know the case was never solved.

The scheme was officially scheduled to be opened by the Queen on 15th October 1965 but the generating turbines were not ready for operation by then, and so trickery had to be resorted to using an electric motor, sound effects and lighting to make it appear as if a turbine was in operation when the Queen pulled the switch. Neither she nor the many dignitaries and media folk present were any the wiser. It was actually about another two months before the work was finished and the first turbine was ready for operation. In 2005 the power station was given a major upgrade costing some £18,000,000 and this allows the output from it to be more flexible and to give another 20% power output.

Leaving the visitor centre we pass the Hydro-electric Board's offices and the power station's outflow and intake and then cross over the power station's tunnel entrance. Above us on the railway line is the Falls of Cruachan railway halt that was reopened in 1998, but it is a summer only request stop and is mainly used by Munro bagging mountaineers and visitors to the Cruachan Hydro-electric Scheme. It is a handy starting or finishing point for climbers of the Ben Cruachan group of mountains. The ones over 3,000 feet, and qualifying as Munros, are the main peak of Beinn Cruachan at 3,695 feet, Stob Dearg 3,611 feet, Meall Cuanail 3,004 feet, Drochaid Glas 3,312 feet, Stob Daimh 3,272 feet, Sron an Isean 3,163 feet and Stob Garbh 3,215 feet.

Running along here above the railway on the lower mountain slopes is the old military road to Bonawe built by Major Caulfield's men in the 1740's. This opened up the route through the Pass of Brander, which before this had simply been a very rocky and extremely difficult to negotiate track. But that had not stopped it from being an important smuggling route for contraband goods. After the union of Scotland and England in 1707 had landed Scotland with the heavy English system of import taxes, the Scots, who had objected to them and resorted to smuggling on a massive scale. The quiet and sheltered inlets of the west coast were ideal places for landing shipments of smuggled goods, such as tobacco from the Americas, wine and brandy from Europe and salt and soap from Ireland. Most of the population either gratefully accepted the benefits that smuggling brought or turned a blind eye to it.

Bunaw, as it was then called, with a hidden anchorage on the far side of Loch Etive, was a favourite place to land goods. They would then be taken across the loch and transported from there by strings of pack ponies through the Pass of Brander up Glen Lochy and then right across the country. Apparently the authorities tried to stop this by stationing an excise-man at Bonawe. In 1788 a collector of taxes stationed there had seized twenty casks of smuggled rum and brandy from James Elliess of Crieff and lodged them in a barn belonging to Captain Robert Campbell of Craig near Dalmally, but then it seems that Nicol Sinclair from Stronmilchan, Peter Sinclair from Creitchouran and John McCallum from Dalmally had broken into the barn and stolen the casks. A warrant was issued for their arrest but I don't know what the outcome was.

Above us at this end of the Pass are the oakwoods of Coille Leitire (Slope of the Wood) with its south facing slope and dry loam soil, which are ideal conditions for growing oak trees. These trees would almost certainly have been harvested for wood to make charcoal during the time of iron-smelting at Bonawe. Charcoal was the fuel used in the furnace and so the iron-smelting company leased suitable woods in the area, felled and coppiced the trees, and then cut the re-grown wood on a sustainable rotation of twenty or more years. In 1803 when Dorothy Wordsworth was travelling through there with her brother William, the poet, she wrote that she had seen a large sailing boat returning from unloading her cargo of bags of charcoal in the Pass.

This whole stretch of country through the Pass and on to the end of Loch Awe was a lonely and little inhabited place before the railway brought new developments. An 1801 map has only two places marked on that stretch of loch-side. These were Leaters, in Coille Leitire and Drissaig near the end of the loch. Just before we drive over a railway bridge there is the entrance and causeway to Innis Chonain, which is an island named after St Conan who was the local Saint and is reputed to be buried there. In more modern times the island was bought by Walter Campbell who styled himself as of Blythewood. He built a mansion house on the island and lived there

ABOVE: *Walter Douglas Campbell, an architect by profession and builder of St Conan's Kirk, bought the island of Innis Chonain from the Marquis of Breadalbane and built a fine mansion house there, where he lived with his mother and sister, until his death in 1914.*

LEFT: *The earliest phase in the evolvement of St Conan's Kirk shows it as having a slated roof in 1903-1908.*

with his family. He also built a small Kirk beside the village in the 1880's but he had dreams for a much grander building and this he began in 1907. In Walter Campbell and his family's time access to the island of Innis Chonain was by a fixed ferry-boat called the Catamaran, which ran on chains or cables and had to be wound back and forward by hand. However in the late 1940's a causeway was built to the island. The mansion house on the island was unfortunately destroyed by fire in 1989 and a new house has been built since then.

Not very far from Innis Chonain is Fraoch Eilean, which appears to translate into Heather Island, but in ancient Celtic legend Fraoch was a young warrior who was persuaded by his girlfriend's mother to fetch her fruit from an enchanted rowan tree that grew on this island, and gave eternal youth to anyone who ate its fruit. But this tree was guarded by a fearsome dragon and it was awakened and in the fight that ensued Fraoch was killed. No magic rowan grows on the island today but for some reason lots of salmonberry, the North-American raspberry, does.

The island has from very early times had the castle of Fraoch Eilean, or Frechelan, on it and this was a MacNachtan, or Mac-Naughton, castle. Their clan history says that King Alexander II granted the lands between the head of Loch Awe and Loch Fyne to them for their help in his campaign of 1222, and that Alexander III later gave a patent that gave Gillechrist, their Chief, and his heirs 'Hereditary Keepership of the Royal Castle on the island of Fraoch Eilean, on condition that he rebuild it and keep it in repair at the King's expense, and fit for him to stay in should he pass that way'. That patent is still in existence today and preserved in the General Register House in Edinburgh.

When Robert the Bruce started his campaign to become King the MacNachtans backed his opponent John Balliol. They fought against Bruce at Dalrigh but legend says that their chief Baron Donald was so impressed by Bruce's conduct during the fight, and his subsequent ordered retreat after losing the unequal battle, that he said that 'Bruce was the man for him', and so he and the clan switched their allegiance to him. They, it is said, supported Bruce through the rest of his campaign including Bannockburn where their chief Donald was killed. But they still seem to have lost out in the big share-out after Bruce took control of the country because they lost control of Fraoch Eilean to the Campbells. Although they did continue to occupy it for some time afterwards the Campbells have owned it ever since. However during the '45 rebellion it is said that the MacNaughtons dusted off their old charter, forcibly took control of Fraoch Eilean Castle, evicted the Campbell residents and made the castle ready to welcome Prince Charlie when he passed that way, but he never did.

Some repair and stabilization work has been done on both the old castle ruins and the four storey tower-house that was built within it in the 1600's. Those walls still stand to a considerable height. The castle also has a pit with a stairway leading down to it and a garderobe (toilet). If this was the dungeon it would seem to have been a rather posh one. Around 1970 some archaeological digs took place at the castle and various items were found including an English silver long-cross penny of the 1250's and a French 1672 Louis the Fourteenth coin. Also found were a section of a decorated cobalt-blue glass bangle from the First Century AD and part of a jet bangle that is possibly even older.

Beside the A85 road ahead a new housing development has recently been built around what had been local man Teddy MacPhee's Filling Station site. On the opposite side of the road, by the entrance to the road that climbs up the hillside to Cruachan Dam, is the hamlet of St Conan's Road, which originally was built as housing for hydro employees. Lochawe Village is narrow and strung-out as it grew up between the loch and the steep mountain slope.

The next place that we come to is St Conan's Kirk, which is a

The magnificent choir stalls of St Conan's Kirk photographed in 1953.

very interesting and complex church and I have heard it described as being like a small cathedral. It is a relatively modern church built by Walter Campbell from nearby Innis Chonain. A church was first built by him here in the late 1800's as a small local church and it was said to have been built there for the convenience of his aged mother. When she died he had a cross erected there as a memorial, and he appointed and paid for a Queen's Nurse to be based locally. In 1907 he began to expand the church into a really splendid building and he then spent the rest of his life planning and supervising this work. He died in 1914 but his sister carried on his planned work until she too died in 1927, and the building work was then carried on by the trustees until the new church was finally opened in 1930. St Conan's is still actually owned and run by the trustees with the help of a trust fund and public donations. It is an amazing building built mostly from local granite and using local tradesmen. An article written in the 1930's says that it was all built from granite boulders that were

S.S. "Countess of Breadalbane" at Loch Awe Station. The roofed, latticed, tower was a water operated, hydraulic lift, designed to transfer luggage up to Loch Awe Hotel.

rolled down the mountainside and then shaped by hand, but I think that that can only be partly true and just some of the granite would have been obtained in that way. It is built in many different styles and periods, incorporates objects from many old religious buildings and also commemorates local people and events. The small Bruce Chapel has an ivory and wood effigy of Robert the Bruce and incorporated in an ossuary is a small bone of his taken from Dunfermline Abbey.

Lochawe Village owes its existence to the building of the Callander to Oban railway line, which was opened in 1880 and the fact that that was the best place to build a steamer terminal and station to serve Lochaweside. The railway with its station and quay gave a great boost to the economy of the loch-side. Tourism boomed and in the summer three steamers sailed daily and connected with the trains.

The loch-side's goods also went by rail and steam cargo boats, which often towed barges of additional cargo. This may have been the reason that the local folks called all the cargo boats barges. One of the cargoes carried by the barges was timber from the loch-side's woods especially during World War One with the big demand for timber resulted in many of the loch-side woods being felled.

Steam sawmills were often set up and the felled logs would either be sawn into planks, sawn square for ease of transport, or simply made into large rafts which were towed, two at a time, up the loch to Loch Awe Station. There they were craned out of the water and loaded on to wagons. I remember Alec MacLeod saying that when he lived at Ardchonnel schoolhouse he used to hear the boats travelling through the night towing rafts of timber on their slow journey up the loch.

The cargo boats on Loch Awe had various owners but the one who is remembered most is Thomas Dow with his barges called the *Eagle* and the *Ben Cruachan*. The *Eagle* had been bought from H&D Cowan and they had advertised her in 1902 as sailing on Mondays and Fridays from Loch Awe Station to Ford and calling at as many piers as required. In winter this service terminated at Eredine and

S.S.M.V. "Glenorchy" formerly S.S. "Ben Cruachan" alongside the floating pier at Lochawe.

103

so avoided the very exposed and stormy last stretch of the loch. I believe that Dow carried on a similar service until he sold his boats and business to David Wilson in 1921.

Coal was an important, though dirty, cargo carried by the loch cargo boats but I have an article from *The Oban Times* of 1928 describing how a well-scrubbed and decorated the *Glenorchy* (the renamed *Ben Cruachan*) took all the Lochawe children on their annual sports and picnic outing down the loch to Eredine. There it seems they enjoyed a great day of sports, ice-cream and roundabout rides at Eredine House's grounds before sailing up the loch and home.

David Wilson sold the business to a Mr Sheriffs who ran it with the *Eagle* and the *Glenorchy*, which he had fitted out with motor engines in place of the steam ones, until the last of the cargo boats on the loch finally ceased running in 1935 made redundant as a result of the more economic road transport.

Thomas Dow had also owned the village store at Lochawe, and when he sold his cargo boats in 1921 he did not retire but ran the store. He did a weekly grocery and general goods delivery service down the loch as far as Kilmaha in an open boat and in all kinds of weather. He was still operating this service in the early 1930's and supplying my family when we lived at Cruachan.

Peter Wight established a joinery business in 1886 which was later taken over by Alastair MacIntyre and continues in the ownership of his family.

In a prominent situation above the station and quay stands the large Loch Awe Hotel, which is now owned by the Lochs and Glens Holidays Company. It was built by Duncan Fraser who appears to have been quite an entrepreneur. It is said that during the building of the railway line he had arrived in the area with a horse and cart and started doing contract work. If so he must have had a mercurial rise in his fortunes as it does not seem to have been long before he had taken over Dalmally Hotel and then built a new one in its place.

Loch Awe Hotel came later and by 1882 he owned and ran the first Countess of Breadalbane steamer, which was one of the two boats that ran on the tourist route from Lochawe to Ford.

Loch Awe Hotel became one of the popular fishing hotels on the loch-side and an angling writer in about 1900 describes how these hotels used their steam launches to tow a whole string of rowing boats and fishers down the loch in the morning. They then drifted back with the prevailing wind, fishing the bays and other likely spots as they went until they arrived back at their hotel in time for dinner. He was already at that time bemoaning the fact that the fishing was not comparable to what it once was be-

Thomas Dow at Lochawe Stores, built in 1833 by James West who was the first of only seven owners of the business which continues there today.

cause of the railway having made the loch accessible to all of central Scotland.

Across the road from the hotel were the hotel's stables and coach houses and after the Second World War when the local hydro-schemes were begun these were converted into a public house to cater for the workers. As they tended to be rather a rough crowd they built a very wide bar-top to protect the bar staff. The Tight Line pub is still in service and it was from here in the spring of 2009 on a dark and misty night that four fishermen set

105

out after midnight in their small boat to return to their campsite across the loch. Unfortunately catastrophe struck and a companion, who had stayed at their campsite, awoke during the night to hear cries for help. He called the emergency services but they seemed unable to organise any local rescue boat as they had their hands tied by official regulations. Before help could arrive from distant Renfrew the men had all drowned or died of hypothermia. This tragedy

A work boat, towing a string of rowing boats with ghillies to be dropped off at various angling spots to which the guests from Loch Awe Hotel would be driven by car.

resulted in urgent calls for a local rescue boat to be based nearby, and a secondhand boat has recently been purchased and is based on Innis Chonain. A register of the names and contact details of local volunteers who could possibly help in an emergency on the loch are being kept thanks to the newly formed Loch Watch Scheme.

On the right, past the imposing Loch Awe Hotel, is the Tower of Glenstrae mansion house built with a tower so as to give a view of Glen Strae. Unfortunately Duncan Fraser, who was by then likely a millionaire, built Carraig Thura mansion for himself and it blocked out this view. These buildings and many others are built of local granite that was quarried from the left-hand side of the Mhoille Glen and over a mile from the road. The quarried stone was transported by a light railway (with a standard guage) that ran from a siding at Drissaig. Next to Drissaig are the granite Cruachan Buildings and these were built to house quarry workers. The quarry was opened in the 1880's by Bonawe Quarries and it produced granite setts for the city's streets and building blocks, and I am sure that it would have supplied most of the St Conan's Kirk granite. In the quarry the granite would have been drilled and then blasted into pieces, but then the splitting and shaping of the blocks would largely have to be done by hand and this required a fairly large workforce. This workforce was mostly housed in a camp at the foot of the glen and for a while convicts from Barlinnie Prison were employed to do this work. In 1901 William Laing, a quarryman who worked there, was charged with the murder of James Lindsay the quarry manager whom he had attacked and killed. He pled guilty to culpable homicide, was found guilty and rather surprisingly was sentenced to only six months detention. The quarry continued operating until the First World War when demand for its products dropped away and it was closed and the railway line was lifted for its scrap steel.

Drissaig, which was the terminus of the light railway which transported granite from the quarry to be worked there into blocks and setts, pictured between 1890 and 1905.

CHAPTER SEVEN

KILCHURN
AND GLEN STRAE

From Drissaig a relatively modern section of the A85 runs across the low-lying, boggy land at the end of Loch Awe and over the River Orchy. Like the railway line 60 years earlier the construction of the road was problematical because of the boggy ground. The building of the long and expensive bridge over the river, known then as the "Yellow Bridge" due to the colour of the sandstone, took longer than anticipated and was not finished at the start of the Second World War. As this was part of a vital route to the naval installations

ABOVE LEFT: *Site preparation for the new road bridge over the River Orchy in 1930.*
ABOVE RIGHT: *The civil engineering challenge being overcome by the builders of the road bridge over the River Orchy. The main bridge structure is of three concrete arches, sitting on concrete piers, with expansion joints on each side of the central arch and on the landward sides of the outer arches. The bridge is paved on the north-eastern side with concrete benches inset at each of the bridge arches. Three flood arches on the south-east bank and two on the north-west together with a cattle underpass cross the marshy land.*

at Oban and Dunbeg and urgently needed to carry large and heavy loads, which the Stronmilchan road and bridges were having trouble coping with, work on the new bridge and road was rushed ahead and finished. It also connected up with the new section of the A819 Inveraray Road that followed the loch-side and cut out the Monument road.

Just over this new Orchy Bridge is the car park for visitors to Kilchurn Castle. The castle is mostly a ruined shell but it is a very popular tourist attraction. The castle can be accessed on foot from the car park under the nearby railway viaduct. The other way to it in recent years was by a steamboat ferry that ran from Loch Awe pier, but the dredged channel to the castle is now silted up and when I went that way in 2006 the boat got stuck in the mud.

Near to the car park there is a stretch of fertile looking ground with quite a lot of the herb spignel growing. Spignel used to be grown as a garden herb with the roots being used as a spice, so the castle's garden may have been around here. If so, this would be where, according to the Dalmally and the Glen booklet, that John MacGregor, the newly appointed Captain of Kilchurn, was instructed to have his gardener grow the red and white kale and onions that were part of his lease agreement. It was not only the Captains of Kilchurn who had to grow vegetables on the Glenorchy lands because in the 1600's, all the tenants and householders on the estate were ordered to have walled, stock-proof kail-yards. This was to grow vegetables and a few trees in them or be fined 10 pounds. Ten pounds was a serious amount of money to a poor crofter-type farmer.

This was just one of a great many estate rules or laws that were laid down by the baron and earl landlords of Glenorchy and all had hefty fines for non-compliance. Some others were 'burning on moors must only be done in March, and with six honest neighbours present whose advice must be listened too'. 'Peats could only be cut with a lowland peat-spade.' 'No swine must be kept.' 'Briar or thorn could only be cut during the waxing of the moon.' This I expect would be because it was believed that sap travelled up plants during a waxing moon and down during a waning one so cutting the bushes during the waxing moon would be deemed to be more effective in killing them. 'No vagabonds or poachers could be given lodgings.' 'Tenants were not to allow rooks, hoodie crows or magpies to nest on their property', and 'it was forbidden to cultivate or manure land within sixteen feet of the River Orchy'.

Another law said that 'no wife should drink at a brewster house unless her husband was present' and the penalty for doing this was a 20 shilling fine. For every chopin (about a pint) consumed, there was a further sentence of 23 hours sitting in the lang gadde, which would appear to be a kind of stocks. Also 'no person, man or woman could drink at such public houses or their premises, unless they had travelled at least eight miles, or come on a horse'. Although the estate itself got much praise for its improving and modern methods, the poor tenant or cottar living there must have had an extremely difficult time complying with its many laws, and any dissent would surely have meant eviction.

Kilchurn Castle is built on an outcrop of rock that is said to have been an island, before silting and the later lowering of the loch turned it into a peninsula. The original castle, now described as a keep or tower-house, is the part on the left as one enters the building. It was built around 1450 by Sir Colin Campbell who was a son of the Campbell chief in Innischonnel Castle, or if legend is to be believed it was largely built by his wife Lady Marriott. The story has it that Sir Colin started to build the castle then went off to fight in a Crusade and left her to continue the work. This 'Crusade' seems to have been to the Island of Rhodes as the Holy Land ones had finished some two centuries before.

Sir Colin had been gone for many years and with no word from

Kilchurn Castle in 1880.

him folks believed him dead but Marriott still hoped that he would return, so when a local chief, Baron Neil MacCorquodale of Phantilands, wished to marry her she put him off by saying that she would marry him when her castle was finished. She slowed down the building work and it is said she had parts of the castle fall down so that they would have to be rebuilt, but the castle was eventually finished and she reluctantly fixed a wedding date.

On the big day everything was prepared and ready and there were a great many guests arriving for the celebrations. Amongst them was a scruffy, bearded, weary traveller who, when he was given a drink by the bride-to-be returned the empty goblet with a ring in the bottom, which she immediately recognised as her husband's and on taking another look at the bearded man realized that he was her husband and flew into his arms. I don't know how much, if any, of the story is true.

It is said in the family's old historical Black Book of Taymouth that Sir Colin 'throch his valiant actis and manheid maid knicht in the Isle of Rhodes, quhilk standith in the Carpathian sea near to Caria and countrie of Asia the Less, and he was three sundrie times in Rome'. The Isle of Rhodes was held in these days by the Knights of St John who were both a military and religious organisation, and Rhodes would seem to have been a European outpost manned for the purpose of holding back the Muslims and infidels to the east. Sir Colin it seems had previously been honoured in Scotland after King James I was murdered at Perth in 1437 and he had helped to hunt down and bring to justice one of the people responsible. For this he was awarded that person's Barony of Lawers land on Lochtayside.

The title to the lands of Glenorchy, where he built his castle, had been given to him by his father who had somehow obtained title to both Glenorchy and Glenstrae lands despite the fact that they were occupied by the MacGregors, who regarded them as theirs but had no official title to them. This was to cause much trouble between them in the future.

The early part of the castle has a number of masons' marks on its stonework similar to the ones that are found at Rosslyn Chapel and so it seems that masons had come from there to work on Kilchurn.

Sir Colin became the guardian of a young Campbell chief from Innischonnel during the time that he was a minor, and he is credited with building both the first Inveraray Castle and the old town of Inveraray. He was succeeded by his son Duncan who enlarged and added to Kilchurn but he was unfortunately killed at the disastrous Battle of Flodden in 1513 along with his clan chief who was by then an Earl. They are both buried together at Kilmun Church near Dunoon for it is said that 'they fought and died valiantly together'.

Some further enlarging and alterations were later done to the castle but from sometime in the mid-1500's it ceased to be the main residence of the Campbells of Glenorchy. They had then started to live in the other castles on their expanding Perthshire lands, which is when a MacGregor of Glen Strae, became for a time the Keeper or Captain of Kilchurn, until a violent feud developed between his people and the Campbells.

In the 1650's Scotland was coming under the control of Cromwell's forces and the Campbells of Glenorchy and others backed his regime. However in 1654 there was a rising by the people loyal to King Charles and Kilchurn Castle was surrounded by a Loyalist force who were about to launch an attack on the castle when a large force of General Monck's troops arrived and drove them off. These troops would almost certainly have come from the Cromwell garrison that was stationed at Inveraray. During the Jacobite rebellion fears of the 1690's, a three storey garrison block that could hold 200 men was added to the castle. This is when the carving above the castle entrance, with its shield, scrollwork, crowns, initials of the Earl and his wife and the date 1693, must have been added.

The castle was garrisoned with Government forces in 1708 but in 1715 the Earl of Breadalbane supported the Jacobites and he manned the castle and raised an army in support of them. But it seems that when things went against them he quickly changed his mind and became a Government supporter. At the start of the 1745 rebellion the castle was hastily repaired using material sent from the Earl of Argyll's new castle that was being built at Inveraray and a garrison was installed.

After 1746 and the Jacobite defeat at Culloden, Kilchurn was no longer wanted as a garrison for troops and it was allowed to fall into disrepair. Its roof was badly damaged by lightning in the 1770's and not repaired, and in the 1800's the roof was stripped to provide timber for estate buildings and the castle then became a ruin. The big 1879 gale that destroyed the Tay Bridge, also blew down one of the castle's towers and its top still lies in one piece inside the castle.

Sometime in the 1800's a cottage was built against the inside wall of the castle, and in the 1880's a Donald Colquhoun and his family moved into it. He was an overseer in the granite quarries that had opened up in Glen Mhoille and he commuted daily to his work by boat and his young children walked to school in Dalmally. One of the daughters, Mary, got married in the castle and a great deal of planning and preparation went into the wedding. The hall in the old keep part of the castle had a temporary wooden floor laid, the walls were whitewashed and the whole place was decorated and given a festive look. On the day of the wedding two hundred guests turned up, which was many more than expected. It seems that one of Donald Colquhoun's sons, also named Donald, drove the Inveraray coach and had been inviting extra guests, but as they had all brought supplies with them there was plenty for everyone.

After the First World War this cottage was occupied by a young woman called Kate Munro. She had been working in the area as a land girl during the war and it appears that she became a drop-out from society. She lived alone in the castle with her dogs and cats and made a living gathering sphagnum moss for use as a dressing for war wounds and for making up wreaths. She obtained fuel by gathering coal on the railway line and she got supplies by rowing to Lochawe in her boat. She lived the life of a recluse and the local children considered her a bit of a witch. She lived in the castle right up to and through the Second World War but in 1946 she went missing and was later found drowned in the loch.

The castle eventually came into state protection and care in 1953 and it is now looked after by Historic Scotland who have stabilized the ruins to make them safe and added viewing platforms and stairs to make the castle more accessible to the public. All trace of the old cottage has been removed. In 1985 the widow of the last Lord Breadalbane sold the castle, which was then the last remaining piece of the Breadalbane and Glenorchy Campbell's once vast properties, to an Australian. He has since died and it has been bought by the local businessman Ian Cleaver who owns several local hotels and runs Highland Heritage Tours, but he of course cannot develop it or alter it in any way.

Leaving Kilchurn Castle we return to the junction of the newer A85 with the old by-passed Stronmilchan road now the B8077. On the hillside above 'veins of lead' are marked on Langland's 1801 map but I do not know of any mining done there. The granite quarries operated a good mile further up and on the left-hand side of the Mhoille Glen. The track of the old railway-line that ran up to these granite quarries is now a farm road and signposted as a one and a third mile walk. It is almost a century since the last quarry steam-engine chugged its way down from the quarries with its wagon loads of setts or granite blocks. This track is now a popular starting point for Munro baggers when they are doing the seven Cruachan peaks. Near the foot of the Mhoille Glen, Langland's 1801 map has Corry Hastle marked, which I think must be a misprint for Corry Castle. I don't know the history of Corry Castle but it probably belonged to the MacGregors and possibly it is their famed Glen Strae stronghold, and the castle that the present Castles farm and estate took its name from.

From the Mhoille Glen an ancient path leads up and over the Lairig Nodha Pass to Glen Noe on Lochetiveside . There is a flat rock on the summit of this pass, and it is here a strange ceremony took place on each midsummer's day, when a snowball from Ben Cruachan and a white calf were handed over by the MacIntyres of Glen Noe to their Campbell landlords as yearly payment for their lands in Glen Noe. This arrangement had been negotiated when the Campbells had taken over the MacDougal's lands on Lochetiveside, and as the Campbells were a very devious lot I have a suspicion that the Campbells did not think that the MacIntyres could honour the agreement, but in the winter the Glen Noe MacIntyres went high up on the steep north face of Cruachan, where the sun did not reach, and there they packed masses of snow into a deep gully to ensure that it lasted into midsummer and they always made sure that they had white cows and calves.

This arrangement lasted for several centuries until in the early

1700's the Campbell chief persuaded the MacIntyres to pay a monetary rent, but this gradually increased over time and eventually became so high that it was uneconomic for the MacIntyre chief to pay it and he and his family emigrated to North America. Many of the MacIntyres stayed on in Glen Noe as tenants of the Campbell-owned Breadalbane Estates, but during later clearances of the people in 1806 they were all forced out, and according to their Clan History 'were scattered to the far corners of the earth'.

Across the Mhoille Burn in the lower reaches of the glen is the modern farm and estate house of Castles. This estate consists of 8,000 acres of mostly steep mountainside and stretches back past the Cruachan Dam and up to the mountain tops. It is now owned by the James Hay Pension Trust Ltd. Above the farm and its modern cottages a burn on the face of Ben Eunaich plunges spectacularly over a precipitous crag into a waterfall called the White Mare's Tail. In 1950 near here Sir Percy Unna, mountaineer, conservationist and the main driving force in the founding of the National Trust for Scotland, was found dead after making a lone mountain foray from Dalmally.

The high ground around here is home to the golden eagle despite the persecution that it suffered for centuries as shown by the 1790's Parish Statistical Account, which says 'Premiums are given in this, and many other parishes for the extirpation of the mountain eagle. Yet still, this bird of prey, so destructive to kids, lambs and game, is common in our wilds and deserts'.

By the roadside past Castles Farm there is a giant electricity substation that is part of the high-powered 275,000 volt electricity line, which runs between the underground power station at Cruachan and Windyhills near Glasgow where it connects to the main South of Scotland electricity grid. This powerful line was routed to avoid almost all human habitation but then Argyll and Bute Council, for some inexplicable reason, built a whole housing scheme directly below it at Glenview. I notice that where the line crosses peaty ground the pylons are becoming very rusty and it appears that some kind of corroding acid vapour must rise from the peat.

Stretching out from that end of Loch Awe the glens of Strae, Orchy and Lochy were once the MacGregors' clan lands, but they held this land by the power of the sword and never had a royal title to it, which was to prove to be their undoing in later years. To tell the MacGregor clan's story properly would require a complete book, and Ronald Williams has done that very well in Sons of the Wolf.

The MacGregors were an ancient and proud clan and according to themselves their lineage goes back to a son or nephew of King Kenneth MacAlpine, the first King of Scotland, but more realistically and historically it can be traced back to one Malcolm, styled as Laird MacGregor of Glenorchy, who with many other clan chiefs swore fealty to the English King Edward at Berwick in 1296. Malcolm's son John, later fought with William Wallace but was captured and died in prison. Malcolm himself is said to have fought with Bruce at Bannockburn and later with Edward, Bruce's brother, in his unsuccessful campaign in Ireland. But if that is so, they were strangely not afterwards granted any land or favours and did not even obtain title to the land that they occupied.

The next MacGregor chief was Gregor of the Golden Bridles who it seems could afford to decorate his horses' bridles with gold. The MacGregor chiefs were in those days people of status and head of the main clan in the area with their chiefs buried by the High Alter in Clachan Dysart (Dalmally) Church. Their chiefs had been the local barons and as such were the administrators of justice with the power of 'pit and gallows', and justice, it seems, was dealt out pretty swiftly. According to the 1790's Statistical Account a person could be apprehended, tried, sentenced and hung, all in the one day. The writer says that this hanging was done on a hillock near the church, and I am told that there is, or was, a hanging tree above Edendonich.

The MacGregors lack of a title to their lands was their downfall because the Campbell Chief from Innischonnel Castle obtained the title to the lands, and in 1432 he granted Glenorchy and Glen Lochy to his second son Colin, which all spelled trouble for the MacGregors. Colin Campbell built his castle of Kilchurn at the head of the loch and calling himself Campbell of Glenorchy, began to settle his own people on what the MacGregors regarded as their land. This resulted in them being evicted or at best becoming tenants of the Campbells. The response of some of the displaced MacGregors was to return, raid and loot their lost land but gradually the Campbell might prevailed and the MacGregor depredations resulted in Duncan Campbell, the next Laird of Glenorchy, and others, being given a legal right to act as they wished 'for staunching thiftrief and other enormities, throw all the realm'. This gave him and the other sufferers the right to pursue and hunt down the MacGregors as outlaws.

Gradually they were forced off most of their land and had to take refuge in Rannoch Moor and other isolated places from where they still returned to loot and raid. This dispossession of their land was not initially the case with the Glen Strae MacGregors because that land belonged to the Innischonnel Campbell Chiefs, now Earls of Argyll, and the MacGregors there had been given a legal lease to it. Glen Strae however became the property of the Glenorchy Campbells and Gregor, the young chief, was also forced to become a fugitive. The Glenorchy chief at that time was Grey Colin and he obtained 'Letters of Fire and Sword' against the MacGregors who he said 'have massit themselves in great companies – and drawn to them the maist part of the broken men of the hale country, whilk at their pleasure burns and slays the poor lieges of this realm, reives and taks their goods'.

The MacGregors, however, had one unexpected and powerful ally in Mary Queen of Scots who heard of their plight and tried to get them land to settle on, but Grey Colin managed to stop this and got the MacGregor Chief outlawed. The Queen was not to be baulked and she had the Chief and all his clan members pardoned for their past crimes. This could have been a whole new beginning for the Clan, but the wilder elements of the Clan could not be controlled and soon Queen Mary herself was deposed and a prisoner in England. This allowed Grey Colin and his son Black Duncan to resume their persecution of the MacGregors, and Gregor their Chief was captured, tried before a court with Grey Colin as judge and beheaded at his castle of Balloch.

The new MacGregor chief was now young Alasdair from Glen Strae and he had an impossible task trying to care for and control the scattered clan, many of whom knew no other life than that of an outlaw. Around 1590 two MacGregors were caught poaching deer by John Drummond, who was the keeper of the King's Royal Forest in Perthshire, and he cut off their ears as a punishment but later a band of MacGregors met up with John Drummond, killed him and cut off his head. They then called in on his sister and asked for food. This she willingly gave them and left them seated around the table but when she returned she found the head of her brother as the centre-piece on the table. It is said that she was driven out of her mind by this cruel act. The MacGregor band then took the head to Alasdair and asked for his protection, which he along with a great many others of the Clan unwisely agreed to. The Privy Council's action was to outlaw the whole clan and they appointed 18 of the Highland chiefs to hunt them down and even men from as far away as the then Shire of Tarbert, in South Argyll, were called to arms to help hunt down the MacGregors, but not all of the clan chiefs wanted to become involved in this as the MacGregors were desperate men who resorted to guerrilla tactics and fought back fiercely.

To try and defuse the situation Alasdair appealed directly to King James VI and Alasdair was granted a pardon for himself and members of his Clan for the murder of the King's Keeper and other crimes, but there were high bail payments to be made, which the Clan could not pay. Many of them continued to rob and plunder sometimes at the instigation of the Earl of Argyll who cynically used them to carry out depredations that would benefit himself, such as a raid against the Colquhouns on Loch Lomond-side where they killed a good number. The Colquhouns appealed to the King taking with them the bloody shirts of the dead. This caused the King to grant a 'Commission of Fire and Sword' and allowed them to call out the fencible men of Dumbarton. They raised, it is said, 300 horse and 500 foot soldiers to attack the MacGregors in their own strongholds. But the MacGregors too had sent out a rallying call and hundreds of MacGregors and others gathered to stop the Colquhoun army.

In the battle that followed they routed the Colquhouns then went on to lay waste to the Colquhoun lands. One of their band, a MacDonald from Glencoe, massacred a large group of prisoners, which was all too much for the King who was just about to set out for England and he gave the order to 'extirpate Clan Gregor and to ruit oot their posteritie and name'. A reward was paid for the head of any MacGregor man produced and if the killer himself was an outlaw he was pardoned for all past crimes. Women and children were also killed, MacGregor houses were burned and their crops destroyed.

Black Duncan imported bloodhounds from Italy and trained them to hunt down the MacGregors, but despite it all the MacGregors and their chief, Alasdair, survived. Their plight however was desperate and when Campbell of Ardkinglas, who Alasdair regarded as a friend, offered to intercede on his behalf Alasdair went to meet him at Ardkinglas but he was seized and bound. However, whilst crossing Loch Fyne he managed to escape and swam ashore. The Earl of Argyll let it be known that he would have him escorted safely across the border to England, which was done but he was promptly seized there by his escort and taken as a prisoner to Edinburgh where he was promptly tried and hanged.

The MacGregors rose again and laid waste the Campbell lands, but it was a last desperate venture and the persecution and killing continued until the Clan was scattered far and wide with many forced to settle elsewhere under new names. Today practically nothing remains of their Glen Strae settlements because the Glenorchy Campbells had everything belonging to them eradicated from that landscape to make sure that they could not return.

Today there is only one occupied place in Glen Strae proper. That is the farm at Duiletter (Black Slope)), which was built during the sheep-farming years. Hill sheep-farming had started in Glenorchy Parish early as is shown by the 1790's Statistical Account for the parish, which says that 'numerous flocks of large and heavy sheep now pasture almost the whole year on these mountains and wilds, where formerly were to be found, and only for the summer months, a few light sheep and goats, small hill horses, as they were called, and some herds of black cattle. Then it was believed that no domestic animal could stand the severities of the winter on the high and stormy grounds, even the goats and sheep were housed and fed in pens during the rigour of the season'. Glen Strae was then part of the Breadalbane Campbell's enormous estates.

Later in 1841 Duiletter had 22 inhabitants but with the break-up of the Breadalbane estates the land was sold off, and sold again and now it is a farming and sporting estate called Glen Strae consisting of some 10,000 plus acres and belongs to a Richard D Schuster. The glen has changed from the bare and virtually barren sheep-cropped state that I remember and now it has more trees and vegetation in the glen and a large and complex system of wildlife ponds in its lower reaches.

There had been two conifer plantations planted in the glen by the Forestry Commission in the 1950's, but that was only after a bitter legal dispute with the Campbell tenant farmer had been won. A forest road was also made, up to the main forest block, at that time and a concrete bridge was built across the Strae. Now a road of sorts continues on up the riverside and glen, to finish near three groups of old ruined shielings. The middle group of ruins called the 'Shielings of the Hazel', suggests a more wooded and productive countryside in past times. They and the others would have been summer dwellings for the folks, mostly youngsters, who herded and tended to the livestock, made butter and cheese and did various other jobs. When these three shieling groups were occupied there would have been three nearby young communities up there at the head of the glen, and I imagine happy days for the young folk who were largely free from the usual family constraints and could mix with many other young folk of their own age.

Most of the farm stock was taken up into the hills in summer to protect the unenclosed crops and preserve the grazing in the lower glens. I think the Glen Orchy people could have had a share of some of these shieling lands and this ancient custom of taking the animals out into the hills in summer would have been carried on from the distant past right up until sheep took over the hills and glens.

These shieling groups are the ruined villages that are signposted at the foot of Glen Strae as being a five mile estate walk. There was in the earlier sheep-farming days an isolated shepherd's house over two miles up the glen from Duiletter Farm and this was accessed by a footpath up the right-hand side of the river. This as far as I know, was occupied up until the 1930's and it was part of a Dalmally postman's delivery round. The house was called Inbhir nan giubhs (Mouth of the Pines). That was because it was at the junction of the Burn of the Pines with the River Strae.

There are no pinewoods there now but in the early 1800's there were still large pine trees growing in that area and they provided the timber for the new Dalmally Church's roof beams. Also in earlier

ABOVE LEFT: *The elaborate construction of the conical timber roof of the octagon in Glenorchy Kirk is of impressive dimensions, with the principal tie-beam spanning the building being 15 metres in length.*
ABOVE RIGHT: *The imposing monument to Duncan MacLaren who rose to become Lord Provost of Edinburgh and Member of Parliament.*

times there were extensive pinewoods in the Strae, Orchy and Lochy glens and so it seems appropriate that pine is the clan badge of the MacGregors. The old empty cottage was in later years used as a bothy by the RAF Mountain Rescue teams when they were on exercise in the area, but there was nothing anyone could do when a low-flying American jet plane flew into the hillside on the right hand side of the glen past the large conifer planting. The large parts of the plane were all buried but small pieces were still to be seen when I later helped plant that conifer wood.

Returning to the mouth of the Strae glen and the B8077 we pass the new-built Strae Bridge Cottage before we cross the old Strae

Bridge, which was built in around 1780, and on a rise above us there stands a very large and finely carved sandstone monument in the form of a Celtic Cross with a bust of Duncan MacLaren inserted into it. He was born in 1800 at Renton in the Vale of Leven but spent his schooldays living with a cousin in one of the now grass-covered ruins at Tullich where the monument is. When he left school he became an apprentice to an Edinburgh firm owned by his relations then later went into business on his own, prospered and eventually became Lord Provost of Edinburgh and a Member of Parliament for there. But apparently he never forgot his young and happy days at Tullich.

Tullich (Knoll) in 1841 had 16 inhabitants and at the present time there is one house called Inverstrae near the old site. Below there, and now blanketed by conifer wood, is Tom Mhargaidh (Hillock of the Market) and this was once the local market site where the twice yearly market fairs were held - St Conans on the third Wednesday of March and St Andrews on the fourth Tuesday of November. These were too early and too late in the year for long distance cattle droving and so it must have been only local cattle that were sold. The November fair was, in later times, the 'term' time or feeing time for hiring farm workers who at that time either worked on a yearly or a six month contract.

CHAPTER EIGHT

STRONMILCHAN AND CRAIG

High up on the hillside are the ruins of the old MacGregor Chief's house of Tigh Mor (Big House), and not much further on, on the B8077, is Stronmilchan, which translates into nose-shaped hill of the greyhounds due to the shape of the hill looking like a greyhound from a certain angle. Stronmilchan is marked on the Joan Blaeu/Robert Gordon map of 1654 and also Herman Moll's 1745 map and it would appear to have been a fairly large-sized farming township. On Langlands 1801 map it was called Stronmagachan, and as magachan means abounding in small rigs, and it had recently in the 1790's been made into crofts each with its own strip of land and house, that would seem to be a new name for it. However it reverted back to its old name because in the 1890's Ordnance Survey Map it is given its Gaelic name of Sron-mhial-choin (Stronmilchan). These new crofts and houses had been pointed out to Dorothy Wordsworth and her brother William in 1803 as they travelled to Dalmally over what is now called Monument Road. She thought they were attractive and innovative, but on driving past them later she realized that up close they were rather ugly and poor looking. She was distressed to see an old woman creeping along behind a cow that was grazing the trough between two rigs and stopping it from eating the crops on either side.

These new crofts at Stronmilchan were created by the Breadalbane Campbells, but later they carried out massive evictions to make way for large sheep runs and farms, and as a result the population of Glenorchy Parish plummeted. The parish minister, the Rev Duncan MacLean says in the 1843 Statistical Account, 'A great and rapid decrease has, however, taken place since 1795. This decrease is mainly attributable to the introduction of sheep, and the absorption of small into large tenements. The aboriginal population of the parish of Glenorchy has been largely supplanted by adventurers from the neighbouring district of Breadbalbane, who now occupy the far largest share of the parish. There are a few, and only a few, shoots from the stems that supplied the ancient population'. He mentions names that have almost disappeared as being, Downie, Macnab, Mac-Nicol, Fletcher and MacIntyre, and says that the MacGregors were gone completely. Then he goes on to say that, 'By this nobleman's mania for evictions the population of Glenorchy was reduced from 1806 in 1831, to 831 by 1841, or by nearly a thousand souls in the short space of ten years'. This leads me to think that the Rev Duncan MacLean must have been a brave man to speak out in such a way about his all-powerful Campbell landlord and Church patron.

Stronmilchan, however, seems to have escaped during these clearances because in 1841 it still had a population of 139 people. In modern times Stronmilchan is still a strung-out development on the old crofting and other sites, and crofting is still carried on and it is still officially a crofting community. By the riverside below Stronmilchan stands the White House, which is now enlarged from the days when it used to be the home and office of the local Breadalbane ground officer or factor. He would have been a much-feared man in his day as his word would have been virtually law for the local tenants.

Across the Allt Donachain we come to Edendonich, which is another strung-out development of now mainly modern houses. The name may mean the 'Hill-face of Donan' who was an ancient holy man and Saint. In 1762 Cambell of Carwhin noted that he had

A thatched cottage, identified by the hill behind as being at Edendonich near the Smiddy, is from an album of "Camera Studies" by the MacDougall family who owned Sonachan Estate between 1898 and 1917.

contracted with John Brown, mason, for building a bridge over the Water of Edindonich in Glenorchy on the line of the public road from Dalmally to Bonawe now being carried on by a party of the military men. Along this road we now have masses of Himalayan balsam growing, which looks very nice when in flower but can become a pest. Past Edendonich we now have the Orchy Bank Guest-house beside the river but a 100 years or more ago this building was a bakers and general merchants selling all kinds of groceries and hardware of every description.

On the left is the road to Craig with at the start of it Smiddy House, which was the local blacksmith's place and up to and during the mid-1900's was occupied by Mick MacDonald who, as well as his smiddy business, ran a mobile shoeing and repair service that covered a wide area.

Craig and its estate land like almost all the land around the area once belonged to the Campbells of Breadalbane and they, in the

127

ABOVE LEFT: *A horse being shod by Mick MacDonald the blacksmith, who travelled widely shoeing horses and repairing farm machinery and was highly regarded in the area.*
ABOVE RIGHT: *Mick MacDonald - "The one that* did not *get away".*

times when it was fashionable and a status symbol to own or lease a sporting estate, built Craig Lodge and let the estate and lodge out to wealthy tenants for the shooting and fishing season. It formed quite a large estate with a good part of it deer forest and with good salmon fishing on the River Orchy, but with the later downturn of the Breadalbane family's fortunes parts of the Craig Estate were sold off to pay debts. After the Second World War a great deal of it was bought by the Forestry Commission and most of that has been planted up with conifer trees many of which are now being felled and the land replanted. The Craig land now consists of a farm of 2,957 acres owned by Donald and Alastair MacLaren.

Back in 1746 James Macnab, a drover living at Craig, was given a safe-conduct permit for himself and his two men to go and buy cattle in Kintail and Skye. It shows how important droving was considered to be in that drovers were still allowed to travel and bear arms in the year of Culloden.

On a present day journey around Loch Awe the only arable crop likely to be seen growing or stored is silage, and although this, in our damp climate, is a very suitable crop to grow, things were all very different in past times when most foods had to be grown on the farm. The Parish Minister of the 1790's lists the main crops as oats, potatoes, Scotch bear (a kind of barley), turnips and hay, and he goes on to say, 'Nowhere are potatoes cultivated with more care or thrive better. For nine months of the year potatoes make a great part of the food of the middling and lower ranks of people, and it may be said with truth that till the general introduction of potatoes into this country so little adapted from soil and climate to the growth of other grain, the poor and lowest classes pined away nearly half of their time in want and hunger'.

Craig Lodge, the old estate mansion house, was bought by Calum Macfarlane Barrow in 1970 and is now run as a religious centre and retreat. During the Bosnian War Magnus, his son, organized and took supplies there to relieve the suffering and this grew and developed into Scottish International Relief, which has since expanded worldwide and is run by Magnus from Craig Lodge and Glasgow.

The organization now has an annual turnover of some £5,000,000 plus and has been renamed Mary's Meals and is doing very good work by helping to feed starving children in many countries. From Craig an old road of sorts once continued up the riverside and past the various old settlements on that side of the glen, but these, with the exception of two, are now long gone and the modern road is on the other side of the river. This is the way that we shall be going and so we return back to the Dalmally Bridge.

The present three-arched Dalmally Bridge and the Bridge of Orchy were built around 1780 less than thirty years after the military roads were built through these places, which is puzzling, as surely these military roads had bridges. The bridges built on such roads by Major Caulfield and his teams were usually substantial stone structures with many still being in use today. Could it be that he had made

The three-arched Dalmally Bridge, above which stands a memorial to the dead of two World Wars was completed in 1780.

use of old estate bridges that were already there before the military roads were built?

There is a concrete abutment for a bridge just above the present Dalmally one, but it is modern and would have been built for the temporary wartime Bailley Bridge that was erected across the river to bypass the old stone one early in the war. In the days before there was a bridge at Dalmally, a ferry plied across the river to the church on its island, and from there a short bridge across the Little Orchy river diversion would have joined the island to the far side.

The church site, on its natural mound on the island, is ancient and there must have been a number of churches or places of worship there through the ages. In the mid-1800's the place ceased to be an island when the Little Orchy was blocked off during the embanking and piling work that was done by the Breadalbane Estates to control the river and prevent it flooding the surrounding land. Quoting from the 1850's Statistical Account it says, 'The River Urchy, which by overflowing its banks when in flood was want to do a great deal of damage, is in course of being embanked for a space of two miles at least. This embankment, which is nearly finished, has done a great deal of good', and it also goes on to say that 'The bed of the River Awe, where it flows out from the lake, was considerably lowered and an immense mass of stones, the accumulation of centuries, was removed allowing the water to escape with greater rapidity. This drainage has done a great deal of good in different places along both sides of the lake, but more especially to the low ground along the banks of the Urchy'. This last part will refer to the 1818 dredging of the River Awe outlet, which lowered the level of Loch Awe by about seven feet.

Just across the Dalmally bridge is the local war memorial built in 1926. It is situated by the roadside on a high outcrop of rock and lists the local men killed in the two World Wars, the highest toll being for the First World War with twenty six killed and six in World War Two.

Glenorchy Kirk and grave-yard is just ahead built on the high ground that would have protected it from the flooding river in the past. The old name for the church and parish was Clachan Dysart meaning a place of religious retreat, but I don't know whether the retreat referred to St Conan, St Maillidh or even St Donan. In 1692 when a list of the fencible men was drawn up, Clachan Dysart Parish was the only one in the area that was fully armed with each man having a sword and a gun.

Glenorchy Kirk, the third on the site, opened for worship in March 1811.

The present church, which was built in 1810, was paid for by the Earl of Breadalbane and designed by James Elliot who also designed and built Taymouth Castle. It is an attractive octagonal-shaped building with a tall belfry tower attached. The roof beams and other wood features are of local pine that came from the last of the old native pines that grew in Glen Strae. It had a considerable amount of restoration work carried out around 1900 and the stained glass window featuring 'The Good Samaritan' was added then. About another 90 years later in 1988 there was a further £200,000 spent on the building to bring it

A faithful representation, by Morag Malcolm, of a medieval sculptured stone in Glenorchy churchyard, representative of the Loch Awe School of carving of the 14th to 15th century, portraying a man armed with a sword and spear.

up to its present state. During that restoration many ancient human bones were discovered buried in the foundations, but these apparently had already been disturbed and after investigation they were again reburied.

The churchyard has many ancient medieval carved stones and these are attributed to the 'Loch Awe School' of carving, which is a modern term to describe the style of stone carving that was done by the local stone carvers in the middle ages. Examples of this style are to be found as far afield as Islay.

One elaborately carved stone of later date appears to have been re-used and commemorates Dugald Lindsay who was minister of the parish from 1689 to 1728. He was an Episcopalian minister and in 1690, when the Synod of Argyll ordered all its churches to adopt the Presbyterian form of worship, he refused to change and eventually a new minister was appointed in his place. This was against the congregation's wishes and no one would have anything to do with the new minister. The only lodging that he could get was with the man that he was replacing. On the Sunday in April 1691 when the new minister was due to conduct his first service a large and hostile crowd gathered in the churchyard. He was surrounded by 12 armed men with drawn swords and forcibly marched off in a procession headed by two pipers. They marched him all the way to the parish boundary near Tyndrum and made him promise never to return before releasing him. It seems that these 12 armed men were not from Glenorchy but were from Glencoe where the people were also Episcopalians and were from that Mac-Donald clan that was to be so brutally massacred less than a year later. This example of people power certainly worked because the Rev Lindsay continued on as Minister at Dalmally until his death 37 years later. As for the deposed minister he unsurprisingly reported back to the Synod that he had 'received verie undutiful entertainment'.

A reminder of the body-snatching days of the early 1800's is to be seen in the churchyard. There is a large iron mort-safe that would have been used to protect the newly buried bodies. Although with Dalmally's distance from cities and medical establishments I would have thought the bodies would not have been in much danger. This mort-safe measures seven feet by six and consists of a heavy iron frame with legs and four heavy iron grids that were set into it and secured with iron straps. It has iron loops around the inside of the frame that would appear to be for iron spikes. The legs on the mort-safe and some other aspects of it I find very puzzling. It would seem that holes must have been dug for the legs to stand in when the mort-safe was fixed over a new grave, then, if my ideas are right, long iron spikes would have been driven into the ground around the grave and the four iron grids laid in the frame and locked in place to prevent the spikes removal. The mort-safe would then be left in place till the body had started to decompose and it was deemed safe to remove it.

This type of mort-safe would have allowed the grave to be filled in at the burial unlike other kinds where the mort-safe was like a cage and the grave was left open, which meant the mort-safe and coffin had to be raised again to remove the mort-safe.

It is now sitting over the grave of John MacLaurin the late tacksman of Clachan and Glenfyne who died in 1828. Tacksmen in general were moneyed middle-class men and his family probably could have afforded to hire the churchyard's mort-safe to protect his body. This mort-safe appears to have been factory made but other mortsafes I have seen, such as the parts of ones that are on display at St Conan's, have all been different styles and it would seem as if some of the local blacksmiths made them to their own design.

Some of the churchyard stones are interesting in the information they give and one illustrates the high infant mortality rate before modern medicines and know-how. 'Archibald, died in May 1801. Three boys, each baptized Neil and a girl baptized Ann. All of whom died in their infancy'. It must have been even worse in earlier times as the 1790's Statistical Account records that smallpox that had killed many children in the past was now eradicated by inoculation. Not everyone died young however and there is a stone in a walled enclosure dated 1798 that commemorates a Capt Robert Campbell, Craig, and is also in memory of an Isabel Campbell who died in 1847, aged 108. One modern stone with gold lettering also has a lapwing in gold and this simple design is somehow very appropriate and pleasing.

CHAPTER NINE

DALMALLY, INVERLOCHY
AND GLENORCHY

Leaving the church car park we cross the old 'Little Orchy Bridge' and then past the Highland Critters gift-shop, with its small wild-life area, to the junction with the A85. On the traffic island at the junction is the Bruce Stone so called because Robert the Bruce is said to have sat on it when he passed that way before the Battle of the Pass of Brander but I am somewhat sceptical of that. Across from the junction is the now very large and florally decorated Dalmally Hotel, which is part of the Highland Heritage Tours Group. The hotel has

Dalmally Hotel in the 1930's, at the road junction from Stronmilchan showing the Bruce Stone in the foreground.

increased in size many times since it was originally built by Duncan
Fraser back in the 1880's, and it now has the capacity to take the passengers from a good many Highland Heritage tour coaches.

In 1803 when James Hogg, the shepherd poet, stopped at the
Dalmally Inn, which was then across the road where the auction mart
now is, he said that the inn was a poor place with some of the windows built up with turf and he was refused a fire in his room to dry
himself as they said that there was a shortage of fuel. The main fuel
used, before the arrival of the railway allowed coal to be brought in
cheaply, was peat and the Rev Joseph MacIntyre writes in the 1790's
Statistical Account that in a wet season when the peats could not be
properly dried there was much suffering among the lower classes in
the winter because of this.

His description of the Dalmally Inn does not agree with James
Hogg's, because he says that 'there is an excellent inn in the parish at
Dalmally. Nowhere in the Highlands has more attention been paid
to the accommodation of the traveller than on the property of Lord
Breadalbane'. Later, in the 1840's, the next Statistical Account says,
'Since then the Inn of Dalmally has been considerably enlarged. A
very comfortable and respectably-kept inn has been built at Cladich,
and another on the south side of the ferry of Portsonachan. The
whole of these places of entertainment are provided with excellent
accommodations, and kept, it is believed, in a manner highly satis-
factory to the public. Our high roads, of which there are several
lines, are maintained in an excellent state of repair. Facilities for travelling have greatly multiplied. Conveyances of every description
from the seated cart to the gay and dashing barouche, and post-
horses are kept at all our inns, more especially at Dalmally'. This
sounds a great deal different from what it was like in James Hogg's
day.

The Free Church was located between Dalmally Hotel and the
entrance to the Glenview Housing Scheme. It was in use up to the

1930's but a ruin by the late 1940's. Two new houses now stand where the Free Church once was. The Glenview Housing Scheme is a council development that was started in the 1950's with 12 houses, a new police house and station, and a forester's house for the expanding Glen Orchy Forest. Six of these new houses were also allocated for forestry workers. Later many more council houses, a new school and a shop were built, but unfortunately many of these are directly below the high-powered Cruachan Power Station line.

In a railed enclosure across the road from the police station is the stone-lined St Conan's well. This was blessed by St Conan and considered to be holy and to have healing powers with early writers describing its waters as salubrious. In later years an iron drinking cup was attached by chain to the well and this is still in existence. During a clean out of the well by the Dalmally Historical Association some years ago a good number of coins from the 1600's onwards were discovered.

An old story is told about St Conan and how he once met with the Devil in order to sort out the local people and see who should have them when they died, but after sorting the good and the bad there were quite a number of middling cases so they each agreed to pick one in turn. However the Devil became over excited and tried to pick out of turn whereupon St Conan rapped him on the knuckles and said 'Na Na, fair play, paw for paw'.

On from the well some older, mostly council built houses, the recently demolished old school site, five reconditioned pre-fab houses from 1947/48 and the local joiner's workshop are beside the road. The old school was built in the early 1800's and so would be the one that a certain John Cameron, nicknamed the Grey Badger, took over in 1843. He had previously been schoolmaster in Kilmichael Glassary School and to get to Dalmally he travelled to Ford, sailed up Loch Awe and then was rowed up the River Orchy to the school.

This Dalmally or Glenorchy School seems to have had a very good reputation in the late 1700's. The Rev Joseph MacIntyre says in the Statistical Account that, 'The school of Glenorchy has long been in great repute, and is well attended. Beside the natives, many children, both from the East and West Indies have been from time to time sent for their elementary education to this seminary where freed from that contagion of vice and bad example, which too often corrupts the morals of youths in towns, they form early habits of virtue, and acquire a vigour and hardiness of constitution less common at their years in warmer climes. Many of those, who in the early period of life, have been brought up at this school have become distinguished as useful professional men in the various situations of society'. He goes on to say, 'During winter the scholars amount to 100 and then an assistant is employed, and even in the summer months, when many of the poorer children are obliged to leave school and go to service, the number attending is seldom under 60'.

The Reverend does not, however, appear to have had a very high opinion of women and says about them and their earnings, which were then less than half that of the men, 'Let not their earnings then, advanced as they are, be grudged but let all who respect the female character, and female utility regret that these earnings are often thrown away on the gewgaws of vanity and fashion. Every man of humanity is pleased to see them clad in decent and suitable apparel but it is painful to observe that what should be support to their future families, and a provision for sickness and old age, is misapplied in the purchase of silks, laces, lawns and tinsel! But the moralist may speculate on this female infirmity as he chooses as far as the lass has cash or credit to procure braws she will step by step follow hard after what she deems grand and fine in her betters'. And on smoking he says, 'Let the men, however, continue to do in this as they choose, but far be it from the fair and respectable females of this vale to disfigure their features, and to destroy their powers of sweet song and cadence by a habit so repugnant to everything engaging and cleanly in woman'.

Above and across the road from the far end of that development is the recently built medical centre, the post office, sorting office and chemist's shop and a new recreation centre and sports complex. Next place is Tullich where the Free Church manse was and the road to Brackley Farm with, at its entrance, the Council Road Department's depot and yard. Brackley Farm has been farmed for three generations by the Crerar family. Some of its old land is now forest but it still has 3,755 acres and is owned and farmed by Sybil (Crerar) and husband George MacPherson. An old road continues on from there to some old ruined settlements and beyond, but these we shall visit on our return journey. Past Brackley's entrance and a new house is the old corrugated-iron fever hospital built in 1898. This is where folks with infectious diseases were isolated and treated. The patients would be treated in a much different way to that described by the writer of the 1790's Statistical Account where he says that before vaccination for small pox was introduced, the treatment meted out to try and cure this terrible disease, was to have great fires burning in a room. Often two or three children lay gasping under a weight of clothes in one bed with every particle of fresh air excluded from the room. Whisky, saffron and heat was administered to the children. The result of this, he says, was that numbers were hurried into an untimely grave and those that recovered were often blinded or suffered other ravages from the disease.

This fever hospital is now a dwelling house and ahead of that is the farmhouse and cottage of Corryghoil, which is a name that translates into coire of the ravine. This is no longer a farm as it was a casualty of modern forestry but it only seems to be poetic justice that the sheep, which drove out so many people in the past, should now have been driven out by the coming of the new trees. Langland's map of

1801 has a mansion house marked at Corryghoil and a stone in Dalmally Churchyard is in memory of one-year-old Margaret Campbell who died at Corryghoil in 1796. There was also a high Corryghoil marked above the mansion house but this may have been where the present old cottage is.

In travelling through Dalmally and its strath one thing that I notice is that one does not find the old burial cairns, standing stones, cup-marked rocks, or hill-top duns that are often so common further south. Although a burial cairn is mentioned in the 1840's Statistical Account, which says 'A cairn of stones was opened some years ago on the farm of Stronmilchan in which was found a stone coffin containing an urn' but apart from that, and a hill-top dun at Barr a Chaistealain, I do not know of any other such ancient historic relics. Why are there so few? Maybe it suggests that the area was not greatly populated in ancient times.

The old sawmill at Inverlochy, on the left at the start of the Military Road through Glenorchy, is thought to have occupied the site of an earlier meal mill and was built and operated on behalf of Breadalbane Estate by Robert George, great, great grandfather of the Livingstone family brought up in the present day Inverlochy which is understood to have been built by their grandfather using the stone from the sawmill building following its demolition before the First World War.

Before we take the winding single-track B8074 road up Glen Orchy we cross the River Lochy and above its old bridge there was once a water-driven meal-mill, which when such local mills became redundant was converted into a sawmill. At the start of the B8074 is the small farm or croft of Inverlochy with its present house beside an old hipped-roof building, which was once the original house and byre. The fact that both Achnafalnich and Arihastlich have similar old buildings suggests that they may have been purpose built estate ones. This old building at Inverlochy could have been the one where an Archibald MacPherson was granted a licence to operate an ale house in 1778.

Ahead by the riverside is a new house called Orchy View but the glen now has very few dwellings in it and this is a legacy of the clearances made with the coming of sheep. One man who had seen this happen was Duncan Ban MacIntyre, the poet, whose home had been

Inverlochy in 1888 shows the house and byre, with a house or barn behind, one of about ten homes in the township at this time occupied by a number of MacIntyre families and others. Similar townships were to be found at Strone and Brackley.

141

near Loch Tulla at the far end of Glen Orchy. He did not like what the sheep invasion was doing to the Highlands and part of one of his Gaelic poems called Song of the Foxes translates as

'My blessings with the foxes dwell
For that they hunt the sheep so well
Ill fa' the sheep, a grey-faced nation
That swept our hills with desolation'

The 1840's Statistical Account describes these events when it says 'Vast tracts of our straths and valleys, of our moors and mountains, exchanged stock and occupants. The deer and the goat gave place to the sheep and in many instances, the intelligent, well-educated, well-descended, and hospitable Highland tacksman with his attached devoted cottars and dependants gave way to the plodding industrious low country farmer and shepherd. One or other of three alternatives was adopted by the unfortunate mountaineer, that of removing to some manufacturing towns of the south, of emigrating to America, or of contenting himself with a small patch of land with the keep of a few cows in some assigned locality in his native strath or valley'.

Although Glen Orchy is still fairly desolate as regards dwellings and people it is now, I think, one of the most scenic glens in the West of Scotland with the tree-lined and ever changing river winding up through it. The birch and other broad-leaved trees that clothe parts of the hillsides soften the effects of the large conifer plantations and the glen's somewhat stark hillsides. However it too is beginning to suffer from the now common West Highland complaint of too many trees and bushes blocking off the views. The river that flows through the glen has long had a reputation as a salmon river and it has a local record of eight salmon caught in one day. A salmon of 42 ½ lb was caught by Peter Anderson in 1947, but the numbers of fish in the river have dropped away and recently it has been the policy to return caught fish.

The first of the old abandoned glen settlements that we come to is across the river at Inverour or to give it its proper Gaelic name Inbhir-odhar. It is marked on Langland's 1801 map but by 1841 it had only four inhabitants and now consists of ruins by the Odhar Burn.

The next place in the glen is Achnafalnich, which is by the road-side and still has one occupied old croft house. Apparently it had two dwellings in 1801 when it was called Achanafaundich but by 1841 its name had changed to Achnasandich and had seven inhabitants. It appears to be the case that in past times folks simply spelt place names as best they could. By the roadside here, there is some tansy growing, and as this is an old culinary herb that was used for flavouring it is likely to be a survival from past times.

Back across the river we have ruin remains for Mollay which was situated down-river from Catnish. Catnish still has an occupied house but access to it is rather difficult. It has to be by a long grass-grown track up the far riverside or on foot across a nearby suspension bridge. This bridge would be considered a big improvement to the previous way of crossing the river, which was by a wooden 'bucket' or box fitted with pulleys that ran on wire ropes slung across the river and was pulled across by hand. The height to which the river can rise in flood can be seen by the debris that often festoons the trees and fences. On one occasion it rose above the suspension bridge and badly damaged it and a reminder of that occasion is still to be seen in the fact that one of the giant concrete anchoring blocks for the bridge's cables is tipped up from the horizontal.

Above Catnish there are ruins marked in the forest called Cat-innis. Further up the glen on this side of the river were the two Bochyles, which according to the Dalmally Historical Association's magazine, *The Quern*, were mentioned in 1683 as having three fencible men. It seems there was an Easter and a Wester Bochyle but at some time Easter Bochyle changed its name to Tom na Gualainn (Hillock of the Shoulder) and Wester Bochyle then simply became Bochyle. In 1792 the parish records had 35 people living in the two places but by 1841 there were only seven inhabitants and by 1872 both appear to have been deserted, which was when the fox-hunting Cameron family came to Bochyle from Strontian. The reasonably well-preserved ruins are the remains of their house and outbuildings, and it is likely during their time that the six-foot high deer fence with its iron posts, droppers and wire was erected around the field there.

This field must have had a great deal of stone-clearing work done judging by the amount of cleared stones that are dumped around the field edges, but I think that that would have been in earlier times when the ground was worked more intensively by the farmers who occupied it.

The Camerons were a family who, over a number of generations, were famous in the district as fox-hunters and some of their grave-stones are in Dalmally churchyard. Bochyle has a small apparently natural mound with a flat top and when I visited the place someone had dug a small exploratory hole in the top and in doing so exposed two broken pieces of old china and the glass base from a small jar. Pieces of patterned china are often found near old settlements and the reason for this, I think, is that they were the playthings of the children.

The Quern has a very comprehensive article and plan by Helen Baney on Tom na Gualainn and I used this to find my way around. There are what appear to be the ruins of two houses and one of them has the obligatory kailyard. A lime-kiln is built into the side of the prominent hillock, which has a naturally sculptured piece of limestone standing upright on top of it. Another hillock nearby has two limestone boulders on it. I do not see any limestone rock around so it may be that the lime-kiln was operated using such 'erratic' lime-stone boulders as its raw material. This kiln still has its very well-built stone bowl but surprisingly it has no opening for drawing out the burnt limestone, which suggests to me that after the burn the burnt limestone was slaked in the kiln and then both the powdered lime and ash shovelled out and spread on the land. A stone wall runs above the old fields and directly above that is a very substantial stone-built sheep fank from the sheep-farming times. This sheep fank and its stone-wall enclosed out-field were planted with pine trees by the estate. Why? I can only surmise that the land around there later became exclusively deer-forest, and the fact that the large field there is now known as 'The Pony Park' because it is said to have been where ponies for stalking were kept, seems to back that up.

Ahead on the river there is a weir with a small hut and solar-panel on the riverside beside it and this powers an automatic water-level measuring device for the Hydro-electric Board. As well as being a good salmon river, the Orchy is also used for canoeing and white-water rafting, but ahead there is a dangerous hazard for either in the Eas Urchaidh or Falls of Orchy. The river here is spectacular as all the water drops down into a narrow chasm in the rocks that looks almost narrow enough to jump across. But this is a dangerous place, a very dangerous place, and at least six people have been drowned there. The river has undercut deep in below the rock at the sides of this channel and anyone going into the river accidentally or otherwise is quite likely to be trapped by the current under the overhanging rock. A forest-road bridge crossing the river gives a good and safe viewing platform for this unique place.

An entry in the 1790's Statistical Account mentions fish-traps that were here at that time and says, 'Four miles below (should be above) the church, at a place called Catnish, shoals of salmon are taken in the Urchy by a simple but fatal device. A bold projecting rock crosses the bed of the river nearly from side to side. Its height is such that few fish can overleap the torrent, which after rain runs forcibly into the pool below. Many salmon, in attempting to leap, fall into a creel, or basket, fixed transversely within the stream. But the great slaughter is effected in a more fraudulent manner. On one side of the river there is an open, of the wideness of a mill-race, betwixt the rock and the bank. Here a wicker gate is fixed that can be opened or shut at pleasure. Many yards above this entry the stream is secured by a like barrier. When the water is high and turbid the fish are let in below, and when the fisherman is satisfied with the numbers that have passed into his toils he shuts the door of his prison, and like a merciless executioner he drags his prey with his spear one after another on shore. Scores, at times, are thus destroyed in the course of a few hours'.

This route that by-passes the main fall is sometimes used by canoeists when the river level is suitable but most canoeists and rafters haul out above the falls and re-launch below them. As a reminder of how dangerous the place is two trees were planted nearby to commemorate Wayne Mulholland, a recent victim who struck a rock when diving from the bridge. Unfortunately these were planted below established trees and both have now died.

The forest road across the bridge is signposted as a mountain-bike track and this follows a road that branches off to the right and leads on through the forest for some 12 kilometres to finish at Bridge of Orchy. The other branch to the left continues up a glen and through Coire Thoraidh where there are some remnant trees of the old native pine woods that once grew in Glen Orchy. These trees have probably survived because they were isolated and not very good for timber. They and that area are now, however, classed as a Caledonian Forest Reserve and are fenced off to protect new seedlings from grazing deer or other animals. Hopefully the trees will regenerate and the place will become a natural pinewood once again.

This road, through the coire, finishes close to a hill loch named on maps as Lochan Coire Thoraidh but it is known locally as Douglas's Loch. Douglas was a gamekeeper from Craig who, some hundred years ago, was digging to try and free his terrier that had become stuck in a natural rock cairn, nearby where it had been sent in to bolt foxes, and unfortunately a rock collapsed on top of him and killed him. The loch has a boat house on it from the Craig Estate time.

After the Second World War the then owner, Captain Oldham, became badly disabled and could no longer walk up to the loch so had a track made up to it and a jetty built, allowing him to drive up and transfer to a boat and go out fishing. The forest road and this old track now gives walkers a circular walk from the falls up through the glen and corrie, past the loch and down this track to the riverside, then back along the riverside, across Catnish Bridge and back to the falls. I thoroughly recommend it as a very interesting walk.

Some way past the Falls of Orchy there are some ruins off to the right, but I have not yet had an opportunity to investigate them. Across the river in the Allt Broighleachan area there are a number of old ruins shown on Ordnance Survey Maps, but these are now largely lost in conifer forest, one of them, Lairigs, is marked on Langland's 1801 map and still had four inhabitants in 1841, one of whom was probably the Archibald Fletcher who is commemorated on a gravestone set against the wall of Dalmally Church, which says that he was born at Lairigs in 1838.

Ahead by the roadside is Arihastlich previously named Cnoc a Tighe (Hillock House). The present house was built as a shooting lodge during the time when these were fashionable. It later became a farmhouse but it has now been renovated and enlarged and has self-catering accommodation. Below there is the cnoc, or hillock, that gave the place its original name and for some reason this is surrounded by a stone dyke. I do not know why this is but a possible explanation comes from the 1700's and 1800's when the 'improving' lairds, such as the Breadalbane Earls, very often put a clause in their farm leases saying that the tenants had to enclose and plant so many trees on the land. The farmers naturally planted these small woods on a poor part of the farm and this may be one such place despite it now being devoid of trees.

Running across past this hillock is a stretch of much sculptured and weather-eroded limestone boulders that are similar to the ones at Bochyle and there appears to be a ridge of limestone bedrock below. The new farmhouse and steadings that take the place of Arihastlich have been built some distance ahead and are called Glen Orchy Farm and this farm, which now consists of 2,789 acres is owned by Norman and Michelle MacLennan. It may have been noticed that I do not list any rebels from Glenorchy Parish who supported the 1685 Earl of Argyll's Rebellion and this is because the Campbell Chief from there was the Earl of Breadalbane who backed the Government and raised troops to fight against his own Campbell Clan Chief's rebellion.

High up on the hillside above Glen Orchy Farm is the large and deep Coire Daimh hollow, which appears to have been gauged out by the ice spilling down from the heights above. There, I think in the 1980's, a gold prospecting outfit did some test borings in the coire and confirmed that these hills had a continuation of the Cononish stretch of gold bearing rock, but the gold is present in such small flecks that it would be a doubtful mining prospect.

Ahead on the river is the Easan Dubha or Black Waterfall. I don't know why it is called black, but it was certainly a black place for a police party of twelve white-water rafters who set off from Bridge of Orchy on a very high flooded river some years ago. They knew about the fall and tried to stop before it but the river was too powerful and they went over the fall with the result that they overturned and two of them, a policeman and a policeman's teenage daughter, were drowned.

James Hogg, the shepherd poet, passed this way on a walking tour one summer's day in 1803 and he mentioned some fine cascades, one of which he fell asleep by but he was not very impressed by the countryside's sheep-farming land as he reckoned that the hills had too much heath. He admitted that he might not be seeing the best of their potential and said 'for who even in the south of Scotland hath not heard of the farms of Soch and Auch'. We shall be passing Auch Farm or Estate later but Soch is puzzling for, as far as I know, no such place exists or existed. It could possibly mean Succoth but I think that it was possibly a joke name made up to rhyme with Auch.

Somewhere in the forest across the river will be the remains of Invervigar, which Langland in 1801 has marked as being just above the mouth of the Bhiocair Burn, but the only ruins marked on modern maps are higher up above the falls. Past the falls on our side an old road runs up the hillside through some modern forest and into the centre of an old estate wood of pine and other conifers, and hidden there are the ruins of Old Arihastlich. *The Quern* has a very comprehensive article and plan of this place and again I used this to find my way around.

The first ruin one comes to is quite a large barn, which has the usual opposite doors to give a through draught for winnowing grain. Nearby is the grain-drying kiln with an attached ruined building, but the kiln part has been filled in at some time. There are the ruins of two houses with their attached steadings and one of the houses is two storey and still has its gable-end with fire openings both below and upstairs. The chimneystack is still standing and Helen Baney, who wrote the article, suggests that this would be the tacksman's house.

Tacksmen leased a large farm or farms and then let the land out in small parcels to the small farmers of earlier days. Most of the rent would have been paid in kind with farm produce, which possibly explains the largish barn and outbuildings at the house. Near this well-preserved house ruin are the remains of a large stone wall-enclosed garden with a surviving sweet-chestnut tree in it. Many of these trees were planted around Loch Awe and elsewhere but unfortunately as they come from sunnier climes they very seldom bear any edible nuts.

In the corner of the garden is a ruined building described as an ice-house but I expected an ice-house to be more underground and have a stone-arched and turf-covered roof for insulation. I was also unable to find the flax pits, which would have been used to ret or rot flax, a process, which combined with a good deal of washing and scutching, left just the fibres behind. The article says that the settlement was abandoned in the late 1780's with the coming of large-scale sheep farming but that house, and its attached buildings, look too well preserved to have been abandoned for so long a time. Also as it is likely that the conifer wood was planted soon after the house was vacated it does not look to me to be over two hundred years old. The name the place is given on some Ordnance Survey maps of Tom Barr an Stalcaidh may hold a clue as it translates roughly into the knoll of stalking or possibly stalker, and it may be that the house became the home of a stalker when the land became a deer forest.

On the river ahead is the Linne Dhubh or Black Channel where the river runs through a deep chasm in the rock, and where there was a 'bucket' river crossing similar to the one at Catnish. This had been built by the estate for transporting the deer carcases and men across the river in the days when the land was deer-forest.

Later when the Forestry Commission bought much of the land in the glen and started planting that stretch the 'bucket' was used for carrying men, fencing material, young trees, tools and many other things across the river. The boundary of that planting ran across the steep slopes of Ben Inverveigh and when a deer fence was being erected there in the 1950's the ground was too steep for tractors or horses to work so much of the fencing material was carried up the steep slopes by men or dragged up by a motor winch.

In preparing the ground for planting trees, crawler tractors were used to plough furrows for planting on, but again the higher slopes were too steep for tractors, and so the ground had to be prepared manually by using a large rutter spade to cut out and upturn turfs to plant on. Most of the forest's workforce in its early days travelled by covered lorry from Eredine Forest and I was often one of them.

In one part of that planting, across the river from the old croft of Invergaunan, the ploughs turned up much old pinewood, tree roots and other forest debris that was in a very fresh state and still showed axe marks on it. This wood had been preserved by the peat and would be from the felling of the native pinewoods in the 1700's when a number of Irish and Scots entrepreneurs had got together to exploit the pinewoods in Glen Orchy.

The Statistical Account from the 1790's says, 'The higher parts of the parish abounded once with forests of the largest and best pines, but these were cut down about 60 years ago by a company of adventurers from Ireland with little benefit to themselves, and less to the noble proprietor of the country'.

The next Statistical Account in 1840 written by the Rev Duncan MacLean gives some more details and says that they had 'felled an immense quantity of timber, which they floated down the Urchay when in flood to the head of Loch Awe where it was hewn into planks, and then floated down Loch Awe in rafts to the Pass of Brander whence it was carted down to the sea and shipped at Bunawe. This, it is said, proved a bad speculation for all parties concerned'.

It does not say however that the trees would have been felled by axe and crosscut saw, sawn into lengths and then dragged to the riverside by horses. Then when the river was running at a suitable level the logs were manhandled into it and there would be many obstacles and problems before the logs reached Loch Awe in an operation that was then described as 'driving the river'. Many logs would become stuck, stranded, or form into a logjam at some obstacle and they would have to be freed and sent on their way by means of a long handled and spiked tool, which was difficult and dangerous work.

The Rev Duncan MacLean says that the logs were then hewn into planks at the loch-side, rafted to the Pass of Brander and then carted to Bonawe, but if you were going to raft the logs you would not hew them into planks. The wood was possibly hewed square at the loch-side for easier transport as there would be very little room to do this in the Pass. I have seen it said that some of the wood was sawn into planks at Bonawe before it was shipped and this would probably be done in sawpits using hand saws. In any case the whole operation must have proved more costly than anticipated. Despite the trees having been bought cheaply at a plack apiece, which was about one twelfth of a penny, the partnership went bankrupt and a lot of the timber did not reach the sea.

Invergaunan is mentioned in 1755 when a Colin Campbell from there was a witness in a court case about a stolen horse. It had six inhabitants in 1841 and at present consists of one old croft-house. Ahead and across the river from there is a ruin that has had a large deer-proof iron railed enclosure around it. This enclosure had been planted with trees but that would not be its original purpose and I think that the ruin would be the abode of a shepherd or stalker. The place had no chimney but chimneys were once luxuries in most high-land dwellings.

On the B8074 road ahead is the Kinglass River, which is a tributary of the Orchy, and across the Orchy from there are an old and new house at Inverveigh that are accessed by a road from the Orchy Bridge. In 1801 seven people were charged with running a distillery in Glen Orchy and it seemed to have been quite a big operation. Two of the men came from Bridge of Orchy, one from Lochearnhead, one from Kingshouse, one from Callander, another, Angus Fletcher from Ardbrecknish and one from Blara-van wherever that might be. The outcome of the case is, unfortunately, not known.

Just across the Kinglass Bridge the track of the old B8074 follows the Orchy to Bridge of Orchy but we follow a new short stretch of road out to the A82, which is a relatively modern and fast road built in the 1930's. Somewhere around this road junction there was once a small settlement called Brecklate but I could find no trace of it. Across the A82 is the Fort William railway line that was opened in 1894 and above that is the abandoned old A82 road, which had once been built as a military road and is now part of the West Highland Way footpath that runs from the outskirts of Glasgow to Fort William and is much used by walkers in the summer.

CHAPTER TEN

BRIDGE OF ORCHY TO TYNDRUM
RETURNING TO DALMALLY
THROUGH GLEN LOCHY

Our route takes us to the right on the A82 up a deep glen. Towering above us on the left is Ben Dorain the beloved mountain of the Gaelic poet Duncan Ban MacIntyre who composed a poem about it entitled In Praise of Ben Dorain. He had grown up nearby and worked in the area but when he was later living in Edinburgh he and his wife would sometimes return and do a walking tour, and on possibly his last visit he composed his 'Farewell to the Bens'. The Rev Joseph MacIntyre wrote in the 1790's 'Beindoran, till lately, was the residence and sanctuary of the roebuck and mountain deer, but now the hunter roams no longer on the hill of the chase, the sheep browse on the heath of the forest, and the sons of the mountain have deserted the inheritance of their race for ages to revisit its springs and glades and secret haunts no more'.

This glen that we are following is part of a very lonely stretch of countryside and in the seven miles between Bridge of Orchy and Tyndrum the only habitations are the small group of houses up ahead at Auch. There the level and green stretch that gave the place its name is very evident. The railway line has had to make a large detour, called the Horseshoe, and cross two viaducts in order to maintain its height and easy gradient.

Auch is a large estate of 13,000 acres but it is mainly high and steep mountainous ground that includes Ben Dorain. All the land to our left stretches as far as Beinn a Chuirn and Loch Lyon. On

154

Langland's 1801 map it is simply called Auch and has a mansion house and what appears to be large gardens but in the 1883 Ordnance Survey map it is given the longer name of Auch-innis-Challain. In the 1841 census the place had 17 inhabitants. At Auch the Kinglass River swings to the left up the long and deep glen called Gleann Achadh-innis-Chailein.

During the hydro-electric scheme days a road was built up this glen and the headwaters of the Allt Kinglass were diverted into Loch Lyon by tunnel to supply extra water for the hydro scheme. I have not been able to get up the glen but the Ordnance Survey maps show a number of ruins of what appear to be old shielings but whether any of them were lived in on a permanent basis I do not know. There is also a burial ground shown that I presume was a private one.

At present the Auch Estate consists of the large Orchy Lodge, a farm and a few cottages that are mainly let out as self-catering holiday accommodation. There is also an old railway cottage high up beside the railway line on the right that was built for a railway linesman. With no road services it would have to be largely provided by the railway. A Glen Coralan runs up near there and Ordnance Survey maps show what appear to be a number of shieling ruins.

From Auch we continue past the ruin of Tigh na Leirge (House of the Slope), which is in a forest planting below, and then up and over the summit of this ancient pass through the mountains. High up on the hillside between Ben Odhar and Meall Buidhe and about 1,200 feet above the summit of the pass there is an old mine adit or tunnel marked on Ordnance Survey maps. However with no road or method of access shown it leads one to suppose that there must have been something valuable and easily transportable mined there. An entry in the 1840's Statistical Account probably has the answer when it says 'Beautiful syenite is found in the farm of Auch on Benbuy, north of Tighandrom'. From the summit of the pass our road drops down alongside the railway and the West Highland Way and then swings away from Tyndrum below through the snow gates that are closed if the weather is so bad that the road over Rannoch Moor cannot be kept open. It then meets up with the A85 Oban road, which we shall follow.

Running up the steep hillside across from this junction is a barren stretch of bare rock and metal-polluted rubble. This scene of devastation was left behind by an abandoned lead mine. Silver was mined there in the 1400's but that appeared to have been worked out. Then in around 1730 a Sir Robert Clifton started lead mining on a lease from Breadalbane Estates, which gave them one sixth of the smelted lead bars produced. The first mining appears to have been mainly opencast work but later shafts were sunk to follow the lead ore and the mining operations were taken over by Breadalbane Estates. Mining however was not carried on continuously and was started and stopped a number of times during the mines long lifetime of some two hundred years. But when working, the mine must have been quite an important local industry and at one time in the latish 1700's it employed some 200 men and women. It was not working around 1800 but reopened during the First World War.

The railway must have helped greatly with the transport of lead and other goods and a branch spur was constructed from Tyndrum to the mine. The mine then carried on working until at least the late 1920's. A works road can be seen zigzagging up the steep face and there are signs of an up and down structure, which is likely to have been a chute for carrying ore down to the crushing plant below. An old photograph from that period shows one large building and some smaller ones at the foot of the hill.

Many years ago I went to investigate the mine and found that a very steep-angled vein of lead ore had run up the hillside and had had tunnel entries to it at different levels. I entered one tunnel and had gone some distance before I found out that I was walking on an artificial floor of rubble supported by rotting cross-beams of wood and so I got out of that tunnel rather fast. I then went into another safer-looking tunnel that had the remains of a rail-track in it but after some distance I was stopped by a rock-fall that had deep water dammed up behind it. These tunnels and other dangerous shafts and openings have recently been fenced off with safety fencing for the public's protection. In the years before and after the Second World War the zigzag road and another one that runs at an angle to the top of the ridge were used as an off-road section for the Scottish Six-Day Motor Cycle Trials.

During wartime there was a small army service camp site beside the A85 road below and I believe that place was the early site of Brodie of Tyndrum's grocery shop. From there we drive past a couple of roadside cottages and then come to Lochan na Bi, which translates into small loch of the pitch (tar). Before other sources of pitch were discovered, pitch came from pine trees and was obtained by drilling holes near the base of the trees and collecting the sap, which was then heat treated to give an end product of pitch. This was the main sealing and waterproofing substance of these days.

Past the loch is the settlement of Arinabea and as the ending is pronounced like the Gaelic bi I am going to stick my neck out and say that this could also be the 'homestead of pitch' rather than of birch, and possibly when this glen was clothed with pine trees there was a small industry manufacturing pitch around there. Not far up a small glen behind Arinabea, the Ordnance Survey maps have a group of what look like shieling ruins called Airighnean na Bi - again the Gaelic word for pitch. Not far ahead and across a young River Lochy a further two groups of shielings called Airigh Badain and Airigh Fhliuch (wet) are shown in the forest planting.

Here in Glen Lochy, the Oban Railway Line runs alongside us on the left and further up the hillside on the right is the old military road built by Major Caulfield and his men in about 1760. The next inhabited place in the glen is Arivain with a farmhouse and four cottages. In 1797 a Duncan McNicol from there went to Inveraray to buy tar and butter to smear his sheep, which was the protection against maggots before sheep dip days. He had bought this and a barrel of herring plus some salt to cure them, and had them in his cart when the Inveraray tide officer (excise man) declared that the salt was being smuggled. He seized the salt and everything else including the horse and cart. However when Duncan McNicol later swore on oath in the JP court that the salt was for use in curing the herring everything was returned to him.

The heavy tax on salt and attempts to evade it appear to have caused a big problem in those days when salt was the main preservative for food. In 1804 four carts carrying bags of salt were stopped by the excise men in Glen Aray and 'seized' but the drivers tumbled the bags of salt off the carts and forcibly drove away. The drivers who were all from the Dalmally area were later charged and brought to court. They were John McNab of Barachastlan, John Ferguson of Kinchrackine and Archibald and John Campbell from Stronmilchan. They were all fined sums ranging from £8 to £25.

Glen Lochy was sheep country before the Forestry Commission bought it and planted conifers on most of it. In the past it would have been largely wooded with pine but it is now planted with Sitka spruce from the west coast of North America.

Across the river from Arivain are the ruined shielings of Airigh Garbh Choirean, and that translates into the shieling of the rough little coire, which is up on the hillside above. All these shielings in the glen appear to mean that the glen was good for summer grazing but did not have much ground suitable for crops. Many of the folks who used these shielings would appear to have travelled a considerable distance with their livestock and some of them could easily have crossed over the hills from Glen Orchy at this point.

Ahead, across a footbridge on the Lochy that gave access to the railway, was the old siding of Glenlochy Crossing, which had a signal box and siding to allow trains to pass on that part of the single track line. About a mile ahead of that is an off road car park for Ben Lui, which is a popular Munro mountain and is also a National Nature Reserve on account of its Alpine flora. It has quite a lot of lime-rich basic rock which calcicole Alpines love and it and some of the other hills around can have surprise finds such as the rare drooping saxifrage. Glen Orchy has some non-flowering twinflower plants, which appear to be missing their usual pine-wood habitat. Travelling in the bottoms of the glens one gets the impression that most of the surrounding hills are covered in conifer trees but this is not the case. If you climb up above the tree line there is a great amount of open hill country left for the hill walker and for the native mountain and hill flora and fauna. There are more shielings marked in the forest across from the car park and somewhere around there was the Easmurag, which is marked on Langland's 1801 map.

The road starts to descend more steeply towards the wide and level Strath of Orchy and we pass a Forestry Commission car park and picnic site that gives access to a walk and waterfall on the River Lochy. Nearby is Strone Farm, which translates into nose-shaped and refers to the hill above. It now consists of the old farm or croft house and a farm building converted into a house. In 1841 it had 24 inhabitants.

The road then snakes down a steepish hill that has seen many accidents, often fatal, and would appear to justify having a 'Danger Accident Blackspot' notice to slow down speeding Dalmally-bound motorists. At the foot of the descent we cross the River Lochy and from there we will be driving on part of the route that we have previously travelled. In the countryside off to the left there are many old and mostly abandoned places still to visit.

The first of these, though not abandoned, is Succoth, which is accessed by a long road from just past the Lochy Bridge. The name Succoth means snout-like hill and this place was said to have been home to the chief of the Loch Awe MacNicols back in the 1600's. It is mentioned in 1755 when a Nicol McNicol and a Patrick Ferguson from there were witnesses in a court case regarding a stolen horse. It is marked as a mansion house on Langland's 1801 map but is not mentioned in the 1841 census and this may be because it was by then a shooting lodge and not occupied in June when the census was taken. It later became a farmhouse but now the land is mostly planted with trees. The main house is now occupied by the Keays , who are both writers, and, I think, the two nearby cottages are also occupied. Access to much of the forested land on that side of the strath is by a forest road that branches off from the Succoth one and goes under the large railway viaduct. An old and much used track and drove route went by the Caorann (Rowan) Pass from Succoth through the hills to the head of Loch Lomond, and this is the way that the high voltage power line to and from the Cruachan Power Station now goes.

Returning to the A85 and on to Brackley Farm entrance we can continue on foot up past the farm over a bridge on the railway and follow a track that leads up the slope to the left and on to Auchtermally, which means the high ground of Maillidh. He was the ancient holy man after whom Dalmally is named. Auchtermally was the main settlement on that side of the River Orchy before the military roads shifted the centre of importance to Dalmally. It had its own school, small farms and a number of tradesmen, and although it was situated quite high up on the hillside it seems to have been a fertile place and had lime-rich rock that was utilised by building a lime-kiln.

From Auchtermally, or as the Ordnance Survey folk now call it, Uachdar Mhaluidh, a track continued to the Teatle Water glen and past the settlement of Barran, which in the past was once home to an overspill of the MacNab family from Barr a Chaistealain and another site for their metal-working. Barran in1841 still had 11 inhabitants but now it appears to be simply used as a working sheep-fank.

The old track then climbed up through the narrow Bealach an Cabrach pass and down into the head of Glen Shira. This is a route that Rob Roy MacGregor would have known well in his cattle-droving days as he had a house near the head of the glen, and being a cattle dealer he would have taken cattle that way to the tryst at Dalmally. In the autumn he would no doubt have taken droves of others by way of Glen Lochy and Loch Earn to the Crieff markets. Further down the Teatle Water from Barran is Blararchaorain whose name is rather a mouthful and translates into 'the cleared ground of the rowan trees'. In the 1841 census it had 17 inhabitants and it is still a working sheep farm but has lost much of its lower land. Nearby in what is now forested land was Dychlie. This was spelt Duchlie in 1841 and had seven inhabitants. Going further back Langland's 1801 map had it as Duchally. Its main claim to fame now seems to be in the name Dych-liemore Forest Estate, which is of 1,170 acres and is owned by the Hon. Rosemary Maitland.

Returning back to the Dalmally area we have Barr a Chaistealain on the hillside above. It translates into hill of the castle and this 'cas-

Close to the Iron Age Dun, on a flat-topped ridge above the station building can be seen the cottages at Barr a Chaistealain once home to the McNabs, who were renowned smiths and armourers to the Campbells of Breadalbane. The last family to live there moved to Dalmally in 1948.

tle' was probably an ancient dun whose ruins can still be seen. This dun is in fact the only one I know of in the Dalmally area. In later years the place became renowned as being the home and workplace of an extended MacNab family who were skilled metalworkers and armourers. The first famous metal worker in the family seems to have been Duncan MacNab who is said to have learned his metal-working and weapon making skills in Italy in the 1400's, and on his return he built his house and workshop at Barr a Chaistealain and was commissioned to do the metalwork for Kilchurn Castle.

These MacNabs prospered and multiplied and many of them carried on the craft of smiths and armourers for the Campbells of Glenorchy and much further afield. Some were also skilled white-smiths who worked with precious metals and did more intricate work in jewellery.When the land east of Brackley was being prepared for tree-planting the ploughed furrows cut through a number of old iron-waste slag heaps on the top of a ridge. These were the residue from iron smelting and would almost certainly be from the MacNab's iron making. Smelting then was done in clay furnaces using charcoal and local ironstone. The reason for them being on top of a ridge was to make use of the wind to blow up the furnaces.

Returning to the A85 past the Dalmally Hotel we head back to-wards the old Dalmally village and the derelict corrugated-iron build-ing that was once called South Church and was the local United Free Church until 1930. When the churches were once again reunited the building then became a church hall. Next to it is the new fire station and the auction mart that is now owned by United Auctions and at times, especially during the autumn sales, a very busy place indeed. It deals in sheep and cattle and is one of the main sheep markets in the country and thousands of sheep pass through its sale-ring an-nually. Its premises and the adjoining field are also where the Dal-mally Agricultural Show is held in early September each year.

The show has classes for sheep, cattle, poultry, dogs, garden pro-

ABOVE: *The judging of a class of Highland bulls at Dalmally Show in 1962 (from the left): "Drumachar the second of Scone Palace" exhibited by Mrs Bowser, Benmore Fold and shown by Benmore shepherd, Mr Donald Stewart. "Gaisgeach of Duart" stock bull in Cladich Fold shown by Mr David Fellowes. "Padruig Ruadh of Achnacloich" bred by Mr E. Nelson and shown at 15 months old, by Mr Duncan MacNab.*

RIGHT: *Archie Black, Duncan Crawford and Malcolm MacKay at Dalmally Show in 2003.*

BELOW: *Dalmally Show in 1991 with Angus MacKay winning the overall championship with his home-bred heifer "Dossan Ruadh the 3rd of Edentaggart" from over 100 exhibits in the Highland cattle section. He is seen here with show stewards David Fellowes and Ernie Crawford.*

163

Glenorchy shinty team, winners of the Munro Shield in 1952 having defeated favourites Dunstaffnage by two goals to one despite being one goal down at half-time. Back row: Tommy Gibson, John Mathieson, Lorn Campbell, Angus Cameron, Robert Craik, Hughie Cowan. Front row: Donald Cowan, Archie Black, Donnie Campbell, Bobbie Cameron, Ian Young, Ian Black.

duce, crafts, baking, shepherd's crooks, photography, children's work and much more. There is an important shinty tournament and there are stalls selling goods, stalls for amusement and of course for refreshment. It is an important farming and social event where one can meet up with a lot of friends and learn how to beat the opposition next year.

Going back a couple of centuries this may also have been where the local New Year's Day shinty matches were held. Matches in these days had few rules and no limit on the number of players on each side, and the match teams were, I think, north side versus south side of the river, and they could be quite rough affairs. The final New Year`s Day match was played in 1932. Shinty is still played in Dalmally and the local Glenorchy shinty team were successful Premier League players. Another old pastime in the area was curling and the

164

present Glenorchy Curling Club was formed by 11 members and admitted to the Royal Caledonian Curling Club in 1879 under the patronage of the Earl and Countess of Breadalbane. The first curling
pond, which would be large enough to host four rinks, was constructed in 1879. A new pond was made on Dalmally hill above
Kinchrackine in 1892 but in 1919 the original pond was restored and
with the appointment of a joiner as Pond Master in 1936, was maintained until 1941. The onset of milder winters meant few games
were played on natural ice and players travelled to Falkirk then later
to Perth Ice rinks though a pond continued to be maintained on the
Wee Orchy and the original curling pond, situated below the Old Police Station, was still being maintained in 1955 but was ultimately destroyed when the Dalmally bypass was built in 1969. Curlers today
travel to Greenock and Braehead in Renfrew.

The bypass cuts off the old village, which grew up beside the
railway station, and just at the start of the old village road is

*A tense moment at Drimsynie as Glenorchy skip Russel Buchanan indicates where
he wishes the final stone to come to rest while two of the opposing team anxiously
await the result.*

Dalmally Station showing the engine shed, with the turntable behind it which allowed the engine to be turned around. There was a "Steamie" a short distance further on where laundry could be done up until the advent of washing machines in the 1960's. Mrs McCormick`s tearoom where hospitality was provided for visiting shinty teams can just be seen on the opposite platform.

Glenorchy Hotel. This has taken over as Dalmally's local pub and eating out place now that the large Dalmally Hotel caters exclusively for organized coach parties. On the left, as one continues through the old village, there was once the police station, then the Territorial Army drill-hall, the railway station with its goods yard and tearoom, and across the road a watchmaker and jeweller, butcher, garage, post office, and grocers. The railway station is still open for passengers as an unmanned halt, but all the other businesses have now gone. A famous son of the village was John Smith who was leader of the Labour Party and he was born at Baddarroch in 1938 when his father was the local schoolmaster.

    This part of Dalmally was built after the coming of the railway in 1877 and that must have been an event that changed the way of life there hugely. For as well as giving the people fast and easy access to the cities and elsewhere it brought in large numbers of tourists and their money. The original plans for the railway showed that it should branch at Dalmally with one branch going to Oban and the other going by way of Loch Awe or Loch Fyne down Kintyre to Campbeltown. However the Kintyre branch plan was blocked in the House of Lords by the Duke of Argyll who did not want a railway running through his land. With the coming of the railway to Dalmally, however, there was an alternative way to transport cattle and sheep to distant markets, and for a time cattle were being driven there from as far afield as Kintyre.

For three years after 1877 Dalmally was the end of the line and an important terminus. A person travelling overnight from London would have taken 14 ½ hours to reach Dalmally and a further 3 hours 50 minutes by coach to Oban. There were problems carrying the line further over the boggy ground at the head of Loch Awe but this was solved by using large bundles of brushwood as a foundation on which to build a causeway. Dalmally Station then became simply a halt that served the local area.

The first station building, which was built of wood, burnt down in 1897 but the replacement was made of sandstone and given a grander than normal design presumably as it was intended that it should become a more important station. Later with the coming of motor cars and lorries the transport of goods and people around Loch Awe gradually changed from being mostly water-borne to being carried on the roads, and this gave more business to Dalmally Station. But the really busy time for the Station was during the Second World War.

Large military camps were built around Inveraray as part of what was then No. 1 Combined Operations Training Centre and Dalmally Station became the supply station for goods and troops going to and from there. This made it a very busy place indeed especially every fortnight when there was a changeover of most of the troops with special trains arriving and a fleet of lorries to collect them. These troops were trained in Inveraray for the landings in North Africa, Sicily and D Day and during this time some 250,000 troops trained and tested equipment around Loch Fyne. Many of them and much of the equipment passed through Dalmally Station. Even in wartime a lot of timber was being felled around the loch-side and this was all being transported by rail. Also there was a lot of passing traffic on the line carrying military supplies to the naval and other establishments around the Oban area.

At this time there was a small Royal Army Service Corp's depot at the A819 Inveraray road junction. It is described as having been a butchers that served the Lochfyneside camps and military establishments but I do not think that it had a slaughter-house, so I presume the animal carcases came by rail and were cut up and delivered to the various cookhouses. Also on the Inveraray road near the junction there was a road-block barrier that in the event of an enemy invasion would have been used to block the road. Presumably this would have been manned by the local Home Guard.

During the 'Cold War' there was an underground nuclear bunker by this road junction that was designed to hold two men. It had supplies to last a month and in the event of a nuclear warning it would have been manned by members of the Royal Observer Corps. They would, if necessary, have stayed in the bunker measuring and monitoring conditions and reporting them back to headquarters through the main telephone lines, which had by then been put underground so that they would hopefully still function after a nuclear attack. But this underground bunker it seems was somewhat subject to flooding and it was finally abandoned in 1968.

There was also, for a period of time, a sawmill and pallet-making workshop opposite the junction run by Bobby Wilson from Portsonachan. That has gone and the Strathorchy guesthouse now occupies the site with the Dalmally Golf Club's clubhouse next door.

ABOVE: *Neil Thompson, David Smith, Terry McNair, John Malcolm and Callum MacFarlane-Barrow wait to tee off at the first in 1987.*

BELOW: *The first golf course, photographed between 1909 to 1911, features in an advertisement for Loch Awe Hotel shortly after it opened in 1881, where the facilities are listed as, electric light, motor garage and golf course.*

The golf club was formed in 1985 at a meeting in Dalmally Church Hall chaired by Trevor Baney, and held its first meeting at Craig Lodge on 20th October 1985 chaired by Archie MacIntyre, club captain in the first three years. The club uses the flat ground beside the river for its course, but this is still prone to flooding despite the large amount of work that was done by the estate back in the 1800's. The club held formal competitions in 1987 when Keith MacIntyre became first Club Champion. Prior to that there was a nine-hole course on Castles Farm land, which was created before the First World War.

From the junction heading back towards Dalmally we pass Lower Kinachreachan on the right which had eight inhabitants in 1841. In the forest is a large boulder with a lady's hand-print carved into it and nearer the present house a Gaelic conundrum carved into a boulder translates into 'He who will know will not know. He who will understand will not understand'. My interpretation would be that he who is impatient and must know it all at once cannot properly know or understand a problem.

Upper Kinchrackine had 57 inhabitants in 1841. A gravestone by the old barn says 'Erected in Memory of Isabella MacVean Wife of John MacIntyre who died at Kincrackine Dalmally 1896 aged 89 and their Daughter Catherine'. I remember the old croft house further on, getting a new slated roof, and below the old 'tin' roof it still had its original thatched roof for insulation. Across the A85 from there is a new housing development and extension to the old Dalmally Village.

CHAPTER ELEVEN

DALMALLY
TO ACHLIAN

Back in the old village and at the junction of Monument Road we find the start of the road that was once the continuation of the village street, and this road was in fact the Dalmally to Inveraray road until the 1930's. Here we cross the Allt na Mhuilinn (Burn of the Mill) where there used to be a water-mill with a storage dam higher up. I think it would have been the local meal-mill.

Beside the road and by the start of the forest there is an old place called Croftintuime that has had many variations and spellings of its name during its lifetime. According to the superb booklet Dalmally, which is the story of the village past and present and from where I gleaned much information, it also had a grocery shop back in the late 1800's.

From there we climb up the Leac na Ceardaich (Slope of the Smith) about which I am ignorant, but somewhere ahead there was once a toll-gate, which means that it must at one time have been an official turnpike road and the dues charged would have helped maintain it. At this road's summit in 1803 William and Dorothy Wordsworth were so entranced by the view of castle, loch and mountain that they sent their conveyance of an Irish jaunting-cart on ahead to Dalmally. They sat there and admired the view while William wrote a poem about Kilchurn Castle that began,

'Child of loud-throated war! The mountain stream
Roars in thy hearing; but thy hour of rest
Is come and thou art silent in thy age'.

Unfortunately, because of the surrounding forest, this view of the castle cannot now be seen and one has to climb up to Duncan Ban MacIntyre's Monument to see a fine view of that part of Loch Awe with its islands and surrounding mountains. Unfortunately Kilchurn Castle is still not visible from the Monument. Glen Strae, Stronmilchan and the start of Glen Orchy are visible and it was at the far end of this glen, near Loch Tulla, that Duncan Ban MacIntyre was born in 1724.

It seems that it was not until Duncan was grown into manhood that he discovered his poetic bent. During the Forty Five Rebellion he had, on the promise of a large fee, taken the place of an elderly local farmer called Fletcher, and equipped with his sword, marched off with the rest of the Argyll Militia to fight the rebels. However at the Battle of Falkirk the Prince's men won the day and routed the

The monument erected in memory of Duncan Ban MacIntyre bears the inscription, "Duncan Ban MacIntyre, The Glenurchay Poet was born in the year 1724 and departed this life in the year 1812".

Government forces. Duncan escaped unharmed but he lost Fletcher's sword and when he was later discharged and returned without it Fletcher refused to pay him. Very annoyed at this Duncan composed a rather scurrilous ballad called 'The Song to Fletcher's Sword'. It was very well received by everyone except Fletcher but he was it seems, with the intervention of the Earl of Breadalbane, forced to pay Duncan his fee.

Duncan then spent many years as a forester or gamekeeper working for the Earl in the countryside around the head of Glen Orchy. He married Mary MacNicol who was a daughter of the Innkeeper at Inveroran. Many of the poems and songs that he composed were about his beloved countryside and its fauna and flora. Possibly the most famous of these is 'In Praise of Ben Doran', but he also wrote Crodh Chailein (Colin's Cattle) referring to the deer as the Campbell Chief's cattle. A translated verse from that reads

So dappled, so varied, so beauteous their hue;
So agile, so graceful, so charming to view
O'er all the wide forest, ther's naught can compare
With the light bounding flocks of my Colin, my dear.

This song was responsible for Robert Burns and his drinking cronies in an Edinburgh pub calling themselves the 'Crochallan Fencibles' due to an old Highlander who drank there who kept singing about Crodh Chailein. But though Duncan Ban was something of a poetic genius he never learned to read and write and all his work had to be transcribed for him.

In 1767 he moved to Edinburgh and became a member of Edinburgh City Guard and during his time there, at the age of 69, he also joined the Breadalbane Fencibles regiment, which suggests he must have been a very fit old man. In 1782 the law banning the wearing of tartan or Highland dress that had been brought in after the '45 Rebellion was lifted and Duncan Ban MacIntyre wrote his 'Song to the Highland Garb' to celebrate it. He was in the City Guard until 1806, which would put him in his early 80's but he never lost his love of his native countryside. He died in 1812 and is buried in Greyfriar's Churchyard in Edinburgh and it was not until 1859 that this large and impressive granite monument to him was built on the hilltop. Queen Victoria is said to have visited it in 1875 and admired the view from there.

On top of the other nearby hillock there is a mobile phone mast but during the last war this hilltop had a Royal Observer Corps post on it for enemy plane spotting. These were rather Spartan structures with a simple low brick wall and a roof that was removed when the building was occupied. Their equipment was simple and consisted of binoculars, a telephone and a theodolite for measuring angles.

The tarmac road surface finishes below the monument and the road splits with the branch on the left going through the forest past Blarchaorain Farm to finish at a transmission mast above the Bealach nan Cabrach Pass. The other one continues on the route of the old military road that passes Ardteatle Cottage but thereafter the road is now unfit for cars. A short distance further on are the remains of an old burial cairn and near this is what I have seen described as a boulder circle with a large split cup-marked boulder in the centre. The ruins of old Ardteatle are to the left of that and it would have probably been occupied in 1841 when the place had 12 inhabitants. A mile or so past there, at Achlian, the road joins the modern A819 Inveraray road that took over from the old and once military one.

CHAPTER TWELVE

ACHLIAN
TO CLADICH

Achlian was once an estate in its own right, and it still has its mansion house, but it later became part of the large Cladich Estates until its land was largely sold off for forestry. What remained was subsequently broken up and this part is now farmed from Achlian Cottage by Willie and Anne MacNicol. Achlian is marked on Timothy Pont's 1580's map and it seems to have once been a thriving place with much of the hillside above having been cultivated in earlier times. By the first census of 1841 the place had 21 inhabitants.

John Campbell, Archie Gillies and Neil Paterson hand clipping sheep at Achlian in the 1940's.

ABOVE: *Recorded at Inishtrynich in August 1941 is an impressive draw of salmon netted at the mouth of the Teatle. Brigadier R.W.L. Fellowes is on the right next to his elder son Neville W.L. Fellowes, John May, Walter Munro, McNicol, unknown, John Cowan with his father at the front.*

LEFT: *Exercising an ancient right, the men on Cladich Estate prepare to net salmon, at the mouth of the Teatle in the 1950's.*

BELOW LEFT: *Drawing in the catch after netting salmon at the mouth of the river Teatle in the 1950's.*

Achlian translates into 'field of the net' and was so called because Achlian had old netting rights on Loch Awe. I remember post
Second World War that Brigadier Fellowes, who owned Cladich Estates, was still exercising that right by having a yearly draw of a net
near the mouth of the Teatle Water.

There is a story told by Mary McGrigor in her booklet History
of South Lochaweside, which tells of how a man who netted there
had, it appears, drawn his net and also fired a shot on Sunday. This
crime was reported to the Minister who duly took him to task and
told him that the Devil would get him, but the man was unrepentant
and said that the Devil complete with horns had popped his head
up as he was drawing his net in, and that he had shot him, which left
him, the Minister, out of a job. I don't know what the Minister made
of this tall tale, but in the 1840's the local minister gave credence to
a very unlikely tale of a Druidic bridge being built across Loch Awe
about three miles from there as he wrote in the Statistical Account
of that time, 'Tradition alleges that a bold attempt was once made
to throw a bridge across Lochawe a little to the north of Cladich.
On the south side of the lake on the farm of Barandryan huge
blocks of stone may in a clear and calm day be traced into the lake
to a considerable distance placed, it is said, at regular distances.
These stones and cairns the foundation on which the intended bridge
was to have rested constitute the sole remains and monument of this
formidable undertaking. These remains are called the Druid's
Bridge'. Modern Ordnance Survey maps have the site of this supposed bridge marked by its Gaelic name of Drochaid na Druidh but
stories such as that lead one to think that many of the Reverend
compilers of the Statistical Accounts were somewhat gullible, and
they also appeared to think that using English names for lochs
etcetera was the only civilized way of doing things.

Leaving Achlian we come to a sheltered bay next to the island
or peninsula of Inistrynich and a pier marked on old maps there

would seem to have been the landing place for the Inishail ferry. A map suggests that it would have been a shorter trip to sail to Inistrynich, but in the days of the ferry that would largely have been an island with swampland between it and the shore. It was only with the lowering of Loch Awe that it became a proper peninsula. Inistrynich means island of blackthorn and a lot of blackthorn bushes do grow nearby, the fruit of which appears to be bigger and not so acidic as the normal wild ones, and so they were possibly once planted stock.

The island is supposed to have had a castle from the late 1300's but no sign of it is to be seen now. It seems that the Clan MacArthur started to decline after the Chief was beheaded by James I at Inverness in 1427. He was known as MacArthur of Innistrynich or Traigh Cladich and seems to have been regarded as a trouble maker by the King. In the rebellion of 1685 Patrick McArthur, the laird of Inistrynich, and four other men from there turned out to support the Earl of Argyll, and the later occupying Government forces looted the place of everything valuable. In 1686, however, Patrick McArthur was successful in claiming compensation of 2,600 merks in a court case against Donald MacDonald of Benbecula and his followers, but I don't know if he ever received his money. This place is probably the Teirivadich that is listed in 1692 as having eight fencible men five of whom were

Brigadier R.W.L. Fellowes with a ghillie stalking on Achlian.

MacArthurs. There is said to have been a monastery at In-

ABOVE: *The stalking pony waits patiently at Inistrynich with lunch for the stalking party packed in panniers.*

BELOW: *Inistrynich, originally a single storey and basement cottage before 1843, had a new wing of the same height with bay windows and a verandah added in 1865, while in 1881 Walter Campbell Muir balanced this to the East while adding a further block of two storeys, basement and two towers, one octagonal and one square. In 1956, Brigadier Fellowes demolished the two storey addition and the towers seen on the far right, to recreate a single storey and basement home pleasingly symetrical on the North and South fronts.*

istrynich but as there was one on nearby Inishail it is not likely there would have been two so close together. It may be that Inistrynich had a monastery while Inishail had a nunnery and that the monastery later moved to Inishail after the nuns had left.

In 1801 there is a settlement marked between the road and the crossing to the island and the island is shown by Langlands as a peninsula. In the 1841 census for Inistrynich an inn with nine inhabitants is given, a farm with 24 and Inistrynich House with 16. This would have been the present Inistrynich House, which was built in the late 1700's. It was downsized and had the roof lowered and other alterations done to it in the 1950's. A small crannog is in the bay to the south of the island.

Ahead by the Allt Fearna (Alder Burn) is Millside, which probably took its name from an old sawmill there. There is a ruined wooden building by the roadside but the old sawmill building is further back and completely hidden in the trees. This still standing but ruined building is built of wood and corrugated iron and has its saw-bench and much else still there. It was originally water-driven and the turbine and rusted iron water pipes are still in place. These pipes are made of riveted sheet-iron and would, I think, date back to about the late 1800's. At a later date an engine to drive the mill has been installed and the concrete mountings for it are in an attached wooden engine-shed. Fred Stewart said that this mill operated and cut wood till about 1950.

Around the Second World War the lady living at Millside Cottage was described as a 'hen-wife' and such 'hen-wifes' were experts on poultry. They used to visit schools and other places instructing in the best ways of keeping poultry. In those days most country places kept hens.

The church building across the road was built around 1736 and replaced the Inishail Church and was built using quite a lot of the stone from the original Church. It served the old Inishail Parish that took in both sides of the loch, and in the late 1700's an aunt of the poet Coleridge, who was touring in the area and attended a service there, wrote about the many folk travelling by boat and coming ashore below the church. That large attendance unfortunately dwindled through time and after the Second World War the church had to be closed and the building was later sold. The bell is now housed at Inistrynich with Mr David Fellowes and an inscription on it reads 'Re-cast in part from the old bell of Innishail and presented to that church by William Muir of Innistrynich AD 1865'.

Up the long hill from there is Dugall's Barn, which is an old field barn that has lately been converted into a dwelling house, and a short distance ahead is Bovuy now consisting of one house but in 1841 there were 56 people living there on sites further up the hillside. Some of the men's occupations were three farmers, two shoemakers and a schoolmaster, so quite possibly the school was there too. Bovuy is marked on Timothy Pont's 1590's map of south-east Loch Awe. He, during his map-making years, did a map-making journey that started near Loch Gilp and took him up the south-east side of Loch Awe mapping and measuring distances by counting the number of paces that he took. I am doubtful if he went all the way as he has marked very little at the Dalmally end and I think that he must have gone back to Lochfyneside from Cladich. In 1685 five rebel supporters of the Earl of Argyll's rising came from Bovuy and seven years later in 1692 there were seven fencible men of military age there.

Below Bovuy and across the Cladich River are stretches of old natural, mainly oak, woods, which would no doubt have been worked and harvested for charcoal fuel in the iron-smelting times of the 1700's and early 1800's. Near the B840 junction a short farm road leads up to what was once a fairly large chambered cairn, but like almost all such cairns most of the stones have been robbed for building and it is now merely a shadow of what it once was.

James Hogg, the shepherd poet, passed this way on a lone walking tour in 1803. He had left Inveraray very early in the morning, intending to breakfast at Portsonachan, then cross the loch and go on to Oban, but he somehow missed the turn off for Portsonachan and when a person that he asked directions from told him that he had gone a mile too far, and that the road he was on led to Tyndrum or the Braes of Glenorchy, he pigheadedly carried on the way that he was going and refused to answer any of his fellow-traveller's questions.

Ahead the modern road bypasses the hamlet of Cladich and then climbs up a long hill and at its summit is the start of the long road into Accurach Farm. The farm is in an isolated but pleasant spot near the Cladich River. There has been a large sheep-farm there since 1802 when it was bought by John Campbell of Airds and merged with neighbouring Boccaird and for many years past the farm has been run by a Campbell family. The place is spelled Auchuruch in a 1692 list of fencible men and in the 1841 census it had 13 inhabitants. A road carries on from Accurach past some old ruins by the riverside to near the old abandoned settlement of Boccaird.

This old hamlet and surrounding lands were part of the MacArthur lands of Lochaweside before these were taken over by the Campbells. In 1685 Niccoll mc Niccoll, a rebel supporter of the Earl of Argyll who came from there, had his livestock of 12 cows confiscated. In 1692 there were three fencible men there but by the 1841 census there were only eight people living in the place. Mary MacGrigor, in an article in the Kist magazine, says that there are the ruins of 11 houses, a church and a school there and she describes how it's being isolated and high up had allowed it to escape the 1846 potato famine that was caused by a blight disease.

So its potatoes were able to feed the neighbouring people but whether it remained free from that fungal disease in all the following years is doubtful because the potato blight plague hung around and persisted for about 10 years.

From Boccaird we return to the A819 and above here was the old road from Glenaray and at a spot where the island of Inishail first came into view was what was called The Cross of Prostration where pilgrims travelling to Inishail threw themselves down at the first sight of the holy isle. Back down to the east entrance to Cladich and the first buildings that we come to on entering that road are what were once Cladich Steadings and date from the late 1800's. These were built in the form of a square and included a cottage and this buildings complex has recently been converted into a housing development.

There was a mill at Cladich which was situated in the field where the telephone box is and I am told that the water inlet and position of the mill is still visible. It was originally a meal-mill but later under the MacIntyres's, a clan who had come down from Glen Orchy in about 1750, it then switched to making Cladich stockings and garters, which were a must for kilt wearers. They were a red, blue and black, which could be varied. Back in the days when stockings were woven and not knitted and garters were a long strip of fabric that was wound round the leg and tied in a knot it seems that these Cladich produced ones were a must-have accessory for any well-dressed wearer of a kilt or Highland dress. These stockings were highly prized and even the Earl of Argyll wore them when the factory was at its peak around 1800.

Cladich is mentioned in an Inveraray court case of 1730 when two people from there were charged with not paying excise duty. One of them, a James Oswald, was again charged in 1734 for illegal brewing. In the late 1700's when Coleridge's aunt was touring, she described Cladich as a hamlet with an inn and rough stone built thatched houses with mud floors and peat fires in the middle of the living quarters, but no chimneys. This hamlet with its inn had probably grown up beside the junction of the Portsonachan Ferry road with the Inveraray to Dalmally military one. The Bridge Cottage building was built as an inn with the part nearest the river being the residential end. One version I have says that Johnson and Boswell stayed at the Inn on their trip to Inveraray, which would make sense on a very wet night.

I am puzzled by the list of Cladich people recorded in the Inn in the 1841 census - Cladich Inn has 16 residents and Cladich one old woman. What has happened to the hamlet of earlier times and why are there 16 people in the inn? These consisted of the innkeeper, his wife and three children then we have an agricultural labourer, a young man-servant, four female farm-servants and four youngish men who were not born in Scotland, two of whom are described as Army with one of them having his wife with him.

Notes taken from the calendar for the first surviving minute book of the Commissioners of Supply for Argyllshire were given to me by Ile Crawford of Blarghour plus many others from former research work: 2nd June 1744 - Bridges to be built over the Waters of Cladich, parish of Glenorchy and Inishail, and Inverliever, Parish of Kilmartin. 5th June 1745 - The bridge over the Water of Cladich 'now near finished'. 'That was quick, built in one year' - - - But it was not finished yet as thirty men and horses adjacent to the Bridge of Cladich 'to work on finishing the Bridge'. Then in June 1750 – 'Mr Douglas to be required to finish the bridge'.

Timothy Pont in the 1590's has no settlement there at all although he has an Avon Clady river marked. The name Cladich is usually taken to mean a stony shore but this is a long way from a shore, which is rather puzzling. Across the Cladich River a road runs off to the right past the new Cladich farm steadings and down to some level fertile fields one of which gets called the aerodrome as it was once used for that. Back on the B840 the old cottage on the left was at one time the home of the local blacksmith with his 'smiddy' behind it, and in later years was home to Fred Stewart whose knowledge I have used. A couple of new houses have been built there and the small Douglas Cottage,

Fred Stewart, assisted by Emma Fellowes, leading "John of Cladich" winner of the top award at Lorn Agricultural Show at Mossfield Park in 1968. Bred at Cladich, this bull was sold at Oban bull sales in 1961 but was later bought back into the Cladich Fold by Brigadier Fellowes and enjoyed many successes in the show ring culminating with the overall championship at Dalmally Show in 1967.

named after the road-man who occupied it for many years, has now been renovated and enlarged.

The Cladich School opposite the road junction has long since been closed and is converted into a private house. The hill by the old schoolhouse was once known as the Saw-pit Brae as a saw-pit operated from there in the days before mechanization. This had a log lying across a deep pit and one man stood on top of this, and another was in the pit below and they sawed backwards and forwards with a long saw between them, which was the way all wood was once sawn.

At this junction we leave the old military road and continue on what was once the Portsonachan Ferry road. Running underground alongside this stretch of road are telephone cables that once carried the Cold War 'Hot Line' connecting the White House and the Kremlin with a direct line. It was dubbed the K K Line because it connected Kennedy and Khrushchev. This line came via Shetland, down and across Scotland, under Loch Awe, on to Gallanach near Oban and across the Atlantic. The idea was to give direct contact between the two leaders and hopefully prevent retaliation in the event of an accidental missile firing or malfunction of some kind. Later the K K Line became a radio link and now with fibre-optic cable and satellite communication this Atlantic telephone cable is no longer in use.

Between here and the loch-side there were two old settlements, which are now no more. I have noticed that there are very few ruins with standing walls around the loch-side and I am wondering if old ruins were deliberately demolished, or was it simply the ravages of time and robbing of stone for dyke-building that was responsible?

These settlements were Drimuirk and Barandryan but the information that I have as to their sites is not clear. Drimuirk is marked on Timothy Pont's 1590's map but its position is vague. It is also marked on Langlands's 1801 map, which is usually pretty accurate but in this case he has Keppochan Burn running into Loch Awe instead of the Cladich River, which does not inspire confidence in his placing Drimuirk midway between the two burns and a third of the way towards the loch. I think that the ruins across Keppochan Burn will be Barandryan and that Drimuirk was somewhere nearer Cladich. There are some ruins not far from the road junction and another ruin is by the roadside at a square of hawthorn and holly trees that was once a garden hedge. Drimuirk had two rebels in 1685 and in 1692 had seven fencible men, and in the 1841 census there were all of 45 people living there so it appeared to be quite busy, and as these included a schoolmaster, the local school was presumably there or nearby. There was also a ground officer who would be the estate factor.

I discovered a strange story about Drimuirk that I had not known. When Archibald, 9th Earl of Argyll, was imprisoned in Edinburgh in 1681 with a view to being beheaded, Mr MacArthur of Drimurcht, parish of Inishail, went to Edinburgh with his ghillie and got into the place of confinement. He dressed his ghillie in a lady's garment and after getting in he dressed Argyll in the lady's dress and MacArthur acted as a page holding up her train when coming out. He had taken two ponies with him, which were shod with the shoes turned around so as to deceive the pursuers. Argyll then returned to Inveraray and MacArthur to Drimurcht. When the Atholeman were trying to get the deeds of the land Macarthur came to Argyll to assist in keeping them and took them home to Drimurcht. The Atholemen found out that he had them and he had to flee across the hills to Aurthur's Seat in Glencoe.

This is the traditional account of the escape of the Earl in the disguise of Lady Sophia Lindsay. Lady Lindsay was married to Argyll's son Charles and was supposed to be saying goodbye to him. He was nearly caught at the outer gate when the guard grabbed his arm. In agitation the earl dropped the train of Lady Sophia, who with singular presence of mind, fairly slapped his face with it, and thereby smearing his features with mud exclaimed, 'Thou careless loon!' Laughing at this the soldier permitted them to pass.

I am afraid that I am doubtful about this story as all the information I have says that Lady Sophia Lindsay and a page took part. If he was involved it must have been in another role.

Barandryan, or to give it its Gaelic name Barr an Droighinn (Hill of the Thorns), had three fencible men in1692 and in 1841 it had 10 residents. Mary McGrigor, in a Kist magazine article, says that in 1529 the lands of Barandryan were granted to Duncan MacKaus, who was Vicar of Inishail Parish, on condition that he and his heirs maintained the chapel on the island, held a weekly mass and prayed for the souls of the King, the Earl and their families. She also says in her History of South Lochaweside that the new Keppochan sheep farm was leased out in 1880 with obligations to purchase the sheep-stock of Drumurk from Ed. McCallum and Barandryan from D & P McCallum, and that probably spelled the end of individual farming in these places.

Driving on towards Keppochan we first pass by a dead, monster-like skeleton tree that has been known and much photographed for the past fifty years. Somewhere to the north of here is a cup-marked stone at grid reference 104 239. Then over the Keppochan Burn (the original Keppochan settlement was higher up and across the road from the later farm) where a number of ruins of buildings and a grain-drying kiln are to be seen. Timothy Pont had the place marked on his 1590's map and in 1841 there were 17 inhabitants but when the large sheep farm of Keppochan came into being that would probably have seen the end of the old settlement. During the Second World War there was a small hutted encampment by the roadside, housing Timber Control workers who were engaged in felling and extracting the trees of the surrounding woods, to help meet the tremendous demand for timber.

Leaving Keppochan, we drive up a steep hill to the road's summit near the Tom nan Freumh hillock, and if we climb the short distance to its top we have a magnificent all-round view of much of Loch Awe and its surroundings. There is a Trig, or rather Trigonometry Point, on top here and these surveying spots were marked by small concrete cairns that had an anchoring point for a theodolite. They were built on many hill-tops, post war, by the Ordnance Survey. Their purpose was to enable accurate triangulation mapping to be done but since then satellite and other simpler methods of surveying can be used and the Trig Points appear to be redundant. Surprisingly, only one of the areas wind-farms is visible from here situated on the hills beyond Loch Nant. The 1851 census has a house listed called Tomnafraive that was presumably named after the hillock and it would seem to have been somewhere around here. It had a family of seven living in it plus one eighty year old relative who was registered as a pauper and receiving one shilling and sixpence a week of poor relief.

CHAPTER THIRTEEN

ARDBRECKNISH

Descending Ardbrecknish Hill we pass the entrances to forest roads on either side, and around Loch Awe there are now several hundred miles of such roads built to extract timber and service the forests. These are all built using local material that is dug on the site or quarried nearby and this is a method that was pioneered and perfected by earlier Forestry Commission road squads.

The first house of the scattered Ardbrecknish community that we come to is the manse or parsonage for the nearby St James's

St. James Episcopal Church, built by James Thorpe of Ardbrecknish and consecrated in 1891, has three fine stained glass memorial windows designed and executed by Charles Kempe (1837 - 1907) commemorating William and Archibald James, sons of James Thorpe and also Edward Codrington who had drowned.

Church. This is the only Episcopalian Church on the loch-side and was built by the local laird Colonel James Thorpe in around 1890. It is still in use, but not continually as it does not have a resident parson and relies on parsons from elsewhere who use the parsonage for a working summer break. There are three stained-glass windows in the church one of which commemorates a son of the church builder who was killed in the First World War. Across the road from the Parsonage is the recently built Hill House belonging to Donald Wilson owner of Ardbrecknish House and its holiday complex and opposite St James's Church is Inishail Cottage, which is now alongside several recently built houses.

In the 1950's a botanist, Dr Kenneth MacLeay lived there and he was responsible for the mapping of plants for the 'Main Argyll' part of the Atlas of the British Flora, which was published in 1961. This was the first country-wide British flora atlas that divided the country into ten kilometre squares and if a species was found in that square it was marked by a dot. As 'Main Argyll' covered all mainland Argyll, minus Kintyre, it was a tremendous task and there were of course omissions and a few mistakes but if early dog-violet is ever found at Balliemeanoch and marsh Helleborine at Braevallich then he will have been vindicated in placing them there.

Another survey by the Botanical Society of the British Isles was done in the 1990's for a new 2000 Atlas and the plant recorder then was Bernard Thompson from Ford. He had recently retired and with the help of his wife Barbara they put in a tremendous amount of time and work on this mammoth task. I can claim to have played a very small part in this survey as I am responsible for a few of the dots around Lochaweside. Above Inishail Cottage there was once a dam on the Alltan Eireannaich burn and the water from there drove a sawmill that was lower down below the road. But this dam burst in about 1910 and its water flooded Ardbrecknish house and did other damage and that appeared to be the end of the sawmill.

Ardbrecknish Hotel in 1966. Steps and a path led to the productive walled garden and hotel jetty.

Ardbrecknish House is a very old building and in its advertising website it says that until recently Ardbrecknish house was described as early 17th century, but on Pont's map of 1590 it clearly shows the West Tower sketched as was Pont's style.

And it goes on to say that Ardbrecknish House is the oldest surviving and still operational building around the shores of Loch Awe and that it has its own resident ghosts. It has of course been much added to and altered since then and it went from estate house, to shooting lodge, to hotel and the place is now run as a holiday complex with self-catering apartments, cottages, chalets, bar, games room, restaurant and boat hire business . The house's old walled garden can still be seen down near the loch-side.

Most of the land between the public road and Loch Awe now belongs to Rockhill Farm and it runs a Hanoverian horse stud and sheep farm. The farm house itself is also a guest-house and has two self-catering cottages and a nearby fishing loch. In the 1851 census there were two Rockhill farms listed the larger occupied by a lady laird who was owner of Ardbrecknish House, which was being let out as a shooting lodge. This lady, Mary Jane Campbell,

"Fern" sits on the slipway in front of the boathouse which, prior to 1907, was the original part of Fern Cottage, later Green Cottage.

who was a widow, describes herself 'as a farmer of 80 acres employing 2 labourers'. She had listed in the farmhouse, a housemaid, dairymaid, cook, shepherd and cowherd.

Down in a bay at the loch-side is the old steamer pier and a boathouse plus a cottage (Fern Cottage) that I believe was built for the captain of Ardbrecknish House's boat back in the days when most of the 'big houses' around the loch had their own boat for pleasure and for conveying themselves and their guests back and forward to the station at Lochawe. Fern Cottage was extended after 1907 to accommodate the estate engineer Harry Hough, his wife Rebecca and later their children, Francis Alexander born in 1911 and Alice Mary born in 1913 both christened in St. James' Church at Ardbrecknish. Mary Hough, later Mrs Luckhurst, returned with her parents to visit Ardbrecknish and Green Cottage in the 1950's. In 1987, having seen an article and photo of the *Alder* which Mary had contributed to the *Scots Magazine,* the present owners made contact and arranged a visit to her home, "Ardbrecknish" in Codrington near Newark whence the Thorpe family had come and where her father had gone to run a steam threshing business. They were interested to find that Mary`s son had made a working steam model of the *Alder.*

Off the point there is Eilean t-Sagairt (Priest Island) and it is said to have once had a chapel and burial ground on it. Ruin remains can be seen there but there are no gravestones to be seen apart from one in memory of a dog. Near there, in the loch at map references 0779 2230 and 0715 2206, are another two of the twenty or possibly more crannog remains to be found around Loch Awe.

At the foot of the steep hill is a burn called Allt' Cuile Riabhaicha and in 1759, "the timber bridge on the Water of Brechnich is to be repaired", according to the Commissioners for Supply for Argyllshire.

ABOVE LEFT: *A workboat named "Alder" was maintained by the Thorpe family to bring in supplies and visitors from Loch Awe station after the Callander and Oban railway had been extended from Dalmally to Oban in 1880. The "Alder" continued to deliver coal to communities on the loch-side until after the Second World War.*
ABOVE RIGHT: *"Fern" at the pier at Fern Cottage, later Green Cottage, was brought to Loch Awe in 1861 by James Thorpe of Ardbrecknish and was the first steam driven, private pleasure boat on the loch. An attempt had been made the previous autumn to bring her from Loch Etive.*

CHAPTER FOURTEEN

PORTSONACHAN

The next place on our way is upper Sonachan and like most places on the loch-side it is of ancient origin. Lady Mary McGrigor, who is a local historian and lives there, says that it had belonged to the Dukes of Argyll but in 1752 it was transferred from the then duke to the Earl of Breadalbane. Then, through a circuitous route, it returned to a Duke of Argyll a century or so later. It then had several owners before

Upper Sonachan, from a painting by J.M. Heathcote who, with H.W. Elphinstone, A.L. Wigram and Geo. Culley, had taken a lease of the house for six weeks in 1855. The painting shows the original Tacksman's house of the mid 18th century when it would have been in the ownership of the Campbells of Sonachan.

being bought by her late husband Sir Charles McGrigor in 1956. The place also had its home farm but most of the land has now been sold off for forestry. Church Cottage at Upper Sonachan was a Free Church in 1851, then converted into a dwelling house in 1914 when it became the home of the Farquarson family, and later that of their daughter Mrs Jean Carmichael. It is now home to Mrs Kirsty Mc-Grigor. Ard Cottage by the roadside there was a school until the late 1800's and I think that the corrugated-iron school, now a dwelling house, that is opposite Portsonachan Hall would then have taken over from it. This hall was built by the Marjoribanks, who were owners of Upper Sonachan, in 1933 but it has been added to and much improved since then. The last improvements and renovations were mainly funded by a National Lottery grant.

Across the burn from the hall are two new wooden houses and the old, but now renovated, cottage of Allt Bhann (White Burn). This for many years past was home to Jim and Pam Gibson, but tragically he and his young grandson were drowned in a boating accident nearby . The house, many years ago, was the home of Charlie Farquarson who was the gamekeeper on the old Sonachan Estate land and he kept spaniels there. Apparently the ghost of one of them still haunts the place.

Sometime in the first half of the 1800's a 'vinegar' or pyroligneous factory operated near there and produced acetic acid as its main product. The 1843 Statistical Account says 'There is in the parish a work for the manufacture of pyroligneous acid in connection with an extensive secret work at Camlochie in the suburbs of Glasgow'. The raw material used in this manufacturing process was wood, which was heated to almost combustion point in kilns. The vapour given off was distilled and then processed into acetic acid with tar, wood-alcohol and possibly other things as by-products. Acetic acid was used in the calico printing industry to fix the colours and the fact that the manager of the plant came from Bonhill sug-

*Donald Sinclair, last of several genera-
tions of spinning wheel makers, pictured
in 1930 opposite his home at
Achnacloiche beneath the larches planted
to mark the Jacobite Rising of 1745.*
© National Museums Scotland.

gests that it would be used in one of the Vale of Leven's calico printing works. It seems that a wide range of woods could be used but there is a tradition of ash trees being felled and they are trees whose trunks could be easily split up for use in the kilns. Mary McGrigor says that the buildings were demolished in 1850 so the factory did not operate for very long unlike the similar Crinan Harbour one that carried on until 1888.

The old cottages above the road have all been renovated and improved including the wooden one that housed the Post Office, which was run by Katie Bell for many years. A number of wooden chalets belonging to Portsonachan Timeshare Club have been built across the slope. The corrugated-iron church has however been closed for many years and the building still lies unused .

Ahead is Portsonachan (the Port of Peace) and it still has the remains of the old steamer pier complete with a red telephone box beside it. This pier was an important port of call for the Loch Awe steamers. Portsonachan Hotel too had its own steamer that ran a service to Loch Awe Station and Taycreggan and also did excursions.

The old ruined, and by then dangerous wooden pier, went out in a blaze of glory one night when the annual bonfire was built on top of it and set alight. Next to it is a concrete hotel jetty and then there is the old stone ferry jetty that must have been the scene of much activity in the past. The Portsonachan Ferry was the main one across Loch Awe and was part of an important route from Inveraray to the west coast and its islands. Before the Callander to Oban railway opened up a new route in 1880 it was the main route and the way that the mail for the west coast and islands was transported.

The first mention we know of the ferry is from the early 1300's when Sir Neil Campbell, Clan Chief and Baron of Loch Awe, granted land at Portsonachan and the ferrying rights across the loch to a MacPhedran for his skill and bravery in saving the chief's son during a gale on the loch. This family of MacPhedrans held the ferrying rights for over three centuries. Then the MacPhederans found

T.S.S. "Caledonia" acquired in 1895 by Thomas Cameron to run ferry services and cruises from Portsonachan Hotel till 1918, replaced S.S. "Kilchurn" which was bought in 1882.

T.S.S. "Caledonia" laden with passengers at the ferry pier at Portsonachan.

that they had not got an heir to pass it on to, so they tried to pass it on to Duncan Campbell of Sonochan and gave him the Title Deeds, but the Duke of Argyll reckoned that as his Superior it should revert to him and he sent some men to take possession of the Deeds, but Campbell of Sonochan did not give it up to him, and two of his sons were killed defending it. The ferrying rights were then given to Campbell of Dunstaffnage to run.

During its long life the ferry must have seen and transported many kinds of people and cargos such as the busy cattle traffic of the 1600's, 1700's and 1800's, horse-drawn coaches, gigs and carts, countless foot passengers and riders, and cargo of all kinds from farm goods to flittings and charcoal fuel for the Bonawe Furnace.

In 1773 it was recorded that the inhabitants of Kilchrenan, being small tenants, cotters and labourers, were only liable for half freight, but freight of black cattle and sheep remained unchanged. During the Covenanting Wars Alasdair MacDonald, or Colkitto as he was usually known, crossed both this and the Portinnisherrich ferry with his large army in 1645 on his way to Inveraray. A hundred years later, in 1745, a hurried messenger crossed on his way to Inveraray to warn of Prince Charlie's landing on the west coast. Dr Johnson and Boswell crossed here too in 1773 but found only a hut for an inn at Portsonachan. They were both very wet and they dried themselves before a peat fire and then had dinner before riding on through the rain to Inveraray. But an account I have read says they spent the night at Cladich.

From at least the late 1700's through most of the 1800's the mail for much of the west coast and islands of Argyll went via Inveraray and the Port Sonachan Ferry. The Lismore and Appin Statistical Account says in 1790 'A runner now goes thrice a week from Appin to Bunaw, and from Bunaw to Inveraray, and returns as often. A letter may come in three days or even two days and a half from Edinburgh to Appin'. Then from 1840 and the start of the Penny Post the quantity of mail increased greatly and it was then transported by an Inveraray coach to the ferry at Port Sonachan, and then onwards by another coach from Taycreggan to Bonawe and Oban from which it travelled up and down the coast and out to the islands.

Charges for the ferry for15th October 1832 were 'A single foot passenger 4d, a single horse and rider 1s, four wheeled chaise and two horses 5s 3d, with four horses 6s 6d, cart and horse 2s 3d, sheep over three 1d 1/2d, a single cow 9d, a bag bale or package 3d'. It was recommended that the fares were reduced considerably but I do not know whether this was successful.

Into the mid-1900's the ferry was still used by the local doctor, district nurse and minister and it continued to run in a reduced way until 1953 when the ferryman was unfortunately drowned. Back in its heyday two boats were operated - a large boat for animals, cargo, carts and coaches and a smaller one for foot passengers. In 1891 the rates for the ferry were, 'a four-wheeled carriage – 5/, cart or

S.S. "Countess of Breadalbane" leaving the Steamer Pier at Portsonachan.

two-wheeled carriage – 2/- 3d, a horse – 9d, cattle per head – 4d, and a foot passenger – 4d'.

A strange incident was claimed to have occurred during a private boat crossing at Portsonachan in the 1840's when the Kilchrenan Schoolmaster, who was also the officer for poor relief, had been summoned to appear with his records at some kind of County board meeting to apparently answer allegations of dishonesty. He said at the board meeting that he had set out very early in the morning with his servant girl rowing him across the loch but somehow on the way he fell overboard and his record books were, it seems, conveniently lost.

Another crook, but one who did not escape justice, was one Robert Clark who appeared to have been the innkeeper at Portsonachan. He was tried at Inveraray Court on a charge of stealing 51 sheep from the neighbouring farms. Suspicion had fallen on him when he had taken a bunch of sheep with various markings on board a Lochgoilhead steamer bound for Glasgow. He was tried before Lord Coburn and a jury at Inveraray in 1840, found guilty, sentenced to 14 years transportation and sent to Van Diemen's Land (Tasmania).

Portsonachan Hotel improved from the 'hut' mentioned by Boswell in 1773 and the 1790's Statistical Account says 'There are two inns in the parish; one of them a very good house with stables and boats at the ferry of Portsonachan'. In 1850 Poltalloch Estate bought over Sonachan land and this included the hotel and ferry rights, and a copy of an advert that I have from sometime after this says 'John McMillan begs most respectfully to intimate to the Nobility, Gentry, and Public in general that, having taken a Lease of the above Hotel, beautifully situated on Loch Awe, which he has thoroughly renovated and repaired he trusts by strict attention to business to merit the favour of all who may honour him with their patronage.

There is good Fishing attached to the Hotel for which no charge is made. NB Post-Horses, Carriages, Dog-Carts, and Boats on a few minutes' notice. Tourists going from Inveraray to Oban, or from Oban to Inveraray by Port Sonachan will find the road eight miles shorter than by Dalmally, and the scenery splendid. Parties staying at the house have their letters from the South at 10 am – the local Post Office being at the Hotel.'

Sometime later Poltalloch Estate built what is basically the pres-

The view towards the Green Isle from Portsonachan Hotel in 1955. In addition to growing flowers, fruit and vegetables, the hotel had dairy cows milked by Duncan and Marion Maclean to provide milk and cream.

Looking towards Taychreggan, with the rose garden in the foreground and the veg-etable and flower gardens to the left, this view from above Portsonachan Hotel was taken before 1965.

ent hotel and leased it in 1873 to Thomas Cameron who had been the head gamekeeper at Poltalloch. He ran the hotel until he died when his daughter took over and ran it till she died in 1930. The MacPhee's then took charge of it until 1946 when it was bought by Colonel and Mrs Young. I remember the Colonel as a very popular and successful host who was liked by all. He always wore the kilt and was also a piper and he woke the guests in the morning by marching up and down outside the hotel playing.

In his time, and stretching back for more than a century, the place had been a very popular fishing hotel. It kept a small fleet of boats and employed ghillies to take the guests out fishing for the loch's numerous trout and salmon. Trout fishing was usually done by fly-fishing from a drifting boat but salmon fishing would generally be done by trolling a lure behind the boat. In the early days the ghillies had to row many miles but in later years outboard motors were used. After the days fishing the ghillie would take the catch back to the hotel, register it in the fishing book and then lay it out for inspection. The hotel and its grounds have now become a time-share development and club with flats in the stable-block across the road, chalets above the old cottages and other time-share buildings in what was the hotel garden. If Johnson and Boswell were to arrive there today they would not likely find any welcoming fire or dinner.

CHAPTER FIFTEEN

SONACHAN, BALLIEMEANOCH, BARR-BEITHE AND BLARGHOUR

Above Port Sonachan there are the robbed remains of an old chambered burial cairn at map reference 050 206. Its old name of Cairn Ban (White Cairn) harks back to a time when it must have been a prominent landmark with its light-grey lichen encrusted stones giving it the name of white cairn. The remains were excavated in 1955 but I have not yet been able to find what, if any, significant finds were made. In the loch at Sonachan there is an old crannog out in the bay and above it is Sonachan Farm and a cottage. The farm is run as a part-time enterprise by Robert Wilson Junior and previously his father, Bobby Wilson Senior, who was a retired sawmill manager and died recently. Bobby lived higher up with his wife Cathy , in a wooden bungalow built above the road called Cnoc-a-Mhuilinn (Hillock of the Mill) as he said that there was once a water-mill nearby. This would have been driven by water from the nearby burn but it must have been taken from much higher up as this burn that runs under the 1875 dated road-bridge is in an exceptionally deep ravine.

The old Sonachan mansion house further on is now largely converted into holiday flats and is also the hub of a holiday complex of chalets.

In the past Sonachan was an estate and like so much land in Argyll was owned by a Campbell family. In 1777 a Donald Campbell owned Sonachan and he was appointed by the Duke of Argyll to be

Sonachan House photographed while in the ownership of Mr MacDougall between 1898 and 1917.

his deputy Vice Admiral in charge of all maritime court cases in Western Scotland from the Clyde to the Pentland Firth. Donald Campbell was also given the power to appoint other deputy vice admirals and he seems to have blatantly favoured fellow Campbells as he appointed five Campbells and one MacDonald to these posts. This favouritism in this and other appointments not surprisingly gave rise to the idea that there was a Campbell Mafia operating in Argyll and elsewhere.

In the 1790's the local Minister writes in the Statistical Account that Mr Campbell of Sonachan 'encloses, dresses and limes extensively for grass-feeds. The farm upon which he resides, besides excellent pasture, gives him more hay than a numerous flock of black-cattle and horses can consume. Sheep he pays particular attention to and has more than

An outing aboard the "Sonachan" a private steam launch maintained at Sonachan House by Mr MacDougall between 1898 and 1917.

once gained the premium given to this country for the best tups'.

In 1850 Poltalloch Estate added Sonachan to their extensive land holdings and the land was theirs till mounting debt forced them to sell off almost all their remaining land after the Second World War. The Sonachan farms were then bought by their tenant farmers. By the loch-side and next to Sonachan House grounds there is now the recently built Argyll Chalets complex.

From Sonachan onwards the public road follows the loch-side but unfortunately, for much of the year, very little is seen of the loch due to the dense 'hedge' of trees and bushes that are growing up between the road and the water. The loch-side would be a much more attractive place if much of this was cleared away. The old original road ran at a much higher level above much of the steep hillside and that is the way that we shall now follow for several miles. There was an old dwelling beside a burn up ahead but I don't know what it was called, though I did know a onetime resident, Duncan Fisher, who had lived there as a boy.

This stretch of loch-side is steep, rough and much wooded and as it is difficult terrain to farm sheep on. It has now mostly been left to revert to nature. In the past it is said to have been a favourite secluded refuge for illegal distillers to work in, and as I do not see the local place-names mentioned in any of the court records of folk charged with this offence, they must have been pretty successful at avoiding detection.

The old road, which is a good scenic walk, goes along above this steep wooded hillside, then past the small Lochan Uaine (Green Lochan) before going through the Bealach Mor (Big Pass) gap in some very rocky hills. The highest of these hills, Tom an Eich Bhain, has surviving stunted aspen trees growing on its precipitous sides where the sheep have been unable to get to them. These and a few trees growing by the present road are the only natural aspen that I know of on the loch-side.

After going through the Bealach Mor the road drops down to a lower level and passes the remains of the ancient settlement of Coula-chouralan. This was mapped by Timothy Pont in in the 1590's when he drew a mansion house there, spelt it Coulwhirrelan and apparently regarded it as an estate. It is spelt Coullchurrellune in 1692 when it had three fencible men and it seems to have had four tenant farmers in Argyll's Census when it had 26 people. The spelling is Coulcheussland in 1841 when it had nine inhabitants and the name, whichever way you spell it, would seem to have come from a holy man called Cairell who I have seen referred to as Saint, Bishop and Missionary. He had a chapel and burial ground dedicated to him nearby at map reference 014 167 that goes by the name of Cill Churelan.

Near here too at a later date was the old Balliemeanoch Middle Farm. This in 1779 had 15 people in Argyll's Census but after the

Poltalloch Estate had bought the land in 1850 they built a new farm-house and steadings lower down beside their new loch-side road and called it Balliemeanoch. This took over the land of Coulachouralan, Balliemeanoch and Penchallich, which is up ahead on the old road. This part of the old road has now been upgraded and is the road to the recently built hydro-electric scheme on the Beochlich Burn.

Poltalloch Estate had sold off Balliemeanoch, Blarghour and Sonachan when its fortunes were beginning to go downhill and these were bought by Mr MacDougall in 1898 to form a new Sonachan Estate. This was then broken up in 1954 and Balliemeanoch, which consists of 5,700 plus acres, was sold to its MacPherson tenant and Balliemeanoch is now farmed by a third generation of that family.

The Penchallich settlement ruins show that there had been a number of fairly large buildings there and a grain-drying kiln, which surprisingly seems to be facing into the prevailing wind. These kilns were used to dry damp grain before it was de-husked and ground into meal. They consisted of a bowl-shaped stone structure with a covered entrance. The 'bowl' had a light flooring across its top on which the corn was spread. A fire of peat was built in the covered

ABOVE LEFT: *In the fank at Balliemeanoch in 1948, Iain MacPherson sits on the wall while his uncle Jock MacPhie leans on the gate and his father John MacPherson looks on.*
ABOVE RIGHT: *Iain MacPherson leads a horse and rucklifter loaded with hay up to the farm steading at Balliemeanoch in 1953.*

entrance so that heat from the fire radiated back into the kiln but smoke and any flames were carried in the other direction by the wind. These kilns must also have had a light removable roof to protect the grain from the weather. Penchallich in 1692 had two fencible men and in Argyll's Census of 1779 it had 10 of which two seemed to be farmers. It is shown on Langland's 1801 map but it is not listed in the 1841 census so it would seem to be deserted by then.

Most of the nearby Beochlich Burn's water is now used in a private hydro-electric scheme. This has a dam quite high up on the burn's course and the water is piped down to a power-station at the burn-side. The scheme does not interfere with the scenic waterfall above the road. During the building of the dam, there was very heavy rainfall and the dam filled up before it was finished with the result that it collapsed, causing a torrent of water to rush down the burns course, carrying trees and all kinds of debris with it. It washed away the walls of the bridge below but not the bridge itself, which says a lot for the sturdy building of the bridge in 1875.

This bridge and the present road from Portsonachan to Ederline Estate were built by the Poltalloch Estate in order to open up the lands that they had acquired on the loch-side. The road scheme would have been a big undertaking and it took about forty years to complete. By 1843 the road approaching the Ederline Estate boundary had only reached Eredine, but later road building squads worked from both ends, and I was told that the two wooden bungalows, that were at Portsonachan and Portinnisherrich were built for road foremen and their families. Below the Beochlich road bridge is an enclosed area bounded by the burn, loch and road, and this was in past times the site of an old stance, or overnight stopping place for driven cattle and later sheep, which also travelled on their own legs to market. Because of this, wethers, which went for mutton, were kept until they were at least three years old, thus ensuring they were big, strong animals that were well able to travel long distances.

The wooden bungalow, seen on the left, at Portinnisherrich is understood to have been built, together with an identical one at Portsonachan, to house the foremen building the new road from each end in the 1940's for Poltalloch Estate.

Across the Beochlich there is Barr Beithe or Birch Hill. That old name was used in the 1950's when Duncan and Phyllis Crawford built their house by the waterfall there. This house has since been joined by another one higher up but the original Barr Beithe, or as it was usually spelled Barbea, was higher up still beside the old road and over by the corner of the ancient wood, which is where its quite well-preserved ruins can still be seen. The old settlement was recorded with one rebel in 1685 and had four fencible men in 1692 and in the 1841 census it had twelve inhabitants, but the place appears to have been deserted by 1895. It once had a school there but since Mr Snodgrass gave it up in 1864 it was empty and Mr MacPherson was applying for the £9 - 00 fee to be given to him for teaching the extra pupils at Ardchonnel School. Lower down and just inside what was the old wood there is now a newly built house called Loch Awe House. The original Barbea is a pleasant spot and a shepherd herding that hill some fifty years ago arranged for his ashes to be interred there when he realized that he was dying of an incurable disease.

The old Barbea and Penchallich woods were worked for charcoal in the days when the Bonawe Furnace was in operation. Evidence of that can be seen in the charcoal burning platforms that are in the woods. When I was in Barbea Wood many years ago a mole had conveniently excavated some charcoal at a platform site. These level platforms are of some twenty or more feet diameter, and have been dug into the hillside to give level working areas for the charcoal kilns to be operated, and they would be used again and again each time the wood was re-coppiced. But there is controversy about the origin of these and other such platforms as Elizabeth Rennie from Dunoon, an amateur archaeologist, and others did a lot of excavating of similar platforms and found the remains of post holes and other evidence that the platforms had once been ancient circular hut foundations long before the charcoal burners came along and used them as convenient working sites. But having said that, I helped in the professional excavation of two such platforms at Taynish Nature Reserve, and only evidence of charcoal burning was found.

Barbea Wood stretches down to near Blarghour, which is a place that means 'the cleared place of the goats' and these goats were, it is said, kept to eat the herbage growing on the side of the steep ravine nearby, and thus prevent the other animals from being tempted to feed in that dangerous place. In 1680 'the 3 markland of Blarghour' was taken over when it was bought for 1,800 mks by the then 9th Earl of Argyll. The same 9th Earl was also planning to dive for the Tobermory treasure boat and had ordered his frigate boat to be made ready for the operation.

The hillsides above Blarghour are quite fertile and show a number of old ruins of habitations that existed prior to the coming of sheep.

Ernie Crawford cutting hay with their first "wee grey Fergie" tractor and adapted horse mower while his brother Duncan forks the hay at Blarghour in the mid 1950's.

Blarghour then, like most large farms, had its tacksman and in the early 1800's this was a John McLachlan who is buried in Innisherrich Grave-yard. Timothy Pont in the 1590's has the place down as Blaircuyn and in 1692 there is a place listed with two fencible men, called Braiegoyll (hill-slope of the ravine) that sounds very much like Blarghour. In 1759, a Hugh Cameron from Blarghour was involved in a court case in In-veraray, over a lame horse he had sold at the Foord (Ford) Market. The verdict was that he had to take the horse back if it did not recover from its lameness within a month. The horse did not appear to recover as Hugh Cameron had to pay £4 plus expenses to the purchaser. In Ar-gyll's Census in 1779 the place had 33 people staying there and they all seemed to be engaged in agriculture. In the 1841 census Blarghour had 20 inhabitants and at the present time the place consists of the farm-house, converted steadings that are now holiday lets and one old cottage that has been enlarged and rebuilt.

Overlooking the stack yard to a harvest of oats stooked in the Low field at Blarghour in the 1950's.

One moonlight night in 1940, during the German bombing of Britain, a lone plane flew around the loch-side for some time and then dropped four bombs, three up Blarghour burn and one that did not explode, in the hills behind Eredine. One was dropped into some large spruce trees just above Blarghour Falls and exploded in the tree tops shattering the trees, killing a deer and shaking some plaster down from the farmhouse roof. But why the bombs were dropped on Lochaweside is puzzling as there were no military targets around the loch and there did not appear to be any installations or possible targets by a loch-side in Argyll that could be mistaken for Blarghour.

These spruce trees above the falls were probably planted with the others in the 1800's by someone who had an eye for landscape and scenery and who also planted spruce trees on the steep sides of all the ravines between Blarghour Burn and Braevallich Burn. Many of these trees, growing often alongside the falls and cataracts in the ravines, are still growing today. The same person too would possibly be responsible for planting the monkey puzzle trees on a number of islands and points by that stretch of the loch-side. The Blarghour Burn that runs in that ravine has now got a small private hydro-electric scheme using its water, and this takes most of it away from the spectacular Blarghour Falls as will a larger scheme that is being built there do in the future. This is rather a pity as these falls of about ninety feet high could be quite a sight, but are now only worth a visit during the time of a flood.

A hundred years or so ago tourist coach trips were being run from Portsonachan to see them and while the passengers walked up to see the falls the coach carried on to turn at a place that is still called 'The Coach Turn'. Here there was a circular bit of road for it to turn around as I am told that a coach and four could not reverse, which will be why

Blarghour Fall or Eas Chuil (narrow waterfall) photographed around 1900.

coach drivers carried horns to warn others of their approach.

I have the Militia List from 1803-04 for the Parish of Dalavich:

Ardchonnel 3, 1 servant, 1 herd, 1 workman. Portinnisherrich 5, 1 shoemaker, 2 smith, 2 ferrymen. Kaimes 7, 2 farmers, 4 fishers, 1 taylor. Smithtown 1, 1 herd. Eredine 2, 2 fishers. Durren 5, 4 farmers, 1 herd. Kilmaha 3, 3 farmers. Cruachan 5, 1, farmer, 2 fishers, 1 crofter, 1 shoemaker. New York 3, 1 vintner, 1 workman, 1 fisher. Barmadie 2, both dealers in cat-

CAMERON'S
GLEN NANT
AND THE
FALLS OF BLAIRGOUR
CIRCULAR TOUR
By Caledonian Railway,
FOUR-IN-HAND COACHES,
AND THE
S.S. "CALEDONIA,"

Via Taynuilt, Glen Nant, Portsonachan, Falls of Blairgour, Loch Awe,
Kilchurn Castle and the Pass of Brander,

Daily from Oban at 9.40 a.m. and 12.35 p.m.

	1st Class and Cabin,	3rd Class and Cabin,
Fares for the Round, ...	11s. 9d.	10s. 3d.
Fares not including the Falls, ...	9s. 0d.	7s. 6d.

Tickets issued and all information given at CAMERON'S Glen Nant
Booking Office, Esplanade, Oban ; or at the Railway Stations.

*Cameron's Tour to visit the Blarghour Falls where a viewing platform enabled
visitors to have a more open view.*

tle. Barinlian 4, 1 dealer in cattle, 1 workman, 1,weaver, 1 taylor. Mill
of Avoch 1, 1 dyer. Drimdarroch 3, 1 workman, 2 weavers. Kilmun
3, 2 farmer, 1 labourer. Glen 2, 1 weaver, 1 workman. Duninerain
3, 1 farmer, 1 tayler, 1 labourer. Kilmun Loch Avich, has simply got
'younger'. Narachan 1, 1 cattle dealer. Duaig 1, 1 farmer. Maolacha
3, 1 farmer, 1 herd, 1 workman.

The next old settlement across Blarghour Burn was Cuilchonnel
and its ruins can still be seen next to the old Ardchonnel Wood. This
woodland was the first part of the new Eredine Forest to be planted
in 1935 and some of these original trees are still growing by the roadside and many are well over a hundred feet high. An ancient hollow
silver fir tree in the wood above is a relic from the previous planting
and is now home to a pair of barn owls.

From the Coach Turn a forest road leads up through the forest and passes an old burial cairn in the younger forest above. Despite its having had a great deal of its stone removed to build two nearby dykes it is still the most complete cairn that I know. It is oblong in shape and some eighty plus feet long and it appears to have had four projecting horns at its corners. A tremendous amount of work must have gone into its construction and its age, give or take a thousand, will be around three thousand five hundred years.

When I was a young fellow working around there, I was told that it was the start of a tunnel to Innischonnel Castle, which is on an island in the loch below, and that someone from Eredine had discovered the start of this tunnel but was unable to go very far into it. This 'tunnel' would be the entrance passage and burial chamber that have been opened up into the cairn and the name J McIsa and the date 1813 carved on the wall of the chamber will be his work. As a curious young fellow and not quite believing this tunnel story, I dug a small hole in one corner of the chamber to see if it continued down as a shaft but it did not. However, I did dig through some charcoal and what I took to be decomposed bone.

This burial chamber and entrance passageway only occupy about a quarter of the length of the cairn and it may be that there is another chamber or chambers still to be discovered. The chamber that was opened has, as far as I know, never been scientifically excavated and this might be worth doing, though the weight of its heavy capstone is now causing one of the chamber's side slabs to collapse, which would make it difficult to work safely without removing it.

CHAPTER SIXTEEN

ARDCHONNEL

Just past the far end of the old Ardchonnel Wood is Ardchonnel Croft. This was an old, originally thatched house, that has been modernised and has been home to three generations of MacIntyres. In earlier days water was obtained from a spring called the Hermit's Well that is situated towards the wood and this name, I was told, was because of a beggar who had used this place beside the old road and spring, as one of a number of begging stances. He would crouch

Mrs Margaret MacIntyre and family at Ardchonnel Croft about 1946.
Archibald MacIntyre with his wife Margaret and family had come from Minard to take up the post of head gamekeeper on Eredine Estate in 1892.

there completely swaddled up and hidden from view but if a coin or other offering was thrown to him a hand came out and seized it.

At the loch-side below the croft is an inlet, with a natural rock landing place alongside, that is called The Brandy Rock. Now with a name like that it is almost certain to have been used in smuggling back in the days when smuggling was almost a way of life, with goods like brandy, wine, tobacco and salt being landed on the quiet west coast, and then being transported across country by routes such as that by Loch Avich across Loch Awe, and then onwards by pack-pony. As the people in the hamlet of Kames had a reputation for smuggling it is likely that it was they who transported the illicit goods over the hill road from Kames to the foot of Glen Aray and possibly into Inveraray, as it were, by the back door. The reason for this roundabout route was that the more straightforward way up Loch Fyne was patrolled by tidewaiters, or excise men, who were difficult to evade.

Beside the croft-house is Ardchonnel Cottage, originally built to house a Church of Scotland Missionary, and a ruined water-mill. This was the local meal-mill and was built sometime in the1600's by a MacLachlan laird whose family were hereditary keepers of In-nischonnel Castle and appeared to have a feu of the loch-side land between Blarghour Burn and Braevallich Burn, and on the far side of the loch between Dalavich, Druimdarroch and Kilmun. The mill obtained most of its water by way of a channel cut across the hillside from Ardchonnel Burn and had a holding pond in a boggy area above with a raceway carrying it onto an overshot mill-wheel. Two millstones are lying beside the mill and it is quite likely that these came from the mill-stone making site that was situated below a small cliff face behind Meall na Sroine above Ardary.

Over a rise from the croft-house is Ardchonnel Farm, which is another farm that was built in the sheep-farming boom years. It now consists of 3,428 acres and is owned by Sir Jamie McGrigor, MSP, the son of Lady Mary McGrigor of Upper Sonachan. He has built himself a new house on the site of the two old cottages that were on the hillside above.

In the 1940's one of these cottages was occupied by Dan Stuart who was usually called the 'Bohunk' and his family. He was a larger-than-life character about whom many stories are told, and who also told me many local stories. He was a bit of a poacher and one story told to me by Alec MacLeod was about how they had gone fishing in the hill-lochs above Loch Awe. They had fished all day and caught a good many fish and were on their way home when Dan told Alec to wait as they approached the top of a ridge. He then crawled cautiously forward and Alec heard the crack of a rifle and Dan exclaiming 'I got the bugger', and only then did Alec realize that Dan had been carrying a poacher's rifle around with him all day. Anyway Dan butchered the deer and they carried the best of it home with them and Dan would no doubt have considered it quite a good day's fishing.

In older times Ardchonnel was a farming settlement and in the 1841 census it had 45 people living there. By the side of the farmhouse there is an old yew tree that will be older than the farmhouse and it will take us back to the time of the MacLachlan lairds. They were the hereditary Keepers or Captains of Innischonnel Castle from, I think, about 1500 and in the early days they probably would have lived there but later they would have moved ashore to their Ardchonnel property. The castle goes back to at least the 1200's and Mary MacGrigor says in her History of South Lochaweside booklet that the first historical reference to a Campbell chief from there was one Gillespie Campbell who was chief about 1250 to 1260. He apparently was succeeded by his son Big Colin, or Cailean Mor, who she says was knighted by King Alexander III in 1280. He was the chief who was killed fighting against the MacDougals on the String of Lorne in 1294. He was succeeded as chief by his son Neil, or

Innischonnel Castle.

Nigel as he was often called, and he like most of the highland Chiefs at that time had originally sworn allegiance to the English king, Edward I, but when Robert the Bruce began his campaign for independence Sir Neil and his men joined him and fought alongside him right through to Bannockburn and beyond.

It would seem though that the Campbells must have lost their castle of Innischonnel to the MacDougals for a time because the MacDougal chief, John of Lorne, wrote to King Edward II in 1308 asking for help against their joint enemies. He said that 'he had a lake twenty leagues long with three castles on it to defend' and this, despite the long length given, would seem to be Loch Awe with Innischonnel, Fraoch Eilean and Finchairn as the castles. Another thing that seems to suggest that the Campbells did not hold Innischonnel then is the fact that there is no mention of Bruce in his fugitive years ever using it as a place of refuge.

After Bruce's decisive victory in The Pass of Brander, however, Innischonnel would have been restored to the Campbells and after

Sir Neil's wife died he married Bruce's sister in 1312. Having Bruce as his brother-in-law no doubt counted in his favour when it came to a share-out of the old enemy lands after Bruce came to power, and this was the start of a Campbell rise to power and importance in the country and their acquisition of much land and property. Sir Neil and his wife were given confiscated lands in Perthshire and he became Constable of the Royal Castle of Dunoon. It would appear that he must have passed his Loch Awe castle and titles on to his son Colin as the young Sir Colin was then granted the lands of Loch Awe and of Ardsheodnish (Kilmartin) in free barony. As a baron Sir Colin and other chiefs would have held Barony Courts at Innischonnel with power to sentence and execute prisoners.

The Coronation of Queen Elizabeth in 1953 was celebrated with a picnic for the local children in Innischonnel Castle.

He was succeeded by his son Archibald and then by a Colin 'Iongantach', which means, wonderful, surprising, strange or extraordinary, and according to the stories told about him he may well have been all of these. It is said, among other things, that before his death he threw all his treasures into the loch lest his sons fight over them. He also went through the army of the Lord of the Isles dressed as a beggar in order to spy out his force's strength before a battle. Also he is said to have obtained a foot hold at Inveraray by begging a small piece of land from the MacVicar owners, as much, he said, as an ox's hide would cover. He then cut the ox's hide into a long thin thong and stretched it around a large piece of land. He also had a narrow escape from the Ardsheodnish MacCallums who tried to burn him in a building. He escaped with his chain-mail so hot that he had to jump into a pool to cool it.

Next chief was Duncan who was styled Lord of Argyll and was made a Lord of Parliament and a Privy councillor by King James I. He was possibly treated favourably by him, as he was one of the twenty one Scottish nobles who had gone to England as hostages, as a guarantee for the payment of a £40,000 ransom for the King's release. He also seems to have been responsible for the enlarging and improving of the castle by adding the whole south-west part. This has the vaulted cellars and store rooms on the ground floor and the great hall and entrance to the dungeon and the kitchen with its massive chimney on the next level. A square tower was also added on to the south corner and a middle bailie was constructed with unusually an entrance either side. When the castle was roofed this did not extend to the outer edge of the walls as a walkway was left around them for defence, which is the reason for the many stone spouts that carry the roof water away from the walls.

Duncan's only son Celestine died in England and his body was brought back as far as Kilmun on the Holy Loch and buried there. When Lord Duncan died he was also buried there and this started the tradition of its being the burial place of future Campbell chiefs. Lord Duncan's young grandson Colin then became Chief and Colin, Chief of Glenorchy, became his guardian. Young Colin, who became the first Earl of Argyll in1457, was also Chancellor of Scotland and Master of the Kings Household. He moved his residence from Innischonnel to Inveraray to give his galleys access to the sea and make travelling around the country easier. His eldest son Gillespie succeeded him as Earl but he was one of the many Highland chiefs who were killed at the Battle of Flodden in 1513 where he and his brother-in-law, the Earl of Lennox, commanded the right wing of the Scot's army.

By about 1474 the castle had ceased to be used as the Chief's residence and it became a prison housing mainly political prisoners who were there ostensibly on behalf of the King. But they were just as likely to be there for the benefit of the current chief as they had developed great skill in manipulating the law to further their own interests.

One of the prisoners held in the castle was Donald Dubh the grandson of the last Lord of the Isles. After the Battle of Bloody Bay on Mull the infant, or his pregnant mother, was taken into Campbell custody and the young Donald Dubh grew up a prisoner in Innischonnel Castle until, it is said, at the age of nineteen or some say twenty one, others thirty years, he was rescued in a daring raid by a band of MacDonalds from Glen Coe. He went on to head a revolt of MacDonalds and islanders against King James IV in1545. It is said that he had 180 galleys and a force of some 8,000 men but they were defeated and he was again imprisoned this time in Edinburgh Castle. Also held captive in Innischonnel was another John MacDonald who was son and heir to James MacDonald of Castle Camus in Skye, and two MacLeans from Duart in Mull, one of whom was the chief from there.

In its early prison days a MacArthur was made Captain of Innischonnel Castle but there was a serious split between him and the Earl. It is said that it was because the Captain was robbing Campbell property. Anyway he was booted out and the office was given to a MacLachlan from Stralachlan and he was also apparently feued the Castle Lands. This was a hereditary office and the family remained Captains of Innischonnel for centuries until the early 1800's, by which time the castle was in ruins. This was despite it being said that during the '45 Jacobite Rebellion their MacLachlan relatives from Stralachlan called in and collected the current castle keeper, and they all went off to fight for Prince Charlie even though the Captain's employer was a staunch Government supporter.

After 1745 the castle became abandoned and ruined and in the 1870's a pair of the last native ospreys nested on top of the castle ruins. That is until one of the birds was shot and its valuable eggs taken by the gamekeeper at Eredine. The ruined castle still belongs to the Duke of Argyll as head of the Campbell Clan but it is in the care of Historic Scotland who maintain the sturdy ruins, make them safe and prevent any further deterioration. The castle is still highly regarded by the Campbell Clan as being the birthplace and home of the Clan and its main stronghold and headquarters for three centuries. When I once mentioned its name to a Campbell from South America she quoted the phrase 'Innischonnel best of all'.

There are several other islands near Innischonnel including a small elongated stony islet to the north-east where two small outcrops of rock have been built up to form a crannog foundation. In the other direction is a tree covered island that is called by the Ordnance Survey, Eilean na Meann (Middle Island) but which I know of as Goat Island, and nearer Dalavich is the small low lying Priest Island. This has a small rocky outcrop in the centre on which are the ruins of a small stone hut or cell. Surprisingly, growing on this dry rock outcrop, is a small patch of bog blaeberry and as I have noticed other moisture-loving plants growing on rocks by the loch-side, it seems that they must be obtaining water by a process of capillary action through the cracks in the rocks.

Ashore here was the old Ardchonnel School, which I attended as a boy and now a dwelling house with Brackenburn nearby. Half a mile further on is Portinnisherrich where for many centuries a cross-loch ferry operated carrying people, their animals and goods. It was part of an ancient route from the west coast, which went by way of the Durran hill road to Inveraray and beyond. According to Walter Weyndling's Ferry Tales, the ferry was used by the Campbell and government forces, pursuing Montrose's army in 1644, after it had sacked Inveraray, but they were again defeated at Inverlochy near Fort William.

The ferry ran from at least medieval times up to the early years of the 1900's and it can be assumed that in its early days, the Campbell chiefs from nearby Innischonnel Castle, would have granted out or controlled the ferrying rights. Indeed there is a charter in existence from 1571 in which the Earl granted, or perhaps burdened, Ian Dow MacGeilreid MacKachray with the ferry contract and the obligation of ferrying the local parish residents and the Earl and his family free.

He also had Portinnisherrich Inn and farm whose lease seemed to be tied in with the ferry. Later the MacLachlan captains of the castle had the ferry rights and also the right to malt and brew, which would have applied to the Portinnisherrich Inn. The 1700's were a busy time for the ferry and the rent charged to Donald Campbell of Portinnisherrich then was £60 but this may also have included the inn and farm. Portinnisherrich's long name translates into 'port of the island of the six-oared (galley)' and this galley would not be a super ferry but one belonging to the nearby castle. It would be kept there because there was no sheltered anchorage at the castle.

A strange case was brought before the Inveraray JP Court in 1749 when James Turner, ferryman at Portinnisherrich, complained that Patrick McArthur, tenant at Cuilchonnel, had taken away the ferry boat, hidden the oars and refused to return them. A warrant to summon Patrick McArthur to court was issued but unfortunately I do not know the outcome of the affair.

The 1571 Charter of Archibald 5th Earl of Argyll grants Iain Dow Geillbreid Mac Kathray of the half mkl of Portinnsherrich to be holder of free alms for ever and to provide a ferry boat on the loch. This was once a busy ferry but its use had dropped off as other better ways were found. In 1891 it carried small parcels for 2d, large ones up to a shilling and a single passenger for 4d. Double fares were charged from an hour after sunset until 6am and only one small boat was available for service.

The island of Innisherrich is a fair sized island lying close inshore and sometimes, with low water, accessible on foot. It has an old grave-yard and the ruins of the local pre-Reformation chapel on it. The reason for the graveyard being sited on an island was probably because of wolves, which had a nasty habit of digging up newly buried bodies. It has now ceased to be used for burials and one of the last people to be buried there was John Scott who was the last of the Scott family to live at Eredine House and who died in 1972. He has a rather striking grave-slab with carvings including a galley and an inscription saying 'There is no death. What seems so is transition'.

I was told a long time ago that the building of the wall around the graveyard had been paid for by someone called Turner from Aus-

LEFT: *From the landing place on Innischerrich, also known as Innis Sea-Ramhach (isle of the six oared boat), we look across to Portinnisherrich site of an ancient ferry and Inn. The chapel on the island dates from the 15th to 16th centuries and in the burial ground a stone commemorates William McAllum who died in 1732.*

S.S. "Eagle" a cargo boat owned by David Wilson preparing to load wool bags at Portinisherrich between 1921 and 1929. This boat was fitted with a derrick to help in handling cargo. S.S. Eagle built in Leith in 1881 for Mr Campbell Muir of Inistrynich, was taken by sea to Bonawe and by road through the Pass of Brander to Lochawe. She was sold to H&D McCowan, Oban and purchased from them by Thomas Dow, then in 1921 by David Wilson and in 1929 by Mr Sheriffs. She continued running until 1935 when she was sold for scrapping but sank in 1936 while laid up at Lochawe Pier.

tralia whose ancestors were buried there. There is a gravestone to Archibald and Helen Turner of Ardchonnel and Duncan, their son, who died later in Australia, which possibly ties in with that. In 1800 apart from the two ferrymen, a shoe maker and a blacksmith also lived at Portinnisherrich and in 1841 the place had 23 inhabitants, an inn and still the blacksmith's smiddy. This inn must have been a pretty busy place as I was told that when the bar-room could not hold the large number of folks wanting to be served a bucket was simply filled with whisky, carried out to the steadings and dispensed there. An estate map of 1806 shows three piers in the bay there and I remember that the wooden pile remains of what would have been a steamer pier were also to be seen further out round the shoreline. At present the old inn building is run as a guesthouse and the steadings and land used in a small sheep-farming enterprise.

From Portinnisherrich the road runs around a headland and then does a loop around Kames Bay to an empty school building and nearby cottage. This school was built, along with the nearby post-war forestry village at Eredine but its intended houses were not all built and like Dalavich, the down-turn in forestry employment, combined with other factors, caused the number of pupils to plummet from some thirty pupils down to one, and so the school was eventually closed.

In the past Kames was a small hamlet with most of the houses above the fields and near to the present forest. In 1779 there were 28 inhabitants and in 1841 there were 41. Some of these houses sur-

Mrs Thomson and pupils of Ardchonnel School in 1964/65. Back row: Jean Kilpatrick, Robin Johnston, Susan MacLeod, Forbes Johnston, William Forbes, Fiona Johnston, Janet MacIntyre, Margaret Toner, Douglas and Barbara McCartney, Marie Toner. Front row: Donald Forbes, Robert Kilpatrick, Duncan and Jane Crawford, Lynn Kilpatrick, Alison Johnston and Norman MacLeod.

vived into the early 1900's but by that time they were in poor condition. When the Scotts bought the estate in 1884 they wanted to demolish them but one tenant, Duncan MacArthur, known as The Coileach (Cockerel) refused to leave his house. This was something the autocratic Mrs Scott would not stand for and one day, accompanied by her maid, she went there when The Coileach was not at home, set fire to the house and burnt him out. This burning someone out of their house might have been acceptable at one time but not in the 1900's. I think that The Coileach must have been well compensated for his loss as, when I later knew him, he was tenant of Ardchonnel Farm.

When I was planting trees in ploughed furrows in the hills above Kames, I came across the ploughed up remains of an ancient campfire and nearby I found a very well-made tanged and barbed flint arrowhead, which is now in the Oban museum collection. There is also the ruined remains of an old dun, or fort, on top of the hillock near the school but as is usually the case most of its stone has been robbed for more recent buildings and dykes. It's probably from the early AD years and is too early for anything to be known about its history.

In 1692 Kames had seven fencible men living there but later, in the 1700's, the place developed a bad reputation for smuggling and the following story is probably from that time. One day an exciseman, or gauger, turned up unexpectedly when one house had a cask of brandy in it and there was no time to hide it. So the woman of the house simply sat on it and covered it with her long skirts but the gauger knew that she was hiding something and tried to move her, whereupon she screamed blue murder and yelled that she was being assaulted and everyone rushed to her aid forcing the poor gauger to flee for his life.

Another story from Kames has it that even the Devil was so annoyed by the noise and behaviour of the people there that he climbed up to the top of the Big Rock hill and threw a gigantic boulder at them, but it fell short and it remains there perched up on top of a small hillock. A more mundane explanation for this giant rock's presence is that it is what is called an erratic and was left behind by the ice.

Argyll's Census for 1779 shows the total number of persons as 28 with three being tenants and the rest made up of a mixed lot of people.

From the old hamlet an old road winds up the hillside to the township's peat bog and from there an old track carries on to the left past the old Kames shielings. Then on by way of the Sgadain (Herring) Burn Loch through the Bealach Glas (Grey Pass) over the moors and down into Glen Aray. Over this route would have gone some of the Portinnisherrich Ferry's passengers, packmen, animals for market, smugglers and in the latter half of the 1700's, Mr Campbell of Carwhin's postal service, which used this route weekly and would have been carrying mail to and from the busy Easdale area slate quarries, that were largely owned by him. The women of Kames too would have used it to carry farm produce such as butter, cheese, eggs and other goods to sell in Inveraray, and on return their creels would have been loaded with small necessities such as salt, tobacco, sgadain in their season and seaweed for fertilizing the fields.

Neil Munro wrote about this route in his story Shudderman Soldier and as he had, as a boy, lived with his grandmother at Ladyfield in Glen Aray and she was a MacArthur from Kames, he would probably have heard a lot about it from her. In a list of fencible men that dates from around 1803-04, when Napoleon was threatening Britain, there were six listed from Kames, four of whom were down as fishermen, and one farmer and a tailor. These fishermen must have had their boats based at Loch Fyne and stayed there during the week. There were quite a few Lochaweside people engaged in fishing, as this was a time of big herring catches and I suppose big money was to be made.

Kames, like most settlements, had its grain-drying kiln, as damp grain had to be dried, before de-husking and milling into meal. This is built into the banking on a rise to the north but this one has an L-shaped baffle wall built around the kiln's fire opening possibly because of Kames' contrary winds, which can blow down from the hills or in from the bay. At present the kiln's sunken stone-lined bowl seems to be making a very good shooting-stance for target practice.

A record was kept of a census taken by the 5th Duke in 1779 for the Argyll Estates. This census was taken as part of his modernisation of the whole estate system, with run-rig farms, tacksmen abandoned and new fishing stations started, amongst many other things to enable a complete reorganisation. Some things did happen but not as complete as he would have wished for. I have some of his figures for the population and they are: Kaimes 28, Blairghour 33, Penchallich 10, Ballimenach 15, Culchureland 26, Barnalean 37, Kenchregan 8.

Across Kames Burn, in the south corner of the parkland and beside the present forest, was the old 'Homestead of the Smith' (Ballegoun). In the past it was sometimes called Smithtown and I think that the name Conithtown on some old maps will be a miss-spelling of that. This appears to have been a smithy from olden times and when a forest road was made nearby it dug through the old slag waste from an iron smelter, or bloomery as they were called, which shows that early blacksmiths also smelted their own iron. In 1692 the place had two fencible men and in 1841 one house and five inhabitants. But it was deserted by the 1851 census and only the partly robbed ruins of several buildings now remain.

CHAPTER SEVENTEEN

EREDINE, DURRAN AND BRAEVALLICH

From Ballegoun an old road leads up and across the hillside past the ruins of a small lime-kiln and further on passes an old stone sheep-fank that served the Eredine to Kames hirsel. It then runs along by Eredine Falls and down through the modern village of Eredine.

Eredine was built as a forestry village in the early 1950's and its houses were let out to young married forest workers who came mainly from the Glasgow area. Like the new Dalavich residents the isolation and lack of amenities was totally alien to them with the result that many of them did not stay long. However a more or less settled community did eventually develop. As in Dalavich, by the 1970's, mechanisation and other factors caused the need for directly employed forest workers to drop away dramatically and most of the workers and their families left Eredine and found other employment. The houses were then mostly sold off to private owners and at the present time no one from there is employed in forestry.

The old mansion house of Eredine was recently a holiday complex but it has now been bought by a descendant of the Scotts who once owned the Estate. They have removed the newer additions to the building taking it back to its original style of house and modernised it. The earliest part of the house is about two hundred years old and it was not properly finished when it was advertised for sale in 1812 along with what was then Durran Estate. This stretched from Kames Burn to Braevallich Burn and was praised for its lands that had good shooting, fishing, extensive oakwoods and many water falls. Oak bark for tanning was a valuable commodity in those days and it was said that the next cutting of the coppiced woods would produce some 400 tons of bark.

The estate did not find any buyers however, and it was 1816 before it was sold for £7,050 to the Malcolms of Poltalloch, along with the neighbouring Ardchonnel and Killinuchanich (Kames) Estate, which went for £9,550. The Malcolms ran it as a sporting and farming part of their vast estate and the record

Archibald MacIntyre served Mr James Henry Scott as head keeper on Eredine Estate for many years from 1892.

A horse and cart being backed up near Eredine steamer pier to unload cargo from S.S. "Eagle".

A family shooting party, with James Henry Scott in the centre, assembled at Eredine House in the 1890's. From left to right are: Colin Scott, older brother of J.H. Scott who worked for Scotts of Greenock, the family shipbuilding business. Colin Cunningham Scott, eldest son of J.H. Scott by his first wife. James Henry Scott, who, with his son Colin, is buried at Eredine. Charles Pinckross. James Yuill Scott, younger son of J.H. Scott by his first wife, who lost his life in the First World War at the Battle of the Somme.

grouse bag for Eredine was 2,004 birds shot in 1903 after it was sold off to the Scott family in 1884.

Around this time there was a small industry making wooden soles for clogs from the alder trees growing by the loch-side at Eredine and elsewhere. These were then transported to Loch Awe Station by steam barge and then probably sent south to the mill towns of Lancashire. On the shore, south of Eredine House, about the place where the clog workers worked their wood for clogs a new house is now being built.

GAME REGISTER.

Date 1894	Grouse	Black Game Cocks	Black Game Hens	Duck	Pheasants Cocks	Pheasants Hens	Woodcock	Hares	Rabbits	Sundries	Beat	Weather	Game
Forward ...	836	52	50	3	5	7	1	184	22	3 Snipe, 1 Teal			
Oct. 28												S.W. occ. rain	Sunday
29	2							1			Walking &c 3	mod. S.W. heavy showers pm	Lewn
30	4	1						3			Walking &c 3+5	S.n.E. flat calm	do.
31												Showery SW wind	Dick and C Short
Nov. 1	1											Showy SW. fair	do.
2		5	7		9	6	4		6	1 Mallard 1 Wigeon	Breach to Eredine & Bock	W fair+ occ show	
3	7						1	34			Red + Pine Kept	Strong SW heavy showers	
4												W close showery	Game day
5		1	1		64	28	4	1	19	1 Blackgame	Lorne Gehain	Strong W. heavy show	
6	2	5	23		13	12	11	1	10	1 Black	Bank at Kames and Ballcowie Wood	fresh W occ heavy	
Forward ...	871	64	61	3	91	53	21	223	57	3 Snipe 1 Teal 1 Wigeon 1 Mallard			

A page from the Eredine Estate Game Register notes all the members of the party pictured above shooting in the autumn of 1894. The end of season totals in that year were: 934 grouse, 67 blackcock, 61 greyhen, 3 duck, 120 cock pheasants, 73 hen pheasants, 103 woodcock, 328 hares and 242 rabbits of which 174 were shot by the keepers, 13 snipe, 1 wood pigeon, 1 teal and 5 roe giving a total head of 1,951.

Occupation of the place, however, goes back to a long time before that and some two millennia or more ago some residents built a crannog in the loch below, presumably in what must have been somewhat troubled times. The later name Eredine means a place of healing and this would be because of a 'hospital' that is said to have been on the point there. But this would not have been a hospital as we know it. It was more likely to have been just the residence of someone who was skilled in healing and treated folks there. This ties in with my being told that some ancient relative of the Dukes of Argyll was buried there, and around 1930 the then Duke had the estate workers at Eredine search for the grave. They dug until they found a stone coffin but did not open it, and after the Duke had seen it, the coffin was covered over again and left unmarked. The fact that this person was buried in unconsecrated ground suggests that they had died of the plague.

Behind the village, high up on a shoulder of Corr Bheinn, is what appears to have been the local quern-making site. Here at a sheet of level and suitably grained rock can be seen where the quern stone's outline was cut into the living rock undercut slightly and then levered free. This quern-making must go back to at least the middle ages before the Ardchonnel water mill came into being. When a watermill was built on an estate the laird of the place immediately banned the use of rotary querns and any people continuing to use them had their querns broken and were probably fined.

From Eredine the B840 road carries on through the forest to Durran. This name probably originates from dubh rinn meaning black point and will refer to the rocky point by the loch-side. Durran was and is a small hamlet, that seems to have grown up at the junction of an old pass over the hills to Lochfyneside, and the route up Lochaweside. This route, over and through the hills, must have been used from ancient times and was part of a route to the west coast and islands via the Portinnisherrich Ferry.

It was used by many people including Colkitto and his army of wild Irish mercenaries, fellow MacDonalds and others in 1644 when he and Montrose sacked Inveraray. Montrose and his army marched down Glen Aray and Colkitto, his second in command, went by way of Durran and the snow-bound hill route in order to do a pincer attack on Inveraray, which they hoped would capture the Earl of Argyll but he still managed to escape by boat down Loch Fyne. Another person who used this route for his nefarious purposes was one Black Duncan, who was a robber; and is said to have 'sat' or waited on the hillside above for suitable prey to approach then he would rush down, waylay and rob them. There are the remains of a ruined stone seat by the old road there that gets called Black Duncan's seat and the highest point on the ridge above is called Suidhe (Seat). This ridge incidentally is now the site of the new An Suidhe Wind Farm which has twenty three wind-driven turbines. The main access road to this is built in from Lochfyneside and the wind farm is mainly visible from the far sides of Loch Awe and Loch Fyne.

Despite the importance of this route through the hills from Durran, it remained a simple track or bridle-path until after 1758, when the manager of the Furnace Ironworks persuaded the road authorities to have a better road constructed from Durran to the Water of Leckan. Presumably this was to help in the transportation of charcoal from Lochaweside to the Furnace Iron Smelter. The road that was made, however, was not suitable for carriages and anyway not everyone was happy about the route. It was not long before the heritor's (landowners) from Dalavich and Kilchrenan were petitioning for a new, better and shorter road to be constructed from the ferry across the hills from Kames to Inveraray. They said that the Durran route was too long and tedious and anyway the Kaimes route was ridden across by Campbell of Carwhin every week. It was surveyed but nothing was done and small sums were spent on the road to improve it. In 1844 the Second Statistical Account included it along with some roads maintained at public expense that it says 'scarcely deserve that name'.

On the hillside some distance up this road and just past the Allt Achadh Fionn a' Bhacain burn at map reference 067 965 there is a cairn on top of a rise. At about 20 feet long this cairn is not very large but it does look as if it has been an ancient burial cairn. Some two miles further on to the left of the road and beside the Durran boundary at Allt nan Sac burn are the remains of the summer shielings of the old Durran farmers. On a slight rise beside these ruins there is a lot of scattered charcoal but I do not think that it was a charcoal-burning site. The name of the burn, Allt nan Sac (Burn of the Load), suggests that this may have been a dropping off and changing place for the Lochaweside and Lochfyneside charcoal ponies. There was probably some kind of wooden storage shed there. Charcoal in transit was very prone to damage and there would have been spillage from burst bags. These shielings would have been used in 1692 when there were six fencible men living at Durran, which then belonged to the MacLachlans, Captains of Innischonnel Castle, but it was sold in 1738 and it had several owners before being bought by Poltalloch Estate in 1815. Durran then had four tenant farmers all called MacKellar. This was still a time of small farmers but things were changing fast and large scale farmers were being brought in to farm the land. In the 1841 census Durran still had 25 people living there and the seven adult male residents are all listed as agricultural labourers and would not have been farming for themselves.

A good many of the old MacKellar inhabitants had firstly gone to Lochgilphead and then emigrated to New South Wales in Australia. A number of years ago a MacKellar family from there turned up keen to see where their ancestors had come from. After getting all the information on the MacKellars from me, seeing the ruins and the one surviving house, they then asked where the people would have been buried and were not deterred when I told them that it would be on the island of Innisherrich. They managed to borrow a boat, row across and find a group of MacKellar stones and on scraping away the moss covering one of them, discovered that it said 'Neil MacKellar Died Durran 1818'. This was the ancestor that they had traced the family back to and they were fair delighted.

The old house that survives was what is now called a 'long-house' with house, byre and stable in one long building. It is now renovated and it has the date 1790 carved into a stone in its wall, but the date is upside down and the likeliest explanation for this is that the date was carved into the stone by someone before it was built into the wall and the builder was not literate enough to know which way up it should have been. Houses at that time were usually built by the people themselves and not by professional builders. Shortly after this house was built in 1796 a Neil McArthur from Durran and three men from neighbouring Braevallich were summoned to appear at the Inveraray JP court charged with contravening the Excise Acts. This summons meant meant they had been distilling and selling whisky. Actually at that time it was legal to operate a still provided it was under a certain size and the whisky was for one's own use. Possibly it was around this time too that the burn between Eredine and Durran came to be known as Bertie's Burn. This came about when some folks at Eredine were having a booze-fuelled party and the drink was running out so they sent a young fellow called Bertie to fetch some more whisky. It seems he decided to sample it and he was eventually found beside this burn dead drunk with an empty bottle of whisky beside him.

By the old roadside south west of this house is a natural stone grave-slab with some large stones beside it. These were probably used to cover the new grave and stop any prowling wolves from digging up the body. I was told this grave belonged to the wife of Black Duncan who, when she was travelling by there, had taken ill and died of the plague. She was buried by the roadside along with all her jewellery. Black Duncan, her husband, would probably have been Sir

Dochie MacDonald leads a horse, pulling a raft of logs ashore at Durran "Dump" timber yard in the 1940's, the raft having been towed across from Inverliever by the workboat "Coilleach" skippered by Jimmy Gillies and with Sandy MacVean at the stern, as there was no roadway on that side of Loch Awe until the late 1950's.

Duncan Campbell, the Glenorchy Chief, who lived around 1600 and appeared to have had several wives.

The present Durran consists of six houses, four of which were built by the Forestry Commission, after they bought over the land in 1934. Most of the surrounding hillsides that were once taken over by sheep are now covered by forest. There were recently another two new industries in Durran. One was a plant nursery that operated on the level ground towards the loch and originally started out growing rhododendrons and azaleas, but then became part of Highland Heathers producing mainly heather. This company has unfortunately just gone into liquidation. The other is a fish farm that rears rainbow trout in cages in the loch and is now part of the Scot Trout group.

During and after the Second World War a sawmill and timber yard were operating by the loch-side below Durran and a great deal of timber was rafted across the loch from Inverliever Forest by the Forestry Commission's work boat the *Coileach-coille* (Woodcock). Launched on Loch Awe in 1936, the *Coileach* was a sturdy 35ft. wooden boat with a 30H.P. Kelvin diesel engine and a shallow draught, allowing it to be run ashore. She was Inverliever Forest's workboat and as there was not a proper road, she was used to ferry men and materials around the Inverliever forest. During and after the Second World War, she was largely employed in towing rafts of timber across Loch Awe to the Eredine side, where it was converted into pit props and during wartime she transported about three quarters of a million cubic feet of timber, equivalent to over twenty thousand tons. Based at Ford, her first skipper was Duggie MacCallum, till he was called up at the start of the war along with the rest of the Territorial Army. Jimmy Gillies then ran the boat throughout the war till Duggie returned from a German prisoner of war camp, having been taken prisoner, along with most of the 51st Highland Division, at St. Valery. In the late 1950's, when a proper road was made through Inverliever Forest, the *Coileach* became redundant and was sold.

We are now crossing the burn into Glassary and I have the Military List of 1803 - 04 which gives an idea of the number of people: Braevallich 4, 1 farmer, 1 shoemaker, 2 shepherds. Ardary 1, 1 farmer. Upper Fincharn 4, 2 farmers, 1 shepherd, 1 fisher. Lower Fincharn 5, 2 farmers, 1 shepherd, 1 weaver, 1 fisher. Ederline 3, 1 Esq. 1, labourer, 1 fisher.

Across the Abhainn a Bhealaich, or Braevallich Burn, is the old settlement and farm of Braevallich. Timothy Pont in about 1590 shows a drawing of a mansion house at Braevallich and he has an exaggerated the scale of the river there with the largest stretch of woodland on that side of the loch shown in its glen. The settlement of Braevallich took its name from the bealach or pass through the hills to Lochfyneside. The name means high-land pass and the pass also gave its name to the burn in the glen, which is called the Abhainn Bhealaich, or Large Burn of the Pass.

A story from the early 1700's is told about a servant girl who was working at Braevallich and had been travelling over the hill track to her home on Lochfyneside probably for her Sunday day off. When it became late at night and she had not arrived some of her anxious family set out to look for her and found her lying dead not far from home. She had been killed by a large wolf that was lying dead nearby and that she had stabbed through the heart with a knife. That is what one version says.

Another version says that the person killed was from Braevallich and that she had been paying a visit to her folk back home there and was returning to her workplace on Lochfyneside, spinning with a hand spindle as she walked, when she was attacked, and that it was with this sharp-pointed spindle that she killed the wolf near Brenchoille. Which version, if any, is true? In these days, when folks were accustomed to walking long distances, seven or eight miles across the hills was not considered far and I have seen an old letter written by a person from Lochfyneside who wished to take a contract peeling oak-bark at Braevallich, and who said that he intended to walk back and forward daily.

The name given to the burn that flows down by Ardchoille is Allt Doire nan Sobhrachan (The Burn of the Oaks and Primroses) and points to the fact that there was more oak wood growing there in the past, and peeling the bark for tanning and felling the trees for charcoal may have been the main reason for its disappearance. Though the water-powered sawmill that is shown by the side of the farm burn in an 1864 map could have played a part in this. It got most of its water via a channel across the hillside from the larger Allt Doire nan Sobhrachan but I do not know how long it operated for.

An old Inveraray Court list of rebels who had supported the outlawed Earl of Argyll, when he landed in Argyll in 1685 and started the Monmouth Rebellion, has two people from the next place, which is Nether Bravallich. They are John McKellar and John Campbell and their livestock of six cows, one mare and four cows was confiscated. A later 1692 list of the fencible men in Argyll lists seven men from what it calls the Bravallichs. The men listed were Donald ban Inroich, John McOlvory, John dow McKellar, John roy McKellar, John McIndoir, John McGouin and John McKellar, Cott-tar. This list shows rather surprisingly that out of seven Braevallich men six were called John.

Braevallich Farm had a tacksman and a stone in Kilmichael Churchyard commemorates a John McKellar, tacksman of Braevallich who died in 1802. A tacksman was a kind of middle-man and often a relative of the landowner and so they were generally middle class and their families could afford to erect gravestones. This explains why there are a fair number of stones commemorating tacksmen in the local graveyards but very few for the many small farmers who lived at Braevallich and elsewhere.

These tacksmen leased large farms, or 'tacks', then divided the low ground up into small farms, which were rented out along with a share of the hill ground where the tenants could keep a certain number of animals. In the summer, to protect the crops and save grass for winter use, most of the farm animals would have been taken out to the shielings in the hills usually by the young folk, who lived there, herded the animals, milked them, made butter and cheese and did other tasks. The Braevallich shieling ruins are out in the large coire at the head of Braevallich Burn. Before the countryside was planted with conifers this coire was quite a pleasant oasis among the hills.

In the late 1700's Braevallich belonged to the Rev Dugald Campbell JP who owned Ederline Estate and was the compiler of the 1790's First Statistical Account for Glassary Parish, however he was forced to sell because of debt to John MacDougal in 1805. Then in 1835 it was bought by Poltalloch Estate for £8,000. This was a time of radical change with sheep farmed in great numbers on the hills. Braevallich was joined with Ardary, Durran, Eredine and Ballegoun to form one large sheep farm. Braevallich was the hub of this large farm and a new farmhouse and steadings were built there, but this large-farm policy meant that there was no place for the small farmers and they had to go. Most of the old Braevallich houses appear to have been where the group of ruins are on the slope up and across the burn from Ardchoille. There are also ruins in the field in front of Ardchoille and Ardchoille itself, now a holiday house that has been renovated and added to, is a very old house that will be pre-Poltalloch.

After the Second World War two large wooden huts were erected beside that old cottage and the place became a hostel for ex-service-men who wanted to try a career in forestry. This was still a time of food rationing with small allowances of meat, so all the live mutton running around was very tempting, and two of them decided to kill and butcher some. They then posted some mutton home to their families but rather inevitably the sheep stealers were caught, charged with stealing two sheep and both fined. Later this hostel housed dis-placed persons from Eastern Europe who were afraid to, or did not wish to return to their own communist-controlled countries and chose to stay and work in forestry.

Beside the burn at Ardchoille is a trout hatchery and fish trap belonging to the Loch Awe Improvement Association but this at present is unused. This organisation was set up in 1992 when Loch Awe lost its free fishing status. Amongst other things it controls the issuing of permits and the policing of Loch Awe and Loch Avich. Permits are issued for brown and rainbow trout, pike and perch but unfortunately the landowners, who formed the majority of the mem-bers, reserved the salmon and sea-trout for themselves. Near the road to Upper Braevallich, a well preserved but ruined grain-drying kiln was to be seen, that would have dried the local grain before it was taken to Ardchonnel Mill, to be ground into meal. However during the tidying up work after the recently built hydro-electric scheme's buried pipeline passed by there, some vandal bulldozed and completely destroyed this kiln. Peat was the fuel used in these kilns and both the peat-bog near the kiln, and the one on a higher level have been extensively worked for peat, which would also have been the main fuel used in the old houses at Braevallich and elsewhere.

When Braevallich became a large sheep-farm there would have been great quantities of wool produced at the annual clipping, and in the early days this would have been transported by a string of pack ponies across the Durran hill-road to Loch Fyne and then shipped

Jimmy Mitchell, Willie Miller, Johnny O'Neill and Charlie Mitchell weeding between the young conifers in Eredine Forest Nursery at Braevallich in the late 1940's.

An aerial view over the plant nursery and part of the trout farm with Durran in the background about 1998.

south. Later, with steam boats on Loch Awe and a rail link, the wool was carted half a mile to the Rubha Riabhach rock, which became known as the Wool-rock, and loaded on to a steam-barge.

Braevallich Farm, in the latter part of the 1800's was farmed by a Charles Bell and then by his son another Charles Bell, who was unfortunately drowned when crossing Loch Awe to visit his son in Barmaddy Farm. Then not long after this Braevallich was sold to the Scotts, who had taken over Eredine Estate, and they ran it as a sporting and farming estate until 1934 when they sold it to the Forestry Commission as potential forest land. A nursery for young trees was started in the field by Braevallich Burn and planting commenced on the hillsides. By the early 1970's there was no hill-ground left on Braevallich Farm. The low-ground, the farmhouse and steadings were then sold to Philip Bowden-Smith and he started the Durran-based nursery, growing rhododendrons and azaleas in polyhouses.

He also founded the present fish-farming enterprise, which then was both land based and in cages in Loch Awe. However as he had no interest in livestock or arable farming the remaining land was leased out to Jamie McGrigor and farmed along with his Ardchonnel land.

There were not many houses built at Braevallich in modern times. In the late 1930's a wooden bungalow for a shepherd was built and Richard Bailley, a contractor from Haddington, built a large wooden house on a site with a superb view of Loch Awe and Ben Cruachan. He and his family used it as a holiday and sporting place. He called it Achacaorann, or Field of the Rowans, but it has changed hands three times since and it is now called Braevallich House. The small wooden bungalow that was built beside it for a caretaker burned down in 2003.

A hydro-electric scheme has recently been built at Braevallich powered by the water of Braevallich Burn and its tributaries. The water is taken from high up in the hills and piped to a power station on the low ground at Braevallich. This hydro scheme has no water storage dam and relies on the flow of water from the burns. At full capacity the station will generate 2.2 megawatts, or sufficient to supply some fourteen hundred houses, but at other times the output will be zero. The outflow from the power-station returns to Braevallich Burn at the point where the old Lochaweside road forded it and unfortunately the work has destroyed what remained of the stepping-stones and ford.

This hydro-scheme would probably have been approved of by Tom Johnston who was the driving force behind the big hydro-electric schemes after the Second World War. He was well known in Braevallich as he was a keen angler and had a fishing hut and boat out in the hills at Loch nan Eilean and even during the war years, when he was Secretary of State for Scotland and was in effect in charge of the country's defences, he would still disappear into the hills for days at a time fishing.

An addition to the first Braevallich hydro scheme is now being built that will also take in the water from the Allt Doire nan So-brachan burn and have another power station near to the present one. Unfortunately this is likely to have a detrimental effect on that burn's spawning fish though extra water will be released down the burn at spawning time. The work has to be monitored by an archaeologist during the construction of the scheme to avoid destroying things like the old grain-drying kiln.

The Parish of Glassary Military List of 1803 – 04 lists the following people who were fit to do military service: Braevallich 4, 1 farmers, 2 shepherd, and 1 shoemaker. Ardary 1 farmer. Upper Fincharn 4, 2, farmers, 1fisher, 1 sheperd. Lower Fincharn 5, 2 farmer, 1 sheperds, 1 weaver, 1 fisher. Ederline 1 Alex. Campbell Esq, 1 fisher, 1 labourer. Fincharn 1 farmer.

CHAPTER EIGHTEEN

ARDARY
AND FINCHARN

From Braevallich the public road runs close by the loch-side with the steep forested slopes of Ardary on the left. Some two miles ahead is a car park and picnic site at the Ardary end of the Leacainn Muir Forest Drive. From there a forestry road has been joined up with a Lochfyneside one in order to form one of Argyll's strategic timber extraction routes to help take heavy timber lorries away from the county's single-track public roads. Its twelve and a half mile length is open to the public, and though somewhat rough, can be a pleasant and interesting drive. It has viewpoints and picnic sites along its length.

Ahead and high above the B840 at map reference NM 937 054 is an old millstone making site where millstones were being fashioned from slabs of rock that were split from a rock face. One damaged millstone with a piece split from its side lies there and another good stone, which was raised out of the peat during forest ploughing, has sunk back in again. An unfinished stone gatepost can be seen and it seems that dressed building stone was also being made there. There are two crude stone shelters there and it may be that the folks who worked the stone were itinerant workers who moved to where their services were needed and lived where they worked.

The land on that part of the loch-side would once have belonged to Ardary and the old settlement ruins are up ahead. The area is now all covered by forest but it was once quite a fertile and thriving place. It belonged to a branch of the MacKellars from at least 1470 when they were given title to it by the first Earl of Argyll. I was told by Dan Stuart that they eventually lost this title by trickery to a laird from Kilmartin who coveted the property but no way would the MacKellar owner sell it to him. This laird, he said, invited Old Ardary as he was usually called and his son to a banquet at his mansion house, but during the meal some of the silver cutlery went missing and was found planted in the pocket of the son. Their host then threatened to have him thrown in jail unless Old Ardary signed over Ardary's title to him. This he reluctantly agreed to and that is how, Dan said, that the MacKellars lost ownership of Ardary. If the story is true this devious and crooked laird would seem to have been Neil Campbell, who had been Kilmartin's Rector and was later Bishop of Argyll and the Isles and who obtained Ardary on the 4th March 1603.

A possible postscript to this could be contained in a newspaper report from 2000 about an auction sale in Wiltshire where a set of silver spoons were sold for £126,500. These were topped by heraldic lions holding shields and had first belonged to Neil Campbell who was Bishop of Argyll from 1580 to 1608. They were bought by a private collector. Could they have been involved in the crooked Ardary deal?

However MacKellars did stay on as tenants in Ardary and possibly this was part of the deal. In 1685 a Duncan MacKellar and a Dugald MacKellar from there joined in Archibald Earl of Argyll's rebellion. After this collapsed they had their livestock, consisting of fifteen cows each, confiscated but whether they suffered any other punishment is not known. The last family to live at Ardary was the MacNaughtons and they lived there until at least 1908. As a boy I went gathering blackcurrants at Ardary and there was then still a surviving root of rhubarb in the old garden.

Ardary's old boundary is also the boundary of the modern Eredine Forest. We then enter the present Ederline Estate's land and up ahead there is Finchairn, the ruined castle of the old barony seat of Glassary. This at 16 metres by 8 metres was a reasonable sized keep but the small loch-side outcrop of rock that it was built on did not allow for any expansion into a larger castle in later times. It must however have been a very formidable defensive building in its day as is shown by the remaining three corners of the building that are still standing. Their walls are up to two metres thick and built up from the sheer rock. The 1840's Statistical Account says 'It stands upon a rock, which rises up from the waters of the lake on one side and is all around steeped and rugged without a pathway so that it is entered with some difficulty'. In the past I think that it would have been easier to access it as a tongue of the castle rock that had extended shore-wards had a gully quarried across it for defence. I think it would have had some kind of removable bridge spanning it for access when the castle was in use.

This castle, or keep, would have been built in the 1200's as a stronghold for the Barons of Glassary and the local Barony Courts were probably held there. Such early stone castles are said to owe a lot to the Crusades and the Knight's Templar's expertise in such matters. After almost 800 years its lime mortar is still about as strong as modern concrete and strangely some of it was finished in a pink cement. Not much is known about its history and it did not appear to have had a very long life. I don't know whether the stories (both the local and Canadian versions) about it being burned down, by a newly married bridegroom, who objected to the chief claiming it to be his right, to spend the wedding night with his bride are true or not.

That story about Finchairn is probably set in the 1400's and tells how the local chief who lived in the castle believed it to be his right to spend the wedding night with any local girl who was married in his barony. Understandably not everyone was happy with this arrangement. One groom, who had got married at Finchairn, slipped away from the wedding celebrations and sometime later someone rushed in to tell the chief that his castle was ablaze. He rushed out and ran towards his castle but was ambushed by the groom who stabbed him to death. The groom and his bride, who was called Una, then fled from the district to escape the wrath of the chief's people.

The Canadian version of the story says that the groom was a Campbell, son of the Campbell Chief in Innischonnel, and that he and his bride fled to Lochaber and settled there. Many generations later, descendants of theirs emigrated to Canada taking the story with them, from whence it has returned back to Scotland. The story was brought over here in recent years by a Mary Campbell from Nova Scotia who claims to be a descendant of the original couple. But none of the Campbell historians, including the late local historian Marion Campbell, knew anything about such a happening and Marion rubbished the story and said that the details were not correct. After some five or six hundred years of being passed on by word of mouth, it would be rather surprising if they were. Still if the groom's father was the big chief in Innischonnel Castle he could have fled there, which suggests that if the rest of the story is true and the bridegroom was a Campbell, he was not the Campbell Chief's son.

Another wedding at Finchairn that ended with much trouble was one where the Craignish Campbells had gone to a relative's wedding at Finchairn. As there had been some bad feeling between them and the bride's people, they had divested themselves of their weapons on arrival to show their peaceful intentions. But sometime during the proceedings an argument and quarrel had begun, it is said, about the bride's dowry and the Finchairn MacMartin men attacked the men from Craignish. They, being unarmed, were forced to flee back towards their own country with the Finchairn men in pursuit, until, at MacMartin's Ford, on the old Ford to Kintraw road, they broke branches from the alder trees growing there and turned and attacked their pursuers. In the fight that followed, a number of men were killed including two brothers who had fought on opposing sides, possibly as a result of one having been fostered out, and they are said to have been buried, along with the other dead, in the old stone circle by the Oban road, which then became known as the 'Grave of the Fools'.

The Finchairn Farmhouse stands on the hill-slope above the castle and it has, in its old stackyard, the ancient cairn that gave the place its name. The name Fianna-Charn means Fingal's Cairn but it is not likely that the illustrious warrior of Celtic mythology is buried there. The Farm was built beside the older loch-side road and along this to the north-east is an old shepherd's cottage, with nearby, some cup marks in the rock. Beside the old road in the other direction there is a large very well built but now ruined lime-kiln.

Finchairn in the past consisted of two settlements and Pont's map of 1590 has them as Finchairn Mor and Finchairn Beg (Big and Little Finchairn). In 1692 they are called Over and Nether and Over Finchairn had 4 fencible men and Nether Finchairn, which was linked with a settlement at Kilneuair, 8. A century and a half on in 1841 Upper had 35 inhabitants and Lower had 13.

On the Ford side of Finchairn the remains of an old fence runs out into the shallows of the loch for a considerable distance. Just beyond the end of this there is a sudden drop and it was there that Mrs Bruce from Ederline caught five salmon in one day. This happened in the latter half of the 1800's and because of this feat the local people dubbed the spot 'Mrs Bruce's Hole'.

A short distance further on is the 'Tinkers Point', which was a favourite camping ground for travelling people in the past and these days fishermen. Nearby there is the remains of a white-quartz decorated well that I was told was used by the travelling folk to perform marriage ceremonies. Close by this old well is a massive flat erratic stone, which was split horizontally into two slabs. The top slab has now been drilled and blasted into two pieces because, I was told, of a legend that said that there was a bar of gold enclosed between the two slabs. This resulted in a quarryman who was staying at Ford drilling the stone and blasting it apart but there was no bar of gold to be found.

Nearby is Kilneuair Church or as it was called in the past, St Columba's Church, in Glassary. A church site is said to have been founded there by the great man himself back in the latter half of the sixth Century and it could be that this was the church referred to as Cella Diuni in early Iona records. The name Kilneuair seems to mean Church of the Yews and it may be that there was a grove of yew trees there pre-Columba and that he adopted and Christianised a site that was already considered sacred.

One of the earliest surviving documents that mentions the

Kilneuair Church dedicated to St. Columba was until 1563 the Parish Church of Glassary.

church, is a Papal mandate from 1423, in which Pope Martin V removes James Scrimgeour from his position as Rector of St Columba in Glassary. It says he did not understand the language of the people and went on to say that 'he had held the Rectorship for one and a half years to the danger of their souls'. Another Vatican order dated the same year appoints Nigel, son of Colin Campbell who was Archdeacon of Argyll, to be rector in his place.

The Scrimgeours, who were originally from Dundee and had become Barons of Glassary through the marriage in the 1300's of Sir Alexander Scrimgeour to Agnes the heiress to the local MacGilchrist lands, appear to have learned to speak Gaelic, as their clan association says that they held the office of rector and vicar at Kilneuair, for most of the 15th and 16th Centuries, but that they had lost ownership of the Glassary lands in the 15th Century. The last of that family's rectors at Kilneuair, a Henry Scrimgeour, did not appear to take his duties at Kilneuair very seriously and he seems to have been downright crooked, as he went gallivanting around Italy and converted to the Protestant religion in 1550. He got married in Geneva and stayed there living on the teinds of Glassary until his death in1572.

Kilneuair Church was originally the main church of the area and its parish stretched from Lochaweside to Lochfyneside and south to Loch Gilp. The local markets were held beside the church. The market site probably had a market cross and latterly this may have been the same one that was at Kilmichael, after that church had taken over from Kilneuair as the main parish church in1563. This market cross known as 'The High Cross of Argyll' was taken to the churchyard at St Columba's Church at Poltalloch but it has been broken and was held together by metal straps. I think it has now been taken away for repair by Historic Scotland. It is said that there was later a margadh dubh, or black market, at Kilneuair where salt and other commodities were sold. So it seems that a small scale unofficial and illegal market continued there and avoided the tax that had to be paid at market crosses.

The ruined church building at Kilneuair shows three different ages of building work. The north-east part is from the 13th Century and is the earliest and the other end is Medieval and the latest. At twenty two and a half metres long and seven and a half wide and quite high, with balconies along its side, it was a fair sized building.

There is a tradition that much of the stone used to build it was taken from the old church at Killevin, by Crarae, and that it was passed from hand to hand along a long line of people stretching from there to Kilneuair. Given the distance this is highly unlikely but there is probably some truth in the legend and stones from there could have been carried across the hill route in stages.

Many of the stones are of a reddish sandstone that is not of local origin. In the south-east wall is a bell-shaped carving near to a recess that was probably used to hold the host and holy water and there is also a piscine, which would be used for pouring away unused holy water. By the doorway there are faint impressions of what is said to be the Devil's handprint, left there when he tried to strike an intrepid tailor who had dared, for a bet, to spend the night sewing a suit of clothes, in the ruined and supposedly haunted church.

There is a large walled graveyard surrounding the church but there are not a great many stones to be seen in it now. It may be that many slabs have become covered over and the few that are to be seen escaped by being raised up higher. The graveyard is also badly overgrown and neglected. At the approach to the church there is a small roofless, much ornamented building from the 1700's, that is often called an oratory but is said to be more likely a burial place.

East of the church there are three interesting stone slabs, which are probably medieval, and as they are side by side, it is likely that they are the stones of some powerful local family possibly the Scrimgeours. One shows a small figure of a knight and has ornamentation and scrollwork. Another has much ornamentation and designs on it including what appears to be a pair of shears - they may symbolize the cutting off of mortal life. The third has had carved and decorated sides but it is badly damaged. Another carved grave-slab to the south-east of the church has a larger chain-mail or aketon clad figure and other carvings. These are all the carved stone slabs that are to be seen outside but recently an ornamented slab showing what may be a woman's figure, has been uncovered inside the church.

The Church ruins have however deteriorated badly in recent years and when the Scrimgeour Clan Association paid a visit to the church in the 1990's they were very concerned about the state of the place and decided to try and organise some remedial measures to stop the collapse of the walls. They wanted to see if the small ornate 1700's building could be repaired, roofed and used to house the best of the grave-slabs and the font from the church. They did get the trees that were growing on the walls cut and some preliminary first-aid work done to the south-east wall but in1996 a large part of the north-west wall collapsed and this has made the job of renovation much greater.

The trees are growing back again on the walls and some treasure hunters or ghouls have also dug a deep hole in the floor of the 'oratory' building. Their proposed renovation project was turned down by the Lottery Heritage Fund, mainly because it was a privately owned property, belonging to Ederline Estate. The Scrimgeour Association are a relatively small body and unable to fund major work themselves but they are still hoping that something can be done by Historic Scotland or others before it becomes too late to save this historic ruin from total collapse. I have been told recently that the Church site has now been handed over to Argyll and Bute Council and this may help matters for future funding.

From Kilneuair an old road went over the hills to Auchindrain and before the introduction of the motor car this was a busy route both for travellers and cattle droving. Some distance up this road, another one branched off to Glasvaar and near its start it passed through the old settlement of Garbhallt or Rough Burn. It is listed in 1692 as having three fencible men but by 1841 it had only one house with three people living in it. Now only ruins remain and beside them a boulder with a ring set in it that is said to have been used by the local minister to tether his horse when he visited.

CHAPTER NINETEEN

EDERLINE
TO GLENNAN

From Garbhallt we return back to the B840 and head towards Ford. Below us is Ederline's old boathouse ruin, and out from there are the remains of the foundation of what has been quite a large crannog. A survey of possible crannogs in Loch Awe was carried out in 1972, using divers of the Naval Air Command Sub-Aqua Club and archaeologists and they were able to identify twenty. One of them was this small flat-topped grassy islet with natural rock at both ends. They found many timbers, some were worked and one large piece that had about one hundred tree-rings and later gave a carbon-date of about 300 BC.

They also found two querns, one a saddle quern and the other a rotary one. A rotary quern would seem to date occupation to well into the first millennium period. Some recent excavations from 2004 on-wards does confirm that the crannog was occupied into Dalradian times. Trenches dug in the crannog mound gave carbon dates of material from about 300 BC up to the 500's AD and items excavated included bracken, hazel nuts, wheat and rye samples, wood chips, twigs, animal bones, charcoal and the bottom stone from a rotary quern. To the south the original survey found what was described as 'three stone heaps' and these may have been foundations for smaller crannogs. I have seen another such stone heap to the north-east.

From the crannog we carry on past the small man-made St Mary's Loch and come to a small ruined stone building built into the banking at the start of an old road. This small stone 'hut' was once home to Dan Stuart, his parents and other youngsters of the family in the 1920's. This old road leads round behind what was Ederline House policies and it would have been a public road, bypassing them, for folks travelling through to Kilmichael and beyond. For the moment we go over the rise in the B840 and down past the entrance to Ederline. Lower down are three modern houses and then the village hall with, across the road, the old school and smiddy, which are now dwelling houses.

Below these is the old lodge or gate-house for the Ederline 'Big House'. The wrought-iron gates opposite are now rusted and the drive overgrown but at one time things would have been very much different. Someone would have had to run out smartly from the gate-house to open the gates for any horse-drawn or motor vehicle going in or out. The lodge and gates are situated close to the old stone bridge over the Ford Burn. This replaced the ford that gave the place its name and would have been built in the 1700's but the date does not appear to be known.

As we have already passed through that part of Ford that lies over the bridge we will return back to the present Ederline entrance and take that private road on foot, past the large modern wooden Bruachan house and on past Ederline Home Farm steadings, otherwise known as the Square, which are built in that form with a house either side of the entrance. In the 1841 census there were 58 people listed as living at Ederline and the adults' occupations were given as: 11 servants, 3 blacksmiths, 2 shoemakers, 1 house carpenter plus a number of labourers and of course the Campbell family owners.

Ederline's name means between two pools or channels and the name is mentioned in the 730's when there is a record of a battle being fought there between the Scots and Picts. The Picts were the victors and it is said they went on to waste the lands of the Scots and all Dalriada is said to have been captured by 741. Near Ederline Loch and below the present Ederline House there are a number of small cairns.

It has been suggested that these are the graves of the dead from that conflict. Taking a big leap forward to 1692 there was both an Ederlingmoir (Big Ederline) and Ederlingbeg (Small Ederline) listed with nine fencible men between them. A hundred years later the Ederline Estate, which then stretched as far as Braevallich, was owned by the Rev Dugald Campbell who was the Parish Minister and a compiler for the First Statistical Account. His parish had Ford Burn and Ederline Loch as part of its boundary and this split the Ford village between Kilmichael and Kilmartin parishes. The Ederline Estate was bought by Henry Bruce in the mid-1800's and run by him until he died. It was then bought over by the Warde-Aldam family from Yorkshire and it is now owned and run by Clare Wilson, a descendant, and her husband. She is the fourth generation of that family to do so and although it is not quite as large as it was in 1790 the estate still comprises 8,700 acres and includes Finchairn land and stretches over the hills to Carron.

Our route through the old 'big house' grounds takes us past the modern 'big house', which is built on a pleasant site overlooking Loch Ederline. It was built after the Second World War to replace the previous house that had been demolished. Just ahead, at the far end of the old 'big house' grounds, there were another set of wrought iron gates at South Lodge but these gates are gone now and the house now called South Lodge does not appear to be old enough, or close enough to the gates, to have been the gate-house. There is a very old stone building beside the gateway but it does not appear to have been a house. The gate-house may have been on the opposite side where there are traces of possible foundations. Not far

Ederline House, the Scottish Baronial style mansion of 1870 was demolished in 1966.

through these gates are the old cottages of Clachandubh and the even older stone bridge across the Clachandubh Burn. This seems to have been the place mentioned in 1759 in a petition to the road authorities, asking for the construction of a bridge across the Water of Clachandow, on the road from Kilmichael-Glassary to the Ford of Stuacraw, saying 'that the river can hardly be forded because of clay pits and sinking sands'. Again in 1763 we have a 'Petition for £30 towards the cost of the proposed bridge over the Water of Clachandow – the most public road in the Braes of Glassary – the only passage for cattle to the Whitsun Market from Mull, Lorn and Lochaweside'. There were 41 inhabitants living beside the bridge at Clachandubh in 1841 in four houses.

Across this old bridge is the Stroneskar farm land and near the bridge is the new and largely self-built house of Duncan and Martina MacNair. Duncan is the third generation of MacNairs to farm that place, which is a very well kept and run farm of 1,200 acres. Rabbits once presented a major problem to farm crops across the district

Clachandubh bridge, which replaced a ford, was completed in 1764 at a cost of £46.

The water driven mill wheel at Stroneskar was fed from a nearby pond which enabled the threshing mill to operate for one hour separating the oats for horse fodder.

and at Stroneskar, in the winter of 1935/36, gamekeeper Dempster Cameron snared three thousand pairs, carrying in twenty-five pairs across his shoulders, each weighing five pounds. The farmhouse and steadings are to the left at the junction ahead but we are taking the road to the right that leads to Glennan.

Below that road there is a small steep-sided hillock that is what the geologists call a kame and would have been left by the melting ice.

According to the local folks this is Gocam-go where a skirmish, or battle, took place between the marauding army of Colkitto and a local force in 1647. Different versions are told as to how Colkitto's encamped army was attacked by a local force led by Big Zachary MacCallum. Some say that he and Colkitto fought in single combat and Big Zachary won but was killed by Colkitto's men, but others say that this happened elsewhere.

Other versions say that Colkitto's force was ambushed as it travelled through and some say that the local men won the encounter and others that Colkitto did. It is all very confusing with versions saying that the staff of Colkitto's standard writhed like a snake when planted in the ground there and the flag flew out against the wind, a coin sprang up out of the earth and Colkitto lost his precious talisman stone in a bog when he cast it for luck. The name of the place too is somewhat confusing. Gocam-go is Gaelic for a sentry or watchman, which might be appropriate for the hillock.

All the stories mention the name Gocam-go, or the Mill of Gocam-go, the site of which appears to be lost and most say that Colkitto had been warned by his old nurse in Islay, or maybe a crone in Ireland, that his luck would run out when he came to a place called Gocam-go, and say that he had just learned the name of the place before the fight.

On studying the site it is evident that the steep-sided hillock surrounded by boggy ground is not a place that a large force would or could camp. The ambush story seems much more likely as the terrain there would be very suitable for that. If Colkitto's straggling force was attacked there the mound of Gocam-go would make a good rallying point and could have become the centre of the action. Whatever happened there, however, one thing is certain and that is that from then on it was all downhill for Colkitto. This fearless fighting man who had been a brilliant commander and tactician fled ignominiously down Kilmichael Glen and then to Islay and on to Ireland. In Ireland he fought in command at his last Royalist battle, was defeated and surrendered on terms but was later killed, shot in the back of the head by someone.

The rocks in the pass where Colkitto was possibly ambushed are rich in lime and there is a good-sized old lime-kiln built into the banking just below the road. I think that this would have been built by Poltalloch Estates during their ownership of the place. The hillsides around are quite fertile and this is probably helped by the bedrock containing lime. Old rig and furrow cultivation can be seen quite high up on much of the surrounding hillsides and while driving south past the Dog-Head Loch on spring mornings, with the low sun shining on the still bare hillside opposite, I had kept noticing that high up there was a patch of ground, with what looked like the remains of a series of close old parallel dykes running up the hillside, with traces of terracing between them. On climbing up to investigate, I found that the dyke-like lines had been caused by rolling large stones into lines while clearing the ground and that the terrace-like effect was caused by manually cultivating the ground between, probably using a cas chrom foot-plough. On the way up I had noticed that the stones and boulders were rather water-rounded to about the three hundred foot contour level and realized that this must have been the height that the sea had risen to after the last ice-age.

Running along below, there is a stretch of level ground and near the modern road, are the remains of three ancient burial cairns, that date back to at least the Bronze Age. The middle one is just across the road from the modern Tigh a' Charnain (House by the Cairn) bungalow. It must have been quite a large cairn but in more modern times the dyke and house builders have robbed most of the stones from handy cairns like it.

Just ahead is Glennan and the remains of the old House by the Stone, which is where we started from and so we complete our circular journey of discovery around Lochaweside.

Glennan, showing the road past the Dog's Head loch by which we set off and the road coming down Kilmichael Glen by which we have returned.

Charlie Mitchell (on the left) with his mother and brother Jimmy in 1985 at their home in Durran.

ACKNOWLEDGEMENT

Dalmally Historical Association would like to thank all those who have generously given of their time, knowledge and expertise that has led to the publication of this book. We would also like to acknowledge and thank all the people who provided such a selection of photographs which have allowed Charlie's book and memories to be so beautifully illustrated and brought to life.

Also thanks to GreenPower and Glenorchy and Innishael Community Council for assistance in funding this project.

INDEX

INDEX